EPHESIANS

THE TEACHER'S OUTLINE & STUDY BIBLE™

EPHESIANS

THE TEACHER'S OUTLINE & STUDY BIBLE™

NEW TESTAMENT

KING JAMES VERSION

Leadership Ministries Worldwide
Chattanooga, TN

The Teacher's Outline & Study Bible™ is written for God's people to use both in their personal lives and in their teaching. Leadership Ministries Worldwide wants God's people to use *The Teacher's Outline & Study Bible*™. The purpose of the copyright is to prevent the reproduction, misuse, and abuse of the material.

May our Lord bless us all as we live, preach, teach, and write for Him, fulfilling His great commission to live righteous and godly lives and to make disciples of all nations.

Please address all requests for information or permission to:

Leadership Ministries Worldwide
PO Box 21310
Chattanooga TN 37424-0310
Ph.# (423) 855-2181 FAX (423) 855-8616 E-Mail info@outlinebible.org
http://www.outlinebible.org

Library of Congress Catalog Card Number: 94-073070
International Standard Book Number: 1-57407-196-3

PRINTED IN THE U.S.A.

PUBLISHED BY LEADERSHIP MINISTRIES WORLDWIDE

1 2 3 4 5 04 05 06 07

LEADERSHIP MINISTRIES WORLDWIDE

DEDICATED

To all the men and women of the world who preach and teach the Gospel of our Lord Jesus Christ and to the Mercy and Grace of God

- Demonstrated to us in Christ Jesus our Lord.

  "In whom we have redemption through His blood, the forgiveness of sins, according to the riches of His grace." (Ep.1:7)

- Out of the mercy and grace of God His Word has flowed. Let every person know that God will have mercy upon him, forgiving and using him to fulfill His glorious plan of salvation.

  "For God so loved the world, that he gave His only begotten Son, that whosoever believeth in Him should not perish, but have everlasting life. For God sent not his son into the world to condemn the world, but that the world through him might be saved." (Jn.3:16-17)

  "For this is good and acceptable in the sight of God our Saviour; who will have all men to be saved, and to come unto the knowledge of the truth." (1 Ti.2:3-4)

1/04

The Teacher's Outline & Study Bible™

is written for God's servants to use in their study, teaching, and preaching of God's Holy Word...

- To share the Word of God with the world.
- To help the believer, both minister and layman alike, in his understanding, preaching, and teaching of God's Word.
- To do everything we possibly can to lead men, women, boys and girls to give their hearts and lives to Jesus Christ and to secure the eternal life which He offers.
- To do all we can to minister to the needy of the world.
- To give Jesus Christ His proper place, the place the Word gives Him. Therefore, no work of Leadership Ministries Worldwide will ever be personalized.

ACKNOWLEDGMENTS AND BIBLIOGRAPHY

Every child of God is precious to the Lord and deeply loved. And every child as a servant of the Lord touches the lives of those who come in contact with him or his ministry. The writing ministries of the following servants have touched this work, and we are grateful that God brought their writings our way. We hereby acknowledge their ministry to us, being fully aware that there are so many others down through the years whose writings have touched our lives and who deserve mention, but the weaknesses of our minds have caused them to fade from memory. May our wonderful Lord continue to bless the ministry of these dear servants, and the ministries of us all as we diligently labor to reach the world for Christ and to meet the desperate needs of those who suffer so much.

THE GREEK SOURCES

1. *Expositor's Greek Testament*, Edited by W. Robertson Nicoll. Grand Rapids, MI: Eerdmans Publishing Co., 1970.

2. Robertson, A.T. *Word Pictures in the New Testament*. Nashville, TN: Broadman Press, 1930.

3. Thayer, Joseph Henry. *Greek-English Lexicon of the New Testament*. New York: American Book Co.

4. Vincent, Marvin R. *Word Studies in the New Testament*. Grand Rapids, MI: Eerdmans Publishing Co., 1969.

5. Vine, W.E. *Expository Dictionary of New Testament Words*. Old Tappan, NJ: Fleming H. Revell Co.

6. Wuest, Kenneth S. *Word Studies in the Greek New Testament*. Grand Rapids, MI: Eerdmans Publishing Co., 1953.

THE REFERENCE WORKS

7. *Cruden's Complete Concordance of the Old & New Testament*. Philadelphia, PA: The John C. Winston Co., 1930.

8. Josephus' *Complete Works*. Grand Rapids, MI: Kregel Publications, 1981.

9. Lockyer, Herbert, Series of Books, including his Books on *All the Men, Women, Miracles, and Parables of the Bible*. Grand Rapids, MI: Zondervan Publishing House.

10. *Nave's Topical Bible*. Nashville, TN: The Southwestern Co.

11. *The Amplified New Testament*. (Scripture Quotations are from the Amplified New Testament, Copyright 1954, 1958, 1987 by the Lockman Foundation. Used by permission.)

12. *The Four Translation New Testament* (Including King James, New American Standard, Williams - New Testament In the Language of the People, Beck - New Testament In the Language of Today.) Minneapolis, MN: World Wide Publications.

13. *The New Compact Bible Dictionary*, Edited by T. Alton Bryant. Grand Rapids, MI: Zondervan Publishing House, 1967.

14. *The New Thompson Chain Reference Bible.* Indianapolis, IN: B.B. Kirkbride Bible Co., 1964.

THE COMMENTARIES

15. Barclay, William. *The Letters of James and Peter*. Philadelphia, PA: Westminster Press, 1958.

16. Bruce, F.F. *The Epistle to the Colossians*. Westwood, NJ: Fleming H. Revell Co., 1968.

17. ——. *Epistle to the Hebrews*. Grand Rapids, MI: Eerdmanns Publishing Co., 1964.

18. ——. *The Epistles of John*. Old Tappan, NJ: Fleming H. Revell Co., 1970.

19. Criswell, W.A. *Expository Sermons on Revelation.* Grand Rapids, MI: Zondervan Publishing House, 1962-66.

20. Greene Oliver. *The Epistles of John.* Greenville, SC: The Gospel Hour, Inc., 1966.

21. ——. *The Epistles of Paul the Apostle to the Hebrews*. Greenville, SC: The Gospel Hour, Inc., 1965.

22. ——. *The Epistles of Paul the Apostle to Timothy & Titus*. Greenville, SC: The Gospel Hour, Inc., 1964.

23. ——. *The Revelation Verse by Verse Study*. Greenville, SC: The Gospel Hour, Inc., 1963.

24. Henry, Matthew. *Commentary on the Whole Bible*. Old Tappan, NJ: Fleming H. Revell Co.

25. Hodge, Charles. *Exposition on Romans & on Corinthians*. Grand Rapids, MI: Eerdmans Publishing Co., 1972-1973.

26. Ladd, George Eldon. *A Commentary On the Revelation of John*. Grand Rapids, MI: Eerdmans Publishing Co., 1972-1973.

27. Leupold, H.C. *Exposition of Daniel*. Grand Rapids, MI: Baker Book House, 1969.

28. Newell, William R. *Hebrews, Verse by Verse*. Chicago, IL: Moody Press.

29. Robertson, A.T. *Studies in the Epistle of James*. Nashville, TN: Broadman Press.

30. Strauss, Lehman. *Devotional Studies in Philippians*. Neptune, NJ: Loizeaux Brothers.

31. ——. *Colossians & 1 Timothy*. Neptune, NJ: Loizeaux Brothers.

32. ——. *The Book of the Revelation*. Neptune, NJ: Loizeaux Brothers.

33. *The New Testament & Wycliffe Bible Commentary*, Edited by Charles F. Pfeiffer & Everett F. Harrison. New York: The Iverson Associates, 1971. Produced for Moody Monthly. Chicago Moody Press, 1962.

34. *The Pulpit Commentary*, Edited by H.D.M. Spence & Joseph S. Exell. Grand Rapids, MI: Eerdmans Publishing Co., 1950.

35. Tasker, RVG. *The General Epistle of James*. "Tyndale New Testament Commentaries." Grand Rapids, MI: Eerdmans Publishing Co., 1956.

36. Thomas, W.H. Griffith. *Hebrews, A Devotional Commentary*. Grand Rapids, MI: Eerdmans Publishing Co., 1970.

37. ——. Griffith. *Studies in Colossians & Philemon*. Grand Rapids, MI: Baker Book House, 1973.

38. *Tyndale New Testament Commentaries*. Grand Rapids, MI: Eerdmans Publishing Co., Began in 1958.

39. Walker, Thomas. *Acts of the Apostles*. Chicago, IL: Moody Press, 1965.

40. Walvoord, John. *The Thessalonian Epistles*. Grand Rapids, MI: Zondervan Publishing House, 1973.

OTHER SOURCES

41. Berry, John, Editor. *Foxe's Book of Martyrs*. Grand Rapids, MI: Baker Books, 1978.

42. Colson, Charles. *The Difference Faith Makes*, on BreakPoint, December 19, 2002.

43. *God's Little Devotional Book*. Tulsa, OK: Honor Books, Inc., 1995.

44. Green, Michael P. *1500 Illustrations for Biblical Preaching*. Grand Rapids, MI: Baker Books, 2000.

45. Jones, G. Curtis. *1000 Illustrations for Preaching and Teaching*. Nashville, TN: Broadman Press, 1986.

46. Knight, Walter B. *Knight's Master Book of 4,000 Illustrations*. Grand Rapids, MI: Eerdmans Publishing Co., 1994.

47. Krivolahvek, Ken. *Rejoicin' an' Repentin'*. Olathe, KS: KLK Ministries, 2002.

48. Kyle, Ted and John Todd. *A Treasury of Bible Illustrations*. Chattanooga, TN: AMG Publishers, 1995.

49. Macartney, Clarence E. *Macartney's Illustrations*. New York, NY: Abingdon Press, 1946.

50. McHenry, Raymond. *McHenry's Stories for the Soul*. Peabody, MA: Hendrickson Publishers, 2001.

51. Price, Charles S. *The Real Faith*. Plainfield, NJ: Logos International, 1940.

52. Reed, John W. *1100 Illustrations from the Writings of D. L. Moody*. Grand Rapids, MI: Baker Books, 1990.

53. Rowell, Edward K., Editor. *Fresh Illustrations for Preaching and Teaching*. Grand Rapids, MI: Co-published by Christianity Today, Inc., and Baker Books, 1997.

54. Smith, James. *Handfuls on Purpose*, 10 vols. Grand Rapids, MI: Eerdmans Publishing Co., 1947.

55. Steele, Jr., Richard A. and Evelyn Stoner, Editors. *Heartwarming Bible Illustration*. Chattanooga, TN: AMG Publishers, 1998.

56. ——. *Practical Bible Illustrations from Yesterday and Today*. Chattanooga, TN: AMG Publishers, 1996.

57. Tan, Paul Lee. *Encyclopedia of 15,000 Illustrations*. Rockville, MD: Assurance Publishers, 1988.

58. Wiersbe, Warren W. *Be Mature*. Colorado Springs, CO: Chariot Victor Publishing, 1978.

MISCELLANEOUS ABBREVIATIONS

& = and

Bckgrd. = Background

Bc. = Because

Circ. = Circumstance

Concl. = Conclusion

Cp. = Compare

Ct. = Contrast

Dif.= Different

e.g. = for example

Et. = Eternal

f. = following

Govt. = Government

Id.= Identity or Identification

Illust. = Illustration

K.= Kingdom

No.= Number

N.T.= New Testament

O.T.= Old Testament

p./pp.= page/pages

Pt.= Point

Quest. = Question

Rel. = Religion

Resp. = Responsibility

Rev.= Revelation

Rgt. = Righteousness

Thru = Through

v./vv.= verse/verses

How To Use

THE TEACHER'S OUTLINE AND STUDY BIBLE™ (TOSB)

To gain maximum benefit, here is all you do. Follow these easy steps, using the sample outline below.

1 Study Title

2 Major Points

3 Subpoints

4 Commentary, Questions, Application, Illustrations
(Follows Scripture)

	B. The Steps to Peace (Part II): Prayer & Positive Thinking, 4:6-9
1. Peace comes through prayer a. The charge: Do not worry or be anxious b. The remedy: Prayer 1) About everything 2) With requests 3) With thanksgiving c. The promise: Peace 1) Peace that passes all understanding 2) Peace that keeps our hearts & minds **2. Peace comes through positive thinking** a. The charge: Think & practice things that are... 1) True 2) Honest 3) Just 4) Pure	6 Be careful for nothing; but in every thing by prayer and supplication with thanksgiving let your requests be made known unto God. 7 And the peace of God, which passeth all understanding, shall keep your hearts and minds through Christ Jesus. 8 Finally, brethren, whatsoever things are true, whatsoever things are honest, whatsoever things are just, whatsoever things are pure, whatsoever things are lovely, whatsoever

1. First: Read the **Study Title** two or three times so that the subject sinks in.
2. Then: Read the **Study Title** and the **Major Points** (Pts.1,2,3) together quickly. Do this several times and you will quickly grasp the overall theme of the Scripture.
3. Now: Read both the **Major Points** and **Subpoints**. Do this slower than Step 2. Note how the points are beside the applicable verse and simply state what the Scripture is saying—in *Outline* form.
4. Read the **Commentary**. As you read and re-read, pray that the Holy Spirit will bring to your attention exactly what you should study and teach. It's all there, outlined and fully developed, just waiting for you to explore.

Teachers, Please Note:

⇒ Cover the **Scripture** and the **Major Points** with your students. Drive the **Scripture** and **Major Points** into their hearts and minds.

(Continue on next page)

⇒ Cover *only some of the commentary* with your students, not all (unless of course you have plenty of time). Cover only as much commentary as is needed to get the major points across.

Do NOT feel that you must...

- cover all the commentary under each point
- share every illustration
- ask all the questions

An abundance of commentary is given so you can find just what you need for...

- your own style of teaching
- your own emphasis
- your own class needs

PLEASE NOTE: It is of utmost importance that you (and your study group) grasp the Scripture, the Study Title, and Major Points. It is this that the Holy Spirit will make alive to your heart and that you will more likely remember and use day by day.

MAJOR POINTS include:

APPLICATIONS:
Use these to show how the Scripture applies to everyday life.

ILLUSTRATIONS:
Simply a window that allows enough light in the lesson so a point can be more clearly seen. A suggestion: Do not just "read" through an illustration if the illustration is a story, but learn it and make it your own. Then give the illustration life by communicating it with *excitement & energy.*

QUESTIONS:
These are designed to stimulate thought and discussion.

A CLOSER LOOK:
In some of the studies, you will see a portion boxed in and entitled: "A Closer Look." This discussion will be a closer study on a particular point. It is generally too detailed for a Sunday School class session, but more adaptable for personal study or an in depth Bible Study class.

PERSONAL JOURNAL:
At the close of every lesson there is space for you to record brief thoughts regarding the impact of the lesson on your life. As you study through the Bible, you will find these comments invaluable as you look back upon them.

Now, may our wonderful Lord bless you mightily as you study and teach His Holy Word. And may our Lord grant you much fruit: many who will become greater servants and witnesses for Him.

REMEMBER!

THE TEACHER'S OUTLINE & STUDY BIBLE™ is the only study material that actually outlines the Bible verse by verse for you right beside the Scripture. As you accumulate the various books of *THE TEACHER'S OUTLINE & STUDY BIBLE*™ for your study and teaching, you will have the Bible outlined book by book, passage by passage, and verse by verse.

The outlines alone makes saving every book a must! (Also encourage your students, if you are teaching, to keep their student edition. They also have the unique verse by verse outline of Scripture in their version.)

Just think for a moment. Over the course of your life, you will have your very own personalized commentary of the Bible. No other book besides the Bible will mean as much to you because it will contain your insights, your struggles, your victories, and your recorded moments with the Lord.

> **"Study to show thyself approved unto God, a workman that needeth not to be ashamed, rightly dividing the word of truth" (2 Ti.2:15).**
>
> **"All scripture is given by inspiration of God, and is profitable for doctrine, for reproof, for correction, for instruction in righteousness: that the man of God may be perfect, throughly furnished unto all good works" (2 Ti.3:16-17).**

A SPECIAL NOTE FOR THE BIBLE STUDY LEADER

Dear Teacher,

The teaching material you hold in your hands gives your church the *maximum flexibility* in scheduling for the church year or for any Bible study program. *The Teacher's Outline and Study Bible*™ (TOSB) has been designed to help you in your teaching ministry. The wealth of material makes the TOSB the most unique Bible study material anywhere. The name says it all:

⇒ The *Teacher's* has been designed just for you, God's dear servant, the teacher of God's Holy word.
⇒ *Outline* makes the material unique as every verse has been outlined—point by point—subject by subject—just for you.
⇒ *Study* allows you, the teacher, to study commentary that has been developed and has drawn upon over forty different sources. At your disposal are well-thought-out points that explain in simple language what the Scripture means. Suggestions for opening and closing each lesson assure that your students will be caught up from the beginning to the end. Practical points of application help you to bring the truth to whatever level of student you are teaching. Gripping illustrations have been interspersed through each lesson, illustrations guaranteed to hold the attention of your students as you drive home the point.. finally, questions that are thought-provoking and discussion-oriented are a part of *every* point in the lesson. Imagine—all the benefits of the time spent collecting this study material are right in *your* hands, waiting for you to glean what *you need* for your next lesson.
⇒ *Bible* is the foundation of *The Teacher's Outline and Study Bible*™. God's Holy Word, outlined for you—verse by verse, point by point, subject by subject—gives you, the teacher, the great advantage of having God's Word outlined, explained, made practical, and illustrated.

"Go ye therefore, and teach all nations"

(Mt.28:19)

OUTLINE OF EPHESIANS

THE TEACHER'S OUTLINE & SERMON BIBLE™ is *unique*. It differs from all other Study Bibles & Sermon Resource Materials in that every Passage and Subject are outlined right beside the Scripture. When you choose any *Subject* below and turn to the reference, you have not only the Scripture, but you discover the Scripture and Subject *already outlined for you—verse by verse*.

For a quick example, choose one of the subjects below and turn over to the Scripture, and you will find this marvelous help for faster, easier, and more accurate use.

A suggestion: For the quickest overview of Ephesians, first read *all the major titles* (I, II, III, etc.), then come back and read the subtitles.

OUTLINE OF EPHESIANS

PAGE

THE EPISTLE OF PAUL THE APOSTLE TO THE

EPHESIANS

INTRODUCTION

AUTHOR: Paul. Few critics deny this. His ministry at Ephesus is covered in Ac.18:18-21; 19:2-41; 20:17-35.

DATE: Probably between A.D. 60-63. The letter was written while Paul was in prison in Rome (Ep.3:1; 4:1; 6:20). Paul probably arrived in Rome in the spring of A.D. 60 or 61. He was under house arrest for two years (Ac.28:30). During his two year imprisonment (either A.D. 60-62 or A.D. 61-63) he wrote the letters that are usually called "The Prison Epistles": Ephesians, Philippians, Colossians, and Philemon.

TO WHOM WRITTEN: Uncertain. There are strong reasons why the words "to the Ephesians" are questioned.

1. The words "to the Ephesians" are not in the oldest and best manuscripts of the Greek New Testament (The Chester Beatty Papyrus, about A.D. 200; the great fourth century Codices Sinaiticus and Vaticanus). The third century writer Origen states that the words "to the Ephesians was not in the original text." Basil and Jerome, of the fourth century, said that the best manuscripts did not have the words in their texts.[1]

2. The letter is the most impersonal of Paul's letters. There is no affection or warm touch in it—no personal greeting—no personal message. This is strange, for Paul spent at least three years in Ephesus (Ac.20:17-35).

3. The indication is that Paul and the recipients of the letter did not know one another. The word "heard" is used instead of the word "know" (Ep.1:15; 3:2).

4. The letters to the Ephesians and Colossians have much the same message. This points toward Paul writing both letters about the same time. In fact, Paul mentions another letter saying it too was being circulated among the churches about the same time that Colossians was being circulated (Co.4:16).

The evidence points to a wonderful truth! The letter is from "Paul...to all those who are saints and faithful in Christ Jesus." It is written to saints everywhere, to all generations. It is written to the believers and the churches of today.

PURPOSE: Paul writes Ephesians for at least two reasons.

1. To reveal the purpose of God for the whole universe. God has shown His purpose through His Son, Jesus Christ, and He is working out His purpose through the church, which is His body on earth.

---

[1] Francis Foulkes. *The Epistle of Paul to the Ephesians.* (Grand Rapids, MI: Eerdmans Publishing Co., n.d.), p.17.

2. To encourage the church to walk in a spirit of oneness and unity: to "be ye kind one to another, tenderhearted, forgiving one another, even as God for Christ's sake hath forgiven you" (Ep.4:32).

Note the word "together" (Ep.1:10; 2:5, 6, 22) and the word "one" (Ep.2:15, 16, 18; 4:4, 5, 6).

SPECIAL FEATURES:

1. **The City of Ephesus**. At its height Ephesus was the most important city along the coast of Asia Minor. Two hundred and thirty cities dotted the coast line of Asia Minor. Many had ideal harbors, but Ephesus was the queen among these coast communities. The city had been founded to command one of the main highways of Asia Minor. Its attraction was not only its natural harbor, but the rich, fertile land that covered the inland area.

Ephesus was, of course, a great commercial city. Its natural harbor and strategic location on one of the main roads of the world made it such. However, in the middle of the first century, the harbor had silted up so badly that trade had declined astronomically from the days of Ephesian glory. There had been attempts to drag the silt out, but the efforts were half-hearted and finally abandoned. The people's hearts were just not in the effort. Part of the reason for this attitude was the successful and profitable trade Ephesus enjoyed from its religious cult. The great temple of Diana, or Artemis, was there. Diana was the goddess who had a grotesque head and many breasts and focused upon the sensual pleasure of the flesh. The worshipping pilgrims found their satisfaction in prostitution with a host of priestesses who promoted the cult of the goddess. A great trade of silversmiths had developed over the years, and tourist commercialism boomed year-round. This accounts for the guild of silversmiths finding the crowds an easy mark for arousing opposition against Paul (Ac.19:24). As the years went by, the great harbor silted up more and more, and the Ephesians depended more and more upon the trade that came from their religion and superstition. The natural harbor of Smyrna, which lay close by, became a more suitable port and began to take away more and more of the commercial traffic of Ephesus. As a result Ephesus became a dying city, living on its past reputation as a religious and philosophical center. The great city of Ephesus had a disease, the disease of sensual unrighteousness, and the disease did its work: it corrupted the people. The people, sensual and self-centered, lost their will and willingness to ply a commendable trade. Thus, the disease of Ephesus proved mortal. The "lampstand" of Ephesus crumbled, and the light of Ephesus died out (see Re.2:1-7, esp. 5).

2. **The Church at Ephesus**. The church in Ephesus had a small beginning. When Paul visited Ephesus, he found only twelve believers in the city. They had been won to the Lord by the immature but impressive preacher Appalls. As a result they had been misinformed on the presence of the Holy Spirit; they seemed to lack a consciousness of the Spirit in the life of the believer and the awareness that He had already been sent into the world (Ac.19:1-7). After Paul's instruction to these twelve, he began to teach in the synagogue. He taught for three months, but the Jews were hardened and refused to believe the gospel. They murmured against the message. Therefore, Paul moved the church into the school of a philosopher, Tyrannus. There he preached Christ for two whole years. During this time it is said that the church was

instrumental in sounding forth the Word throughout all Asia: "So all they which dwelt in Asia heard the Word of the Lord Jesus, both Jews and Greeks (Ac.19:10).

The Lord worked special miracles by Paul in Ephesus and the church witnessed some amazing things. From all evidence, the spectacular was necessary in order to get through to the people. As always, God did everything He could to reach a people. These experiences show the great love and movement of God toward man (see Ac.19:11-20). In viewing these accounts, we must keep the background of the city in mind. Ephesus was a hot bed of Oriental magic and superstition. The people were an emotional and sensual lot, easily moved to feelings. They were a devoted people, an expressive people, a loving people, and equally a lovable people (Re.2:1-7, esp. 4).

As Paul preached and God worked miracles, many believed and the church grew mightily. The believers gave great evidence of changed lives by living for Christ right in the middle of an immoral and pagan society. On one occasion, the church demonstrated its new found faith by building a great bonfire and setting aflame all of its pagan and magical literature.

3. **The Great Message of Ephesians is "Reconciliation."** Paul deals with the major problem of man—the problem of division, disunity, and disharmony. He deals with the major divisions and dissensions throughout the universe.

a. Man is seen divided against God (Ep.2:1f).
b. Man is seen divided against man (Ep.2:11f).
c. Christians are seen out of harmony with Christians (Ep.4:1f).
d. Christians are seen out of harmony with God (Ep.5:1f).
e. Family members are seen divided against family members (Ep.5:22f).
f. Slaves (employees) are seen divided against masters (employers) (Ep.6:5f).
g. Man is seen out of harmony with cosmic powers (Ep.2:2; 6:10, 11-12; 3:10, 15; see 1:10, 20-21. See also Ro.8:18 for man's division against nature).

This terrible and terrifying division is said to hound and haunt man and to demand his constant attention and struggle. Paul's answer is one-fold. And it should be noted, his answer is one of the great revelations of Scripture. "[God] having made known unto us the mystery of his will...that in the dispensation of the fullness of times he might *gather together in one all things in Christ*, both which are in heaven, and which are *on earth*" (Ep.1:9-10).

Christ is the answer to division, to disunity, and to disharmony. He is the One who breaks down all barriers; He is the One who reconciles all things.

a. He reconciles man to God by the blood of the cross (Ep.2:4-13, esp. 13).
b. He reconciles man to man by bringing all men together into one body, His church (Ep.2:13-22; see 1:22-23).
c. He reconciles Christians to Christians by the power of the Holy Spirit and by giving individual gifts and functions for each member to perform (Ep.4:1-32).
d. He reconciles believers to God by the power and fruit of the Holy Spirit (Ep.5:1-21).

e. He reconciles family members to family members by giving the example of Christ's love for the church (Ep.5:22-24).
f. He reconciles slaves (employees) to masters (employers) by putting both on an equal footing before Christ (Ep.6:5-9).
g. He enables man to overcome the cosmic and spiritual powers and the evil forces of the universe by the armor of God (Ep.6:10-18).

4. **The Great Picture of Ephesians is "God's Redemptive Purpose."** His redemptive purpose reads like a theological picture of four scenes.

a. Scene 1: God's Election (Ep.1:3-14). Before the earth was ever founded, God chose (the literal word is "elected") believers in Christ. He chose all who would trust and commit themselves to Christ.
b. Scene 2: God's Reconciliation (Ep.2:1-18). All things are out of harmony; all is presently out of order. Division, disunity, and disharmony reign now. But the day is coming when God is to gather all things together, as one, and place them before Jesus Christ in His Kingdom—all things that are in heaven and earth (Ep.1:9-10). Christ is the center and the cord that binds all things together. He is the great Reconciler, the One to whom all things can look for salvation and peace—eternally.
c. Scene 3: God's Body, His Church (Ep.2:19-3:13; see 1:22-23). God has a body, a body of people that He is supernaturally *recreating*. He is *recreating* them to experience the great truth of reconciliation and peace and to carry the message to all other men. Christ is God's instrument of reconciliation, and the church is Christ's instrument of reconciliation.
d. Scene 4: The Church, the Followers of Christ (Ep.4:1-6:20). The followers of Christ are to walk worthy of such a glorious life by being reconciled as one. They are to live together in unity and harmony, and they are to carry the message of reconciliation to a world swallowed up in division.

5. **The Great Similarity to Colossians**. There are more than fifty-five verses that are exactly the same, and twenty-five verses that are very similar. This means that of the one hundred and fifty-five verses in Ephesians, seventy-five are closely connected with Colossians. Both Ephesians and Colossians begin with a doctrinal section and end with a practical section, and both were apparently delivered by the same man, Tychicus (Ep.6:20; see Co.4:7).

Such similarity is to be expected. Paul wrote both while in prison in Rome, probably one right after the other.

6. **Ephesians has been called "The Queen of the Epistles."** It is a book greatly loved; it is probably loved more than any other book by most people. With strong wings it soars among the heights of theological thought and glides upon the winds of the greatest of truths.

It is like the delivery of a great sermon that holds a person spellbound. It is like the greatest of prayers that draws a person into the very presence of God. It is like a great doxology that leaves a person with a deep sense of worship.

THE EPISTLE OF PAUL THE APOSTLE TO THE

EPHESIANS

	CHAPTER 1 **GREETING: THE CALL OF GOD, 1:1-2**
1. God's call to Paul **2. God's call to the church & its believers** a. To the saints & the faithful	Paul, an apostle of Jesus Christ by the will of God, to the saints which are at Ephesus, and to the faithful in Christ Jesus:
b. To receive grace & peace	2 Grace be to you, and peace, from God our Father, and from the Lord Jesus Christ.

Introduction
GREETING: THE CALL OF GOD
Ephesians 1:1-2

Study 1: **THE GREAT CALL OF GOD TO BELIEVERS**

Text: **Ephesians 1:1-2**

Aim: To seek and respond to God's call upon your life.

Memory Verse:

"But ye are a chosen generation, a royal priesthood, an holy nation, a peculiar people; that ye should show forth the praises of Him who hath *called* you out of darkness into His marvelous light" (1 Peter 2:9).

INTRODUCTION:
You've heard that God has a plan for the believer's life, a plan for every one of us. Yet when it comes to you personally, perhaps you have not really understood what God wants you to do with your life. How often have you asked:

⇒ Is there supposed to be more to life than this?
⇒ When will God show *me* His plan for my life, just what He wants me to do?
⇒ Why doesn't God tell me in plain speech what He wants me to do with my life?

God wants us to understand His call upon our lives, but to understand, we must investigate His call. Note how Paul begins this letter to the Ephesians. He begins with one of the greatest subjects imaginable—the call of God. Nothing could be any more meaningful to a person than to be called by God Himself, the sovereign LORD and Majesty of the universe.

Ephesians 1:1-2

Outline:

1. God's call to Paul (v.1).
2. God's call to the church and its believers (vv.1-2).

1. GOD'S CALL TO PAUL (v.1).

Paul says that he was "an apostle of Jesus Christ by the will of God." Note four significant points.

1. Paul was greatly privileged. There is no greater privilege in all the world than the privilege of serving Jesus Christ. Jesus Christ is the very Son of God Himself, the Supreme Lord of the universe in all its enormity. No matter how far out the universe reaches and no matter how many universes there are, Jesus Christ is the *Majestic Lord* of all. He rules and reigns as God Almighty.

2. The word "apostle" means one called and sent forth on a very special mission. The mission given to Paul was that of a messenger. The Lord Jesus Christ called Paul to proclaim the glorious message of salvation to the world.

The point is this: Jesus Christ is not only the Sovereign Lord of the universe, He is the Savior of the world. God so loved the world that He gave His only Son to save the world. Any person who believes in Jesus Christ will not perish but have everlasting life (Jn.3:16). *Christ needs messengers* who will take the glorious news of salvation to the world. This was the call of God to Paul: to be a messenger of Jesus Christ to the world.

> **Application:**
> Christ needs messengers. Many hundreds of years have passed and the world still has not been reached with the glorious news of Jesus Christ, God's very own Son. There will be great sorrow to the man who has been called and does not go! If God calls us, we must go or else face a terrible day of accountability.

> **"Ye have not chosen me, but I have chosen you, and ordained you, that ye should go and bring forth fruit, and that your fruit should remain: that whatsoever ye shall ask of the Father in my name, he may give it you" (Jn.15:16).**

3. Paul was possessed by Jesus Christ. The supreme Lord and Majesty of the universe had humbled Himself to come to this earth and to save it. God's very own Son has given man the privilege of knowing Him in the most personal way, as his Savior and Lord. Paul knew Christ—knew Him personally—knew Him as his Savior. Imagine knowing the Son of God personally! No greater privilege could exist. Paul knew this; therefore, he surrendered his life completely to Christ. All he was and all he had, Paul turned over to Christ. He was possessed and obsessed with Christ. He lived for Christ and for Christ alone. Christ was Paul's Savior, but He was also his Lord and Master. He was not his own to do as he willed; he was Christ's, to do only as Christ willed.

> **"Then said Jesus unto his disciples, If any man will come after me, let him deny himself, and take up his cross, and follow me" (Mt.16:24).**

4. Paul was called by the will of God. Who he was and what he was doing was God's will. His work and employment were chosen by God, not him. He had not chosen the ministry because it was a good profession to enter nor because some friends thought he would make a good preacher. He was a minister because God had called him to be a minister.

APPLICATION:
How many of us can say that what we are doing is God's will? How many of us are sure that our work and profession are of God, that we are right where God wants us? Are we working and serving where God wants us or where we want to be? Are we in God's will or out of God's will?

> **"I delight to do thy will, O my God: yea, thy law is within my heart" (Ps.40:8).**

ILLUSTRATION:
How many of you know the story behind the hymn, I Surrender All? All of us can relate to this story as it was told by composers J.W. Van DeVenter and W.S. Weeden:

> *For many years I had been studying art. My whole life was wrapped up in its pursuit and the farthest thing from my mind was active Christian service,...My dream was to become an outstanding and famous artist.... The Spirit of God was strongly urging me to give up teaching and to enter the evangelistic field but I would not yield. I still had the burning desire to be an artist. This battle raged for five years. At last the time came when I could hold out no longer and I surrendered my all—my time and my talents. It was then that a new day was ushered into my life. I became an Evangelist and discovered that deep down in my soul was hidden a talent hitherto unknown to me. God had hidden a song in my heart and touching a tender chord He caused me to sing songs I had never sung before.*
>
> *I wrote "I Surrender All" in memory of the time when, after the long struggle, I had surrendered and dedicated my life to active Christian service for the Lord.*

All to Jesus I surrender, All to Him I freely give;
I will ever love and trust Him, In His presence daily live.
I surrender all, I surrender all,
All to Thee, my blessed Savior, I surrender all.[1]

QUESTIONS:
1. Have you been called by God to be a messenger of Jesus Christ to the world?
2. Have you surrendered to God's call to share Christ with the world?
3. Paul was possessed and obsessed with Christ. Are you? What kind of life does a person live if he is possessed by Christ?
4. When were you first aware of God's call upon your life?
5. Why is it important for you to know God's plan and will for your life?
6. Have you fully surrendered to God's call? If not, what can you do that will help you to surrender all?

2. GOD'S CALL TO THE CHURCH AND ITS BELIEVERS (vv.1-2).

This is Paul's greeting to the church, and it is very similar to the usual greeting he gave to all churches. Note the depth of meaning in what he says: he is actually covering the scope of God's call to a church and its believers.

1. God calls believers to be *saints and to be faithful*.

---

1 Alfred B. Smith. *Al Smith's Treasury of Hymn Histories.* (Greenville, SC: Better Music Publications, Inc., 1985), p.53.

a. In the Bible the word "saint" does not refer to just a few people who have done great works for God. The word "saint" means set apart, consecrated, sacred, and holy. A saint is a follower of the Lord Jesus Christ who has been set apart to live for God. The saint has given himself to live a consecrated, sacred, and holy life—all for the glory of God. Note that believers are *saints* in both senses:

⇒ Believers are *saints* in the sense that they have been given a new heart by God: a heart that is renewed and recreated in righteousness and true holiness.

"And that ye put on the new man, which after God is created in righteousness and true holiness" (Ep.4:24).

⇒ Believers are *saints* in the sense that they are set apart to live consecrated and holy lives in this world.

"As obedient children, not fashioning yourselves according to the former lusts in your ignorance: but as he which hath called you is holy, so be ye holy in all manner of conversation [behavior]" (1 Pe.1:14-15).

b. The word "faithful" means a person who has placed his faith in the Lord Jesus Christ. The faithful person is a person who has looked upon the Lord Jesus Christ and…

- believed that Christ would save him
- counted Christ worthy of his trust
- placed his confidence in Christ and His Word
- entrusted his salvation into the hands of Christ
- committed his life to Christ

Very simply, the faithful are those who have surrendered and set their lives apart to Jesus Christ, trusting Him to save them. This is the very first call God gives to people: to be the saints and the faithful of the Lord Jesus Christ.

APPLICATION:
Every human being should make absolutely sure that God counts him among the saints and the faithful of the world. Unless he is so counted, there is no escape from the enslavements and corruptions of this world; and most tragic of all, his end is death, eternal death.

"And as Moses lifted up the serpent in the wilderness, even so must the Son of man be lifted up: that whosoever believeth in him should not perish, but have everlasting life" (Jn.3:14-15).

2. God calls believers to grace and peace. Grace is probably the most meaningful word in the language of men.

a. Grace means all the favors and gifts of God. It means all the good and perfect gifts of God, all the good and beneficial things He gives us and does for us, whether physical, material, or spiritual (Ja.1:17).

"In whom we have redemption through his blood, the forgiveness of sins, according to the riches of his grace" (Ep.1:7).

b. Grace means the favor of God showered upon men—men who did not deserve His favor. When the early Christians looked at what God had done for men, they had to add a deeper and much richer meaning to the word *grace*. For God had saved sinners, those who had acted against Him, men who were...
   - "without strength" (Ro.5:6)
   - "ungodly" (Ro.5:6)
   - "sinners" (Ro.5:8)
   - "enemies" (Ro.5:10)

   No other word so expresses the richness of the heart and mind of God. This is the distinctive difference between God's grace and man's grace. Whereas man sometimes does favors for his friends and thereby can be said to be gracious, God has done a thing unheard of among men: He has given His very own Son to die for His enemies (Ro.5:8-10).

   1) God's grace is not earned. It is something completely undeserved and unmerited.

      "For by grace are ye saved through faith; and that not of yourselves: it is the gift of God: not of works, lest any man should boast" (Eph.2:8-9).

   2) God's grace is the free gift of God. God extends His grace out toward man.

      "But God, who is rich in mercy, for his great love wherewith he loved us, even when we were dead in sins, hath quickened us together with Christ, (by grace ye are saved)" (Ep.2:4-5).

   3) God's grace is the only way man can be saved.

      "If through the offence of one [Adam] many be dead, much more the grace of God, and the gift by grace, which is by one man, Jesus Christ, hath abounded unto many" (Ro.5:15).

ILLUSTRATION:
Do you struggle with God's call upon your life? You can find great comfort in the presence of other Christians. For example, this is a story that could happen in any Christian church when God's people fulfill their call.

"Unemployed!" In the eyes of many, Bobby became just another impersonal statistic to join the ranks of the unemployed. At one moment, he had a secure position in his company; but the next moment saw him with his pink slip in hand—the victim of an unforgiving economy. For many people like Bobby, they would have to go it alone. But this was not Bobby's testimony.

Bobby found himself surrounded by people in his church who understood God's call upon their lives. Because God had called them, they were to live like saints and be faithful to His call as they became a vessel of God's grace and peace.

They were sensitive to Bobby's struggles and reached out to him in practical ways. Several of them committed to pray for him on a regular basis. Others in the church began to network with the business world in seeking the right career job for Bobby. Still, there were others who used their spiritual gift of encouragement to minister to Bobby when he needed another boost.

Like a light bulb that brightens a dark room, Bobby began to see for himself that God had a special call upon his life. God had not called him to trust in a career. Instead, God had called him to trust in the One who provides everything—including careers.

QUESTIONS:

1. Paul knew he was an apostle of Christ because it was God's will. In your life, have you made major decisions concerning your career choice without God? Knowing what you know now, what changes would you have made?
2. What has been your greatest struggle in doing the will of God?
3. How would you explain the call of God to a non-Christian friend? Does God have a plan for them also?
4. Do you know anybody like *Bobby*? What could you do to help someone like him?
5. Are you truly faithful? Why do you think God wants you to be faithful?
6. What are some traits of a faithful person? How does a person show that he is faithful to the Lord?
7. Have you been obedient to God's first call: trusting Christ to save you? Have you surrendered to Him and set your life apart for His purpose? If not, you are invited to do so now. God loves you and He has a plan for your life. Allow Him to work His will in your heart by inviting Jesus into your life. (Then go and tell a friend about your decision).

SUMMARY:

The Christian's greatest blessing and privilege is to be called by God. God has set us apart to be faithful messengers. In review of these two major points, we learned about:

1. God's call to Paul
2. God's call to the church and its believers

In light of God's call to you, you must now respond in obedience.

PERSONAL JOURNAL NOTES
(Reflection & Response)

1. The most important thing that I learned from this lesson was:

2. The area that I need to work on the most is:

3. I can apply this lesson to my life by:

4. Closing Statement of Commitment:

	I. THE ETERNAL PLAN OF GOD FOR THE CHRISTIAN BELIEVER, 1:3-23 **A. The Blessings of God (Part 1), 1:3-7**		
1. God's great blessings are heavenly blessings	3 Blessed be the God and Father of our Lord Jesus Christ, who hath blessed us with all spiritual blessings in heavenly places in Christ:		
2. God has chosen us to be holy & blameless a. How: In Christ b. Purpose: To live before Him in love	4 According as he hath chosen us in him before the foundation of the world, that we should be holy and without blame before him in love:		
		5 Having predestinated us unto the adoption of children by Jesus Christ to himself, according to the good pleasure of his will, 6 To the praise of the glory of his grace, wherein he hath made us accepted in the beloved.	**3. God has adopted us as His sons** a. Predestinated—foreordained, planned—to adopt believers: Was His will b. How: By Christ c. Why: To praise His grace
		7 In whom we have redemption through his blood, the forgiveness of sins, according to the riches of his grace;	**4. God has redeemed us—forgiven our sins** a. How: By Christ's blood b. Source: His grace

Section I
THE ETERNAL PLAN OF GOD FOR THE CHRISTIAN BELIEVER, Ephesians 1:3-23

Study 1: THE BLESSINGS OF GOD (Part One)

Text: **Ephesians 1:3-7**

Aim: To lay hold of the spiritual blessings of God.

Memory Verse:

"Blessed be the God and Father of our Lord Jesus Christ, who hath blessed us with all spiritual blessings in heavenly places in Christ" (Ephesians 1:3).

INTRODUCTION:

Have you ever heard about a person who did not trust banks, so he hid his money some place in his house? Story after story is told about large sums of money being found in mattresses or hidden under floors. More than once, we have heard of people who went lacking in meeting their basic needs during their life. After their death, fortunes were found that had never been touched.

Do you own treasures that you do not use? Many Christian believers do. Many believers live in spiritual poverty when God intended them to live like royalty.

And this brings us to the point of this Scripture: before we met the Lord, He had already invested an eternity of spiritual blessings for the Christian believer. This Scripture deals with God's plan for the world, His eternal plan; it deals with the great blessings of God which He pours out upon those who trust His Son, Jesus Christ, as their Savior.

EPHESIANS 1:3-7

OUTLINE:

1. The power that exalted Christ as the Supreme Head of the church (v.3).
2. God has chosen us to be holy and blameless (v.4).
3. God has adopted us as His sons (vv.5-6).
4. God has redeemed us—forgiven our sins (v.7).

1. GOD'S GREAT BLESSINGSS ARE HEAVENLY BLESSINGS (v.3).

Throughout history God has used two methods of blessings to deal with man. Before Christ, God dealt with man by blessing him with material blessings. He promised Abraham and Israel land and wealth and fame. But Israel misused and hoarded the material blessings. Instead of sharing its blessings with other nations, Israel isolated itself and claimed superiority and God-given rights over other nations of the earth. However, since Christ, God deals with man spiritually, blessing him with spiritual blessings.

Five things should be noted about this.

1. Spiritual blessings *are of the Spirit.* It is the Spirit that controls man and the circumstances that surround him. A man may feel bad; he may be down, depressed and oppressed; but if his spirit is strong, he arises and conquers his feelings. He controls and overcomes the oppressing circumstances, and he lives a victorious day. But if his spirit is weak, whether at work or at play, he often wallows around in self-pity, grumbling and griping and living a defeated day. And too often the days stretch into weeks and months until a person's life is down more than it is up—all because the spirit is too weak to conquer. Thus, the major blessings of God are bound to be blessings that are spiritual—that enable a person to control his life.

2. Spiritual blessings are the very opposite of temporal blessings. They are the *blessings of the inner man*, the blessings of the immortal. But of all blessings, they are the most glorious and satisfying. They are the blessings that erase the loneliness, alienation, and purposelessness of man. They are the blessings that give man an abundance of life.

3. Spiritual blessings are vastly superior to material blessings. They are *permanent and perfect and eternal,* lasting forever. They are of the very same nature as God Himself. Spiritual blessings exist and can be experienced both upon earth (the physical dimension of being) and in heaven (the spiritual dimension of being).

4. Spiritual blessings are found only *in Christ.* Jesus Christ has been raised from the dead and exalted to the right hand of God the Father. He is in heaven, surrounded by all the heavenly atmosphere and blessings. All heavenly blessings are His; therefore, if a person is to experience the spiritual blessings, he must be *in Christ.* If a person is *in Christ*, then he sits *in heaven* with Christ. How is this possible? In God's mind, *faith in Christ* makes a person just like Christ: holy and righteous and acceptable for heaven. Therefore, when a person believes in Christ, God's mind sees the person in Christ; God sees the person identified with Christ, seated in heaven. And being seated in heaven, the person can experience all the blessings of heaven.

5. God dealt with man in material blessings first because man had to learn several things.
   a. *An earthly inheritance does not last.* It is subject to being lost or stolen. We either watch our material possessions deteriorate or else we leave our material possessions behind for others.
   b. *An earthly nation and material inheritance cannot bring peace and security.* Peace and security are of the spirit. Earthly nations and material things are of the earth, of a corruptible nature. Thus nations and material things do not solve the spiritual struggle that man senses within his own being. Neither can nations and material things erase the spiritual divisions between men and between man and God.

c. *Man has within his inner being a basic selfishness and greed.* Man finds a tendency, an unregulated urge, that desires and seeks the material and hoards the corruptible to the neglect of the spiritual.
d. *Man must undergo a basic change of character to be freed of this urge*, this tendency that causes so much bondage, disruption, and division within one's self and between men. Man must be *born again*, made into a *new creation*, created into a *new man*—spiritually, permanently, perfectly, eternally. And such a spiritual creation must be performed by Someone much greater than himself. Man must be recreated by the hand of God Himself.

APPLICATION:
There are no spiritual blessings outside of Christ and heavenly places. In practical terms this means that there is nothing apart from Christ that can satisfy those who love Jesus. Any passion that does not end with Jesus Christ as the destination is simply a counterfeit distraction.

> **"Thou wilt show me the path of life: in Thy presence is fullness of joy; at Thy right hand there are pleasures for evermore" (Ps.16:11).**

If we can not find what we need at His right hand, we have no need of it at all.

ILLUSTRATION:
Will your blessings be there when you need them? Warren Wiersbe shares this humorous illustration with us:

> *One of the funniest cartoons I ever saw showed a pompous lawyer reading a client's last will and testament to a group of greedy relatives. The caption read: "I, John Jones, being of sound mind and body, spent it all!"*
>
> *When Jesus Christ wrote His last will and testament for His church, He made it possible for us to share His spiritual riches. Instead of spending it all, Jesus Christ paid it all...He wrote us into His will, then He died so the will would be in force. Then He arose again that He might become the heavenly Advocate (lawyer) to make sure the terms of the will were correctly followed!*[1]

QUESTIONS:
1. What are some of the material things of this world that men strive for? Do Christian believers get caught up in this also?
2. How can we turn from our basic desire to satisfy our material desires and urges?
3. Do you believe that you have access to all of God's spiritual blessings? How is that possible?
4. Who or what is the source of all spiritual blessings?

2. GOD HAS CHOSEN US TO BE HOLY AND BLAMELESS (v.4).

Just imagine! God determined before the world was ever created that He would have a people…
- who would be "in Him," that is, in His Son, Jesus Christ
- who would be "holy and without blame"
- who would live "before Him in love"—forever and ever

---

1 Warren W. Wiersbe. *The Bible Exposition Commentary*, Vol.2. (Wheaton, IL: Victor Books, 1989), p.10.

This means a most wonderful thing: God wants us to be with Him. God does not want us separated from Him, gripped by sin and shame, sorrow and pain, death and hell. God wants us to live forever and ever with Him. In fact, note that God has determined that some will live with Him and Christ. He has "chosen us"—chosen believers—to live with Him. No amount of rebellion and rejection, cursing and denial of Him will stop His purpose and plan. God will have a people who will live with Him, and He will continue to choose us until He has the number He has intended.

Now, note the great blessing of God: that we should be holy and without blame before Him.

1. The word "holy" means to be set apart and consecrated to God. It is the same word that is used for "saint" in verse one.

> **"Having therefore these promises, dearly beloved, let us cleanse ourselves from all filthiness of the flesh and spirit, perfecting holiness in the fear of God" (2 Co.7:1).**

2. The word "blameless" means to be free from sin, dirt, and filth; to be above reproach and without blemish; to be without fault and defilement.

> **"That ye may be blameless and harmless, the sons of God, without rebuke, in the midst of a crooked and perverse nation, among whom ye shine as lights in the world" (Ph.2:15).**

God has chosen the believer to be perfect. But note: the believer's perfection is *in Christ and in Christ alone*. No man—not even a believer—can live a perfect and sinless life. No man is righteous or ever will be. Jesus Christ is the only Person who has ever lived a sinless and perfect life; therefore, He is the only Person who has the right to live with God. Our only hope of ever living with God is to *believe in Jesus Christ*—believe so much that God will take our faith and count it as the righteousness of Christ.

QUESTIONS:

1. How does it make you feel to know that God chose you?
2. Are you choosing God by separating yourself from the sins of the world and drawing closer to Him?
3. What is your obligation to God in light of all that He has done (according to verse 4)?
4. What is the ultimate goal of being holy and blameless?
5. What kinds of barriers keep you from living a life of holiness?

3. GOD HAS ADOPTED US AS HIS SONS (vv.5-6).

Note: our adoption was predestinated, that is, foreordained. This is most striking when we consider how sinful and depraved we are and how much we have cursed, rejected, and rebelled against God. The fact that God wills and finds pleasure in adopting us and that He counts it as good is too much to believe. Yet, this is exactly what He says. Now note two significant things.

1. The word "foreordained" does not mean that God chooses some persons for salvation and everyone else for eternal punishment. Scripture teaches the exact opposite.

> **"For God so loved the world, that he gave his only begotten Son, that whosoever believeth in him should not perish, but have everlasting life" (Jn.3:16).**

The word "predestination" means to destine or appoint before, to foreordain, to predetermine. The basic Greek word means to *mark off or to set off* the boundaries of something. The idea is a glorious picture of what God is doing for the *believer*. The boundary is marked and set off for the believer: the boundary of being adopted as a child of God. The believer shall be adopted, made just like Christ and conformed to His very likeness and image. Nothing can stop God's purpose for the believer. The believer may struggle and suffer through the sin and shame of this world; he may even stumble and fall or become discouraged and down-hearted. But if he is a genuine child of God, he will not be defeated, not totally. He will soon arise from his fall and begin to follow Christ again. He is predestinated to be a brother of Christ, to worship and serve Christ throughout all eternity.

> **"In whom also we have obtained an inheritance, being predestinated according to the purpose of him who worketh all things after the counsel of his own will" (Ep.1:11).**

2. The word "adoption" means to *place as a son*.
3. Adoption is by Jesus Christ and by Him alone. God accepts us because we believe and trust His Son Jesus Christ. He tells us plainly that He wants His Son to have many brothers and sisters who will love, worship, and serve Him both now and forever. Therefore, when a person wants to live for Jesus Christ—wants to live for Him so much that he *entrusts all he is and has to Christ*—God takes that person's trust and adopts him, makes him a brother or sister to Jesus Christ.

> **"For ye have not received the spirit of bondage again to fear; but ye have received the Spirit of adoption, whereby we cry, Abba, Father" (Ro.8:15).**

4. God's purpose in adoption is that we might live forever—live to the praise of the glory of His grace.

> **"That in the ages to come he might show the exceeding riches of his grace in his kindness toward us through Christ Jesus" (Ep.2:7; see Ep.1:18).**

ILLUSTRATION:

Have you ever known children who were orphans? They did not have a family, a home? In most cases, they are destined to a childhood without loving parents to care for them and to love them. It surely has to be one of the most lonely feelings known to man.

How many of us had our hearts broken for the orphans of a foreign country in misery? Some adults have been so moved by the need that they have packed suitcases and flown to other nations seeking to adopt a needy child. What kind of child did they adopt? A child who was not in their normal circle of influence. A child who could not care for himself. A child who was drained of love. A child who had no hope at all.

And yet, these adults wanted to make a difference and share their love with children who did not even speak the same language. These loving adults took the initiative and gave, and they continue to give to these children whom they have now legally adopted.

And so it is with our heavenly Father. When we were separated from Him due to our sin, separated because we were out of His will, we became orphans with eternal needs. We were drained of love until we met Love. And we were orphaned children with no hope until we met God the Father. But He sent us His Son to care for our every need.

God, our Father, took the initiative and came to us and adopted us just because He loved us and because He wanted to "according to the good pleasure of His will" (Ep.1:5).

QUESTIONS:
1. What qualities did God pick out in your life that forced Him to adopt you? (Hint. The answer is zero. Why is this so?)
2. How meaningful is the fact that you have been adopted by your heavenly Father?
3. As you think about adoption, can you think of someone that you would like to join the family of God? What steps can you take to lead that person into the family of God?

4. GOD HAS REDEEMED US—FORGIVEN OUR SINS (v.7).

The word "redemption" is one of the great words of the Bible. It conveys the idea of deliverance or setting a man free by paying a ransom. For example, a prisoner of war or a kidnapped person is ransomed or redeemed, or a convicted criminal is freed from the penalty of death. In every case the man is powerless to free himself. He cannot pay the penalty demanded to liberate himself from his situation or bondage. Note several significant facts.

1. Man has been captivated or kidnapped by several forces.
   a. *The force of sin*. All men sin and cannot help but sin. Man is sold under sin. Sin has captivated him (Ro.3:23; 7:14).
   b. *The force of corruption and death*. The whole creation is corrupt (Ro.8:21). Everything wastes away; it deteriorates, decays, ages, and eventually dies. Corruption and death have captivated man. (See 1 Co.15:42, 50; Ga.6:8; 2 Pe.1:4; 2:12, 19.)
   c. *The force of Satan*. All unbelievers are under the power and influence of Satan. He has blinded their minds to the gospel (2 Co.4:4). He works in the children of disobedience (Ep.2:2). They are captivated by him (1 Jn.5:19).
2. Three key ideas are included in the concept of redemption.
   a. *Man needs* to *be liberated, delivered, and set free*.
   b. *Man is unable to liberate himself*. He has no energy, no power, no ability to free himself.
   c. *God* has *redeemed man by the blood of His Son Jesus Christ*. God Himself has paid the ransom for man's release—the ransom of a life for a life. God gave His own Son so that man might be set free. This is extremely important to note: when a man *truly* calls upon the Lord to save him, God buys him right out of the marketplace of this corruptible life (Ro.10:13). God redeems him once for all, purchases and removes him from further sale. He is redeemed eternally (see Ga.3:13; 4:5; Co.4:5).

3. God redeems man because of the riches of His grace. He loves man with an unbelievable love—a love so great that it spurs Him to do whatever is necessary to save man.

"Even as the Son of man came not to be ministered unto, but to minister, and to give his life a ransom for many" (Mt.20:28).

A CLOSER LOOK:

(1:7) **Forgiveness**: the word "forgiveness" means to send off, to send away, to release, to let go. The word for "sin" means transgression, trespass, a falling by the way, or deviating from the way. All men...

- have transgressed the law of God
- have deviated from God
- have fallen from the way of God

Therefore, all men stand guilty of breaking the law of God, and the penalty for breaking the law is death. However, the blood of Jesus Christ brings forgiveness to men. How? Jesus Christ died for man. He took the penalty of sins and bore the punishment Himself. He was able to do this because He was the Perfect and Ideal Man, and as the Ideal Man, He could stand for and represent all men. When He died, He died as the Ideal Man, as the Representative for all men. Any person who really believes that Jesus Christ died for him is forgiven of his sins.

"Him hath God exalted with his right hand to be a Prince and a Saviour, for to give repentance to Israel, and forgiveness of sins" (Ac.5:31).

ILLUSTRATION:

Do you think you are worth the price that God paid to ransom you? The Bible says that you did not come cheap. For example:

Suppose you are standing outside of a great auction room...and you hear a clerk say, "He paid $25.00 for a picture, another man paid $600,000.00 for one." You know quite a lot about the two pictures: The twenty-five dollar picture may be any one of 10,000 little dogs done by amateur artists who paint...hoping to get paid for them. The six hundred thousand dollar picture—was it a Gainsborough, Rembrandt, Reubens?... You can judge the painting by the price that is paid for it.

We can judge ourselves by the price Christ paid for us...when I form conclusions that are justified from other portions of the Scripture—how great was my sinfulness, the depths of my nature and the height of His love.[2]

QUESTIONS:

1. Do you believe that God's grace is sufficient to forgive even your worst sin? Why or why not?
2. According to Scripture, how does redemption come to the Christian?
3. What price did God pay to redeem you from sin's bondage? What price did you pay? Who paid the greater price?
4. Can you tell a person how he can have his sins forgiven, how he can be redeemed? What is the value of being able to do so?

2 Donald Grey Barnhouse. *Let Me Illustrate.* (Grand Rapids, MI: Fleming H. Revell, 1967), p.262.

EPHESIANS 1:3-7

SUMMARY:

It humbles us to know that we had absolutely nothing to contribute to our salvation: Jesus paid it all. God chose us. We are blessed because of God's love that loved us before we even knew Him. In light of this great news, we need to remember:

1. God's great blessings are heavenly blessings.
2. God has chosen us to be holy and blameless.
3. God has adopted us as His sons.
4. God has redeemed us—He has forgiven our sins.

(THE BLESSINGS OF GOD continues in the next passage.)

PERSONAL JOURNAL NOTES
(Reflection & Response)

1. The most important thing that I learned from this lesson was:

2. The area that I need to work on the most is:

3. I can apply this lesson to my life by:

4. Closing Statement of Commitment:

B. The Blessings of God (Part 2), 1:8-14

1. God has given us wisdom & understanding

2. God has revealed the mystery of His will to us
   a. To reveal His purpose in Christ
   b. To bring the ages to a climax
   c. To gather all things together in heaven & earth
   d. To put all under Christ

3. God has given us an inheritance, chosen us
   a. The fact: He destined us by His will to receive the inheritance
   b. The inheritance: "That we might be," that is, exist eternally
   c. Why: That we should exist to His glory
   d. How to receive the inheritance
      1) By hearing the Word
      2) By trusting in Christ

4. God has sealed us with the Holy Spirit
   a. He is the guarantee of our inheritance
   b. Why: His glory is to be praised

8 Wherein he hath
abounded toward us
in all wisdom and
prudence;
9 Having made known
unto us the mystery
of his will, according
to his good pleasure
which he hath pur-
posed in himself:
10 That in the dis-
pensation of the ful-
ness of times he
might gather to-
gether in one all
things in Christ, both
which are in heaven,
and which are on
earth; even in him:
11 In whom also we
have obtained an in-
heritance, being pre-
destinated according
to the purpose of him
who worketh all
things after the coun-
sel of his own will:
12 That we should
be to the praise of his
glory, who first
trusted in Christ.
13 In whom ye also
trusted, after that ye
heard the word of
truth, the gospel of
your salvation: in
whom also after that
ye believed, ye were
sealed with that holy
Spirit of promise,
14 Which is the ear-
nest of our inheri-
tance until the re-
demption of the pur-
chased possession,
unto the praise of his
glory.

Section I
THE ETERNAL PLAN OF GOD FOR THE CHRISTIAN BELIEVER, Ephesians 1:3-23

Study 2: **THE BLESSINGS OF GOD (Part Two)**

Text: **Ephesians 1:8-14**

Aim: To gain assurance of the great blessings of God.

Memory Verse:

"In whom also we have obtained an inheritance, being predestinated according to the purpose of him who worketh all things after the counsel of his own will" (Ephesians 1:11).

INTRODUCTION:

We live in an age where knowledge is king. Through the inventions of video, fax, computer, and other technologies to come, instant knowledge is at our fingertips. But for the Christian believer, knowledge is not the end; it is only a means to the end (knowing God and learning more and more about God). Without wisdom, we will be poor stewards of the knowledge that we collect.

God gives us wisdom and understanding in order that we might be able to comprehend His will, His inheritance, and His sealing us with the Holy Spirit. This is the purpose of this great passage of Scripture: to teach us the great blessings of God. Four blessings are covered in this passage and four were covered in the former passage. Note the four to be covered now, and as we study His Word, let's ask Him for His help in being a good steward of knowledge.

EPHESIANS 1:8-14

OUTLINE:

1. God has given us wisdom and understanding (v.8).
2. God has revealed the mystery of His will to us (vv.9-10).
3. God has given us an inheritance: He has chosen us (vv.11-13).
4. God has sealed us with the Holy Spirit (vv.13-14).

1. GOD HAS GIVEN US WISDOM AND UNDERSTANDING (v.8).

Note that both blessings come to us through Jesus Christ. Common sense tells us that God will give His wisdom and understanding only to those who honor Him and His Son.

1. The word "wisdom" means seeing and knowing the truth. It is seeing and knowing what to do. It grasps the great truths of life. It sees the answers to the problems of life and death, God and man, time and eternity, good and evil—the deep things of God and of the universe.

This wisdom is found only in Jesus Christ and is promised only to those who search after Him with all their hearts (1 Co.1:30; 2:10-16; Ep.1:8; Ph.2:5f; Ja.1:5).

> **"O the depth of the riches both of the wisdom and knowledge of God! how unsearchable are his judgments, and his ways past finding out!" (Ro.11:33).**

2. The word "prudence"(or "understanding") means seeing how to use and do the truth. It is seeing the direction to take. It is understanding, insight, the ability to solve day-to-day problems. It is a down-to-earth practical understanding of things.

> **"That the God of our Lord Jesus Christ, the Father of glory, may give unto you the spirit of wisdom and revelation in the knowledge of him: the eyes of your understanding being enlightened" (Ep.1:17-18).**

QUESTIONS:

1. Who is the wisest person you know? What makes him so wise? How did he become so wise?
2. Whose wisdom do you seek most of the time? The world's or the Lord's? Where is your time spent more ?
3. What happens when the wisdom you have lacks understanding?
4. What practical difference does wisdom make in your life?

2. GOD HAS REVEALED THE MYSTERY OF HIS WILL TO US (vv.9-10).

This is the key thought and great theme of Ephesians. (William Barclay has an excellent description of this point, and he should be consulted by the person who wishes to study the point in depth. *The Letters to the Galatians and Ephesians*, p.96f.) Remember: in the Bible a mystery is not something mysterious and difficult to understand. Rather, it is a truth that has been locked up in God's plan for ages until He was ready to reveal it to man. When the time came, He unlocked the truth, opening it up to man. A mystery is a truth revealed by God that had never before been known. The mystery of God's will can be simply stated: God is to gather together and unify all things in a spirit of peace and harmony—all things, both visible and invisible. All things are to be brought to a peaceful and eternal state under the authority and glorification of Jesus Christ. God is moving history toward that climactic consummation.

Paul's great thought in verses 9-10 says several things. (It is impossible to list all the points beside the Scripture in the outline.)

1. *God has an eternal purpose and plan for the world,* and it is His pleasure to bring it about. He joys and rejoices to bring it about, and what He does is good. It is all good.

2. *There is terrible division throughout the universe.* The need for God "to gather all things in heaven and earth" indicates division (see Ep.6:12). Note the terrible divisions seen throughout the world:

⇒ Man is seen divided against God (Ep.2:1f).
⇒ Man is seen divided against man (Ep.2:11f).
⇒ Christians are seen out of harmony with Christians (Ep.4:1f).
⇒ Christians are seen out of harmony with God (Ep.5:1f).
⇒ Family members are seen divided against family members (Ep.5:22f).
⇒ Slaves (employees) are seen divided against masters (employers) (Ep.6:5f).
⇒ Man is seen out of harmony with cosmic powers (Ep.2:2; 6:10, 11-12; 3:10, 15; see 1:10, 20-21. See also Ro.8:18 for man's division against nature).

The fact that God's primary concern through all the ages has been to harmonize the divisions shows how devastating and horrible the division really is.

A CLOSER LOOK:

(1:9-10) **Reconciliation**: Jesus Christ is the answer to division, to disunity, and to disharmony. He is the One who breaks down all barriers; He is the One who reconciles all things.

⇒ He reconciles man to God by the blood of the cross (Ep.2:4-13, esp. 13).
⇒ He reconciles man to man by bringing all men together into one body, His church (Ep.2:13-22; see 1:22-23).
⇒ He reconciles Christians to Christians by the power of the Holy Spirit and by giving individual gifts and functions for each member to perform (Ep.4:1-32).
⇒ He reconciles believers to God by the power and fruit of the Holy Spirit (Ep.5:1-21).
⇒ He reconciles family members to family members by giving the example of Christ's love for the church (Ep.5:22-24).
⇒ He reconciles slaves (employees) to masters (employers) by putting both on an equal footing before Christ (Ep.5:5-9).
⇒ He enables man to overcome the cosmic and spiritual powers and evil forces by the armor of God (Ep.6:10-18).

3. *There is to be a consummation, a climax of history*—a *fulness of time*, a new order—in which all things will be unified and harmonized and brought to a peaceful state under the authority of Jesus Christ. History is in the hands of God. The word Paul uses is *dispensation* which literally means "household arrangement." The idea is that the universe is a house under the management of God. God is handling, planning, arranging, and administering all things toward a climactic consummation for Christ and His followers. In that climactic day, all disharmony, division, and evil will be subjected and harmonized under Christ. A new, perfect, and eternal creation will be established for the Lord and His followers throughout the universe.

> **"But when the fulness of the time was come, God sent forth his Son, made of a woman, made under the law, to redeem them that were under the law, that we might receive the adoption of sons. And because ye are sons, God hath sent forth the Spirit of his Son into your hearts, crying, Abba, Father" (Ga.4:4-6).**

4. *Jesus Christ is God's appointed Head over the new creation and new order*. He is God's *Head over the church*, which is God's new creation in the present world and order of things (Ep.1:22-23). And He is to be God's *Head over the new creation* in the future world and order of things (Ja.1:18).

> **"And [God] hath put all things under his [Christ's] feet, and [given] him to be the head over all things to the church, which is his body, the fulness of him that filleth all in all" (Ep.1:22-23).**

5. *The church is the Lord's instrument of reconciliation and peace*, His representative body upon the earth. As the instrument of the Lord, the church is to do two things.

a. The church is to take Christ and His message of reconciliation and peace to the world. Through "His body, the church," all division and disorder among men are to be condemned, and His message of harmony and peace is to be proclaimed.

b. The church is to practice reconciliation upon the earth. "In the church" all laws, barriers, and divisions are to be done away with. They are to be nonexistent. The church is to be a speck, an embryo of heaven upon the earth.

> **"To wit, that God was in Christ, reconciling the world unto himself, not imputing their trespasses unto them; and hath committed unto us the word of reconciliation. Now then we are ambassadors for Christ, as though God did beseech you by us: we pray you in Christ's stead, be ye reconciled to God" (2 Co.5:19-20).**

ILLUSTRATION:

Is your church making a difference for the cause of Christ? Beware of the subtle trap that substitutes material wealth for God's true work.

> *There is a story of an artist who was asked to paint a picture of a decaying church. To the astonishment of many, instead of putting on the canvas an old, tottering ruin, the artist painted a stately edifice of modern grandeur. Through the open portals could be seen the richly carved pulpit, the magnificent organ, and the beautiful stained glass windows. Within the grand entrance was an offering plate of elaborate design for the offerings to missions. A cobweb was over the receptacle for foreign missions!*[1]

What a tragedy! To have a beautiful, grand facility for believers to enjoy and give nothing toward the spread of the gospel to the lost of the world!

QUESTIONS:

1. How easy is it to leave behind God's will and replace it by doing religious things? What kinds of things replace God's will which are done in the name of God?
2. Why is it important for the church to be the Lord's instrument for peace and reconciliation upon earth?
3. What do you think your role is in the church? What can you do to bring about God's will upon earth, God's will for all people to live together in peace and to be reconciled both to God and to one another?
4. What practical things can you do to bring unity to your church?
5. According to Scripture, exactly what is "the mystery" of God's will?

---

1 *Gospel Herald.* Walter B. Knight. *Three Thousand Illustrations for Christian Service.* (Grand Rapids, MI: Eerdmans Publishing Co., 1947), p.133.

3. GOD HAS GIVEN US AN INHERITANCE: HE HAS CHOSEN US (vv.11-13).

Note several significant points.

1. The inheritance or heritage was predestinated, that is, foreordained. God works all things out after the counsel of His own will. He must, for only God knows what is best. And nothing could be better than to be given the greatest inheritance possible: that of being made the very heritage of God, the very possession of God.

2. The inheritance is clearly stated in the words "that we *should be*," that is, that we should exist eternally. God gives the believer an eternal *state of being*—an eternal existence. In fact, the word "inheritance" means *heritage*. God takes the believer and makes him His own heritage and possession. He is given the glorious privilege of *being*, of living and existing forever as God's most *cherished possession and heritage*. He becomes the most precious gem and treasure of God. This is the believer's inheritance, his heritage.

> **"Yet they are thy people and thine inheritance, which thou broughtest out by thy mighty power and by thy stretched out arm" (De.9:29; see Ex.19:5).**

3. The reason God makes us His inheritance is that we should exist to the praise of His glory. We shall live forever in the new heavens and earth as the perfect demonstration of His glory. The fact that God would take sinners—totally depraved sinners—and save them will cause praise upon praise to be heaped upon His name. His unbelievable love will be seen and glorified forever and ever by all creatures—both of heaven and of earth, both visible and invisible, both now and yet to be. All shall stand in stark amazement at God's spectacular glory—the glory of His eternal grace and love shown to the world in His dear Son, Jesus Christ.

> **"For here have we no continuing city, but we seek one to come. By him therefore let us offer the sacrifice of praise to God continually, that is, the fruit of our lips giving thanks to his name" (He.13:14-15).**

4. How does a person receive the inheritance? This verse says there are two ways (v.13).

a. By hearing the Word of God. A person has to hear the Word of God before he can ever know the truth, the glorious gospel of salvation. He cannot believe in Jesus Christ unless he first hears about Christ.

> **"So then faith cometh by hearing, and hearing by the word of God" (Ro.10:17).**

b. By believing and trusting in Jesus Christ.

> **"Verily, verily, I say unto you, He that heareth my word, and believeth on him that sent me, hath everlasting life, and shall not come into condemnation; but is passed from death unto life" (Jn.5:24).**

APPLICATION:
In order for an inheritance to be realized, someone has to die. For our benefit and for His glory, our Father gave up His Son to die. Consequently, those who are in Christ have become His most precious possession. What is our part in this glorious transaction? We must claim it to be ours!

ILLUSTRATION:
Through God's infinite wisdom, He has given His Son an inheritance. Because of God's mercy and grace, we have been made joint-heirs with the Son. Listen to this striking story of how one man received his inheritance.

> *A man who was blessed with wisdom, virtue, and wealth had only one son. He offered him the best education, sending him to Jerusalem to learn. He made certain the young man's every need was met.*
>
> *Shortly after his son left, [the father] became sick and died. His death caused immense grief throughout the community, for he was a benefactor for both rich and poor....*
>
> *When the period of mourning was over, the dead man's executor opened the man's will and read it aloud. To the astonishment of everyone, the man left all of his property and wealth to his slave. There was a final clause that his beloved son should have the privilege of choosing only one thing out of the entire estate.*
>
> *Immersed in grief over the loss of his father, the young man asked his teacher to assist him in selecting one thing from his father's estate. In the meantime, the slave began to live the life of a wealthy man.*
>
> *When the teacher read the will, he at once discovered the intention of the father. "We must leave at once for your home," the teacher told the pupil, "where you will take possession of all your property."*
>
> *"But I am a pauper," the boy cried. "All I have are the clothes on my back and one item from my father's house."*
>
> *"I suggest," the teacher said, "that you choose your late father's slave out of his estate, and with him will go over to you all he possesses, since a slave can own nothing, and all he has belongs to his master."*
>
> *"That indeed was your father's clever device. He knew that if the will were to state that all was left to you, the slave, in your absence, would take for himself all the valuables on which he could lay his hands. Whereas, if he thought all belonged to him, he would take care of everything that was left. Your father knew that the one thing he gave you the power to choose would be no other than his slave, and with him you will become the just and rightful owner of everything."*[2]

This young man's father was very clever. But our Heavenly Father is even wiser. Have *you* claimed your inheritance?

QUESTIONS:
1. God has given you a priceless inheritance. What godly inheritance should you plan to give to your family and friends?
2. How do you receive God's inheritance? What is the end result of receiving God's inheritance?
3. What kind of value does God place upon you?
4. How do you feel when you think of being God's possession?
5. How do you feel about claiming your inheritance? Do you believe that your role in claiming your inheritance is passive or aggressive?

4. GOD HAS SEALED US WITH THE HOLY SPIRIT (vv.13-14).

The word "earnest" means pledge, guarantee, a down payment. The Holy Spirit is given to the believer in order to give the believer perfect assurance of his salvation. We

2 William R. White. *Stories for the Journey.* (Minneapolis, MN: Augsburg Publishing House, 1988), pp.86-87.

know that we are redeemed—that we are God's cherished possession—by the Holy Spirit who lives within us.

Again note: Why does God give us such a glorious guarantee as His own wonderful presence? That His glory might be praised eternally.

> **"The Spirit itself beareth witness with our spirit, that we are the children of God" (Ro.8:16).**

ILLUSTRATION:

Have you ever heard of a lay-a-way plan? For example: *a dollar down will secure your lay-a-way for Christmas*. This phrase is spoken in hundreds of stores as merchandise is set aside until it has been paid for in full. If payments are made on a timely basis, the customer picks up the merchandise and is finally able to enjoy what has been previously laid away.

Of course, for a variety of reasons, some people fail to make the scheduled payments and consequently lose what they wanted.

In the same sense, God has a lay-a-way program. However, His program is a guaranteed payment for the believer. In fact, we are not allowed to pay on anything that He has done. The cross took care of it all, and the most wonderful thing has happened: the Holy Spirit has been given to us, given as a pledge or down payment of God's great promise to us, that we shall live forever with Him.

APPLICATION:

Are you laying away things for this earth or treasures for heaven? Material things, position, and pride are not allowed in heaven. Remember Jesus' words:

> **"Lay not up for yourselves treasures upon earth, where moth and rust doth corrupt, and where thieves break through and steal: but lay up for yourselves treasures in heaven, where neither moth nor rust doth corrupt, and where thieves do not break through nor steal: for where your treasure is, there will your heart be also" (Mt.6:19-21).**

QUESTIONS:

1. Are you aware of the Holy Spirit's presence in your life? If not, how can you gain the assurance of His presence?
2. If you are a Christian believer, you have a lay-a-way account already set up in heaven. What "treasures" can you lay up that will be there eternally?
3. Have you ever worried about the assurance of your salvation? How does this verse help assure you?
4. What difference does knowing that you are truly saved affect how you witness to the lost?

SUMMARY

Where is knowledge leading you? Remember, knowledge is not to be an end within itself—it is to lead the believer into a deeper relationship with the Lord. As we know Him better, we will better understand what He has done for us and what He requires of us. Review the four great blessings of God covered in this passage:

1. God has given us wisdom and understanding.
2. God has revealed the mystery of His will to us.
3. God has given us an inheritance, that is, made us the heritage of God.
4. God has sealed us with the Holy Spirit.

Remember: there are eight great blessings of God, four covered in the previous Scripture and four in this passage.

EPHESIANS 1:8-14

PERSONAL JOURNAL NOTES
(Reflection & Response)

1. The most important thing that I learned from this lesson was:

2. The area that I need to work on the most is:

3. I can apply this lesson to my life by:

4. Closing Statement of Commitment:

EPHESIANS 1:15-18

C. The Knowledge of God to Be Gained by the Believer, 1:15-18

1. The basis for knowing God: Faith & love
   a. A strong testimony
   b. An ever-present need for prayer: To grow in the knowledge of God

2. The need: A growing knowledge of God, the God of Christ & the Father of glory
   a. By the spirit of wisdom
   b. By the spirit of revelation
   c. By an enlightened heart

3. The results of knowing God
   a. One knows God's calling
   b. One knows God's inheritance
   c. One knows God's power, v. 19

15 Wherefore I also,
after I heard of your
faith in the Lord Jesus, and love unto all
the saints,
16 Cease not to give
thanks for you, making mention of you
in my prayers;
17 That the God
of our Lord Jesus
Christ, the Father
of glory, may give
unto you the spirit of
wisdom and revelation in the knowledge of him:
18 The eyes of
your understanding
being enlightened;
that ye may know
what is the hope
of his calling, and
what the riches of
the glory of his inheritance in the
saints.

Section I
THE ETERNAL PLAN OF GOD FOR THE CHRISTIAN BELIEVER, Ephesians 1:3-23

Study 3: **THE KNOWLEDGE OF GOD TO BE GAINED BY THE BELIEVER**

Text: **Ephesians 1:15-18**

Aim: To grow more and more in the knowledge of God.

Memory Verse:

> **"That the God of our Lord Jesus Christ, the Father of glory, may give unto you the spirit of wisdom and revelation in the knowledge of Him" (Ephesians 1:17).**

INTRODUCTION:
Do you ever get distracted as you follow the Lord? All of us can relate to this story:

> *It was a fog-shrouded morning, July 4, 1952, when a young woman named Florence Chadwick waded into the water off Catalina Island. She intended to swim the channel from the island to the California coast. Long-distance swimming was not new to her; she had been the first woman to swim the English Channel in both directions.*
>
> *The water was numbing cold that day. The fog was so thick she could hardly see the boats in her party. Several times sharks had to be driven away with rifle fire. She swam more than fifteen hours before she asked to be taken out of the water. Her trainer tried to encourage her to swim on since they were so close to land, but when Florence looked, all she saw was fog. So she quit...only one-half mile from her goal.*
>
> *Later she said, "I'm not excusing myself, but if I could have seen the land, I might have made it." It wasn't the cold or fear or exhaustion that caused Florence Chadwick to fail. It was the fog.*
>
> *Many times we too fail, not because we're afraid or because of the peer pressure or because of anything other than the fact we lose sight of the goal. Maybe that's why Paul said, "I press toward the mark for the prize of the high calling of God in Christ Jesus" (Phil. 3:14).*

Two months after her failure, Florence Chadwick walked off the same beach into the same channel and swam the distance, setting a new speed record, because she could see the land.

And so it is with the knowledge of God. There are many distractions that leave us in a fog. It is vitally important that the believer not lose sight of his one great goal: that of knowing God, of knowing Him personally, of growing in the knowledge of Him more and more. [1]

Paul had just declared the eternal plan of God for the world (vv.3-14). It is crucial that believers come to know the God of this plan in the most personal and intimate sense. This is the great subject of this passage: the knowledge of God. It is absolutely essential…

- that believers grow more and more in the knowledge of God
- that the world come to know God as their personal Savior

OUTLINE:

1. The basis for knowing God: faith and love (vv.15-16).
2. The need: a growing knowledge of God, the God of Christ and the Father of glory (vv.17-18).
3. The results of knowing God (v.18).

1. THE BASIS FOR KNOWING GOD: FAITH AND LOVE (vv.15-16).

The Ephesian church had a strong testimony, a testimony so strong that it was being buzzed about all over the world. Their testimony and its strength had reached the ears of Paul. And note what it was that he had heard:

⇒ He had heard about their faith in God's love (that God had sent His Son to save the world) and about their loyalty to the Lord Jesus in carrying the message of God's love throughout the world.

⇒ He had heard that they were ministering to the saints of God—demonstrating a great love for God's people.

It was this fact—their strong testimony of faith and love—that stirred Paul to write the Ephesians. He knew that the Christian life must never sit still. A person has to grow or else he slips backward. Therefore, Paul wanted the Ephesian believers to grow in their knowledge and power of God. He had just shared the great blessings of God which were theirs when they first came to know God (see Ep.1:3-14). Now he wanted them to grow in these blessings, the blessings of knowing God and experiencing the power of God. Therefore, he told them that he prayed for them. In fact, he never ceased to ask God that they might grow in the knowledge and power of God.

ILLUSTRATION:

Sometimes our days are filled with a lot of good things, yet we often neglect to do the best things. Think about this fact as the following illustration is shared:

Film maker Walt Disney was ruthless in cutting anything that got in the way of a story's pacing. Ward Kimball, one of the animators for Snow White, recalls working 240 days on a 4 1/2-minute sequence in which the dwarfs made soup for Snow White and almost destroyed the kitchen in the process. Disney

---

[1] Craig B. Larson, Editor. *Illustrations for Preaching and Teaching*. (Grand Rapids, MI: Baker Books, 1993), p.96.

thought it was funny, but he decided the scene stopped the flow of the picture, so out it went.[2]

APPLICATION:
We can lose our focus if our priorities are not in order. Programs and organizations will never replace the basis of faith and love. The temptation is strong to work "240 days a year" on pumping up programs and organizations at the expense of love and faith. Anything that distract us from knowing God is like unusable, cut film on the Editor's floor. Put your effort into what God considers to be important: faith and love.

QUESTIONS:
1. What practical things can you do to improve your testimony of faith and love?
2. What are some *good things* in your life that you need to replace with *best things*?
3. What is the secret of a church having a strong testimony of faith and love? In what sense does your church's testimony affect you? How does it affect the lost?

2. THE NEED: A GROWING KNOWLEDGE OF GOD, THE GOD OF CHRIST AND THE FATHER OF GLORY (vv.17-18).

Note that the God we are to know is clearly identified. He is not the god of our own minds and thoughts and hands—the god we conceive when we picture what God is like.

⇒ The God we are to know is the God of Jesus Christ, that is, the God whom Jesus Christ worshipped when He was on earth as a Man; the God whom Jesus Christ came to reveal to men. There is no other God—not a true and living God. If we are to really know God, we must come to know the God whom Christ worshipped and revealed.

⇒ The God we are to know is the Father of glory, that is, the only true and living God. He is the Supreme Majesty and Sovereign LORD of the Universe—the One who is the Supreme intelligence and power of the universe and who has created all and rules over all—the One who is omnipotent (all powerful), omnipresent (present everywhere), and so expansive that His very being and presence reaches out beyond the stars, embracing all that is or ever will be. He is the One who declares that He has "set His glory *above* the heavens" (Ps.8:1).

This is the God we are to know. As stated, He is the only living and true God, the God and Father of our Lord Jesus Christ, and the God of glory. Believers must grow more and more in the knowledge of Him; they must have an ever-increasing knowledge of Him.

Three things are essential if believers are to grow in the knowledge of God. And remember, these things are so important that Paul prayed unceasingly for God to give them to the believer.

1. First, to grow in the knowledge of God a believer must have the *spirit of wisdom.*
   a. Note the phrase "the spirit of wisdom." What the believer needs from God is *a spirit...*
      - that reaches out and grasps after wisdom
      - that hungers and thirsts after wisdom
      - that seeks and seeks after wisdom

[2] Craig B. Larson, Editor. *Illustrations for Preaching and Teaching*, p.186.

b. Wisdom can best be understood by the single words *what* and *how*. Wisdom means knowing what something is, what is behind something, and what can be done. It is knowing how to use or relate to something. Therefore, spiritual wisdom means…
- knowing who God is and how to relate to Him
- knowing the truth and how to use it
- knowing what to do and how to do it
- knowing how to live more and more fruitful lives—for the glory of God and for the welfare of men

c. Wisdom differs from knowledge. Knowledge is the grasping of facts, but grasping facts is not enough. Much more is needed: a person must know how to use the facts. That is where wisdom comes in. Wisdom knows how to use the facts. The point is this: it is not enough to know the facts about God; a person must know God personally. He must know how to experience the facts about God. He must use the facts to develop a personal relationship with God—a growing relationship—a relationship that is intimate, that grows deeper and deeper. This is the meaning of the word "knowledge": a personal and intimate relationship with God; a personal experience with God. It is not an intellectual knowledge of God, but an experiential knowledge of God.

APPLICATION:
If the believer is to grow in the knowledge of God, he must seek the wisdom of God more than anything else on this earth. It is the person who hungers and thirsts after God and His righteousness that is filled.

"Therefore whosoever heareth these sayings of mine, and doeth them, I will liken him unto a wise man, which built his house upon a rock" (Mt.7:24).

2. Second, to grow in the knowledge of God a believer must have the *spirit of revelation.*

a. Again, note the phrase "the spirit of revelation." It is the Holy Spirit who reveals God to the believer. This is made abundantly clear by Scripture.

"But as it is written, Eye hath not seen, nor ear heard, neither have entered into the heart of man, the things which God hath prepared for them that love him. But God hath revealed them unto us by his Spirit: for the Spirit searcheth all things, yea, the deep things of God. For what man knoweth the things of a man, save the spirit of man which is in him? even so the things of God knoweth no man, but the Spirit of God. Now we have received, not the spirit of the world, but the spirit which is of God; that we might know the things that are freely given to us of God" (1 Co.2:9-12).

The believer is indwelt by the Spirit of God (Jn.14:16-17; 14:26; 16:12-15; 1 Co.6:19-20; 2 Co.6:16). The Spirit of God dwells in him to teach him the deep things of God. But note what the believer must have in order to grow in the knowledge of God: "the spirit of revelation"…
- a spirit that drives after God
- a spirit that seeks to know God
- a spirit that hungers and thirsts after God above all else

b. The word "revelation" means to manifest; to reveal; to unveil; to uncover; to open. It is the work of the Holy Spirit to reveal the knowledge of God to Christians. In fact it is the work of the Holy Spirit to reveal the meaning of all truth to the Christian (Jn.14:26; 16:12-15). This is clearly seen in 1 Co.1:9-16 where the wisdom of the world is contrasted with the wisdom of God. A spiritual Christian sees (through the Spirit revealing to him) the meaning behind world events as well as day to day experiences. He understands who and what is behind the events of history and human experience. Therefore, he gains a growing knowledge of God day by day.

APPLICATION:

1) If the believer is to grow in his knowledge of God, the rich and deep things of God must be opened up to the believer. But the things of God are like everything else that is worthwhile: they are not handed over to men on a silver platter. A man must seek to learn more and more about God. He must seek to have the truth of God revealed to him.
2) Lehman Strauss points out that human philosophy says, "Know thyself."[3] However, Jesus said, **"And this is life eternal, that they might know thee the only true God, and Jesus Christ, whom thou has sent" (Jn.17:3).**

   To know yourself is very important. But the greatest thing in all the world is to know God personally and to know that you will live with God forever. God and eternal life are the summits of knowledge. It is better to know that you will never die than to know all there is about yourself and lose that knowledge at death.

3. Third, to grow in the knowledge of God, a believer must have the *eyes of his heart enlightened*. This is a beautiful description of the heart: "the eyes of the heart." The heart must be opened so that the light of God can be seen and grasped. An open heart is the responsibility of both the believer and the Holy Spirit.

⇒ The believer must open his heart and focus its affection, intelligence, and will upon knowing God.

⇒ The believer must seek the Holy Spirit to enlighten and flood his heart with the things of God.

> **"For God, who commanded the light to shine out of darkness, hath shined in our hearts, to give the light of the knowledge of the glory of God in the face of Jesus Christ" (2 Co.4:6).**

QUESTIONS:

1. A man cannot know God apart from God's help. What help does God provide for us in order to know Him?
2. Why do you think that some Christians lack knowledge of the God of the Bible? What kind of false picture do they have of God?
3. What are you told to do in order to know God?
4. How can you continue to improve your knowledge of God?

3. THE RESULTS OF KNOWING GOD (v.18).

The results of knowing God are threefold.

1. *A believer comes to know the hope of God's calling*. What is the hope of the believer's call? It is what has already been covered in the great spiritual blessings of God (Ep.1:13-14):

---

3 Lehman Strauss. *Devotional Studies in Galatians & Ephesians*. (Neptune, NJ: Loizeaux Brothers, 1957), p.132.

⇒ We should be holy and without blame, living before Him forever and ever in love (v.4).
⇒ We should experience what it means to be adopted as children of God—forever and ever (vv.5-6).
⇒ We should experience eternal redemption and forgiveness of sin (v.7).
⇒ We should possess the wisdom and understanding of God (v.8).
⇒ We should live in the perfect heaven and earth where there will be no more division but only peace and unity in Christ Jesus (vv.9-10).

Very simply stated, God has called us to stand before Him in the name and righteousness of Jesus Christ—to stand before Him just as Jesus Christ stands before Him: perfect. It is evident that we are not perfect—not now, not yet. But the day is coming when we shall be. Right now we experience the blessings of God only in part, only imperfectly. But when the glorious *Day of Redemption* comes, we shall be made just like our Lord Jesus Christ, righteous and perfect, enabled to live in God's presence, worshipping and serving Him forever and ever. This is the believer's hope; this is the believer's calling.

> **"The Spirit itself beareth witness with our spirit, that we are the children of God: and if children, then heirs; heirs of God, and joint-heirs with Christ; if so be that we suffer with him, that we may be also glorified together" (Ro.8:16-17).**

2. *A believer comes to know God's inheritance*—His inheritance in the saints. Believers are themselves the inheritance, that is, the heritage and possession of God. When we come to know God, we learn who we are—the glorious position God has given us: He has made us His very own possession and heritage.

3. *A believer comes to know and to experience the enormous power of God.* In discussing this glorious result, Paul explodes into a discussion of God's power which was clearly shown in what God did for Christ. (Because of its length, God's power is discussed in a separate subject in the next outline.)

> **"Now unto him that is able to do exceeding abundantly above all that we ask or think, according to the power that worketh in us" (Ep.3:20).**

ILLUSTRATION:

There is a story that will help us better understand the need to have a heart knowledge of the Lord and not just a head knowledge.

> *The master musician was finally ready to listen to the results of his students' efforts. He had done all that he could do to teach them to play the music. Now, the moment had come for his prize student to play his instrument.*
>
> *Bill was a very talented fellow. He had mastered every note of the difficult composition and did so with great pride. On cue, he proceeded to show off his talent as the notes flew out of his instrument. When he had finished his piece, he took a deep breath and asked his teacher, "Well, what do you think professor? Did I pass?"*
>
> *To Bill's amazement, his professor was not pleased with his performance. Using phrases filled with passion, the master musician said, "You played all of the notes...but, you did not play the music."*

It is not good enough merely to know the truth; we must live it!

APPLICATION:
Has your goal in life been to play all of the notes in trying to know God? Or have you come to the place in your Christian journey of wanting to go beyond the notes and play the music?

Yes, the notes we play are an important part, but *how* we play them is the key to knowing God. We must go beyond a technical check-list and pursue the knowledge of God for one simple reason: we love Him and want to really know Him more and more each day.

QUESTIONS:
1. In your quest to know God, what are some things that have gotten in the way?
2. How can you resolve the problems that "fog" your effort to know God? (Think of some practical things that you can do today.)
3. What are the results of knowing God?
4. Why is it important for you to know God?
5. Do you think it's possible to know everything about God in your lifetime?

SUMMARY:

How is your focus now? In order to keep it sharp, the Christian believer cannot be satisfied with a superficial knowledge of God. Our passion to know the Lord is built upon three pillars of truth:

1. The basis for knowing God: faith and love
2. The need: a growing knowledge of God, the God of Christ and the Father of glory.
3. The results of knowing God.

If the basis of your relationship with God is faith and love, then you will have a desire to grow in your knowledge of God. You will sense and experience God's call, inheritance, and power.

PERSONAL JOURNAL NOTES
(Reflection & Response)

1. The most important thing that I learned from this lesson was:

2. The area that I need to work on the most is:

3. I can apply this lesson to my life by:

4. Closing Statement of Commitment:

1. The power that is available to believers a. Is a great power b. Is measured by God's power in Christ's exaltation **2. The power that raised Christ from the dead** **3. The power that took Christ to heaven & seated Him at**	**D. The Power of God Available to the Believer: Demonstrated in Christ's Exaltation, 1:19-23** 19 And what is the exceeding greatness of his power to us-ward who believe, according to the working of his mighty power, 20 Which he wrought in Christ, when he raised him from the dead, and set him at his own right hand in the	heavenly places, 21 Far above all principality, and power, and might, and dominion, and every name that is named, not only in this world, but also in that which is to come: 22 And hath put all things under his feet, and gave him to be the head over all things to the church, 23 Which is his body, the fulness of him that filleth all in all.	**God's right hand** **4. The power that exalted Christ above all creatures: In this age & in the next age** **5. The power that exalted Christ as the Supreme Head of the church** a. Christ—the Head b. The church—His body c. The church—His instrument

Section I
THE ETERNAL PLAN OF GOD FOR THE CHRISTIAN BELIEVER, Ephesians 1:3-23

Study 4: THE POWER OF GOD AVAILABLE TO THE BELIEVER: DEMONSTRATED IN CHRIST'S EXALTATION

Text: Ephesians 1:19-23

Aim: To claim and live victoriously in God's power.

Memory Verse:

"And what is the exceeding greatness of his power to us-ward who believe, according to the working of his mighty power" (Ephesians 1:19).

INTRODUCTION:
After a powerful storm of nature strikes an area, many homes experience a power failure.

> *"Where were you when the lights went out?" then becomes the topic of conversation. The storm's ferocious hands, winds, and water are hurled at earth like a demon loosed from hell. It takes men years to connect the various parts of our land with electrical lines linked to sources of power. In one devastating night, all of their work can be swept up and scattered into a chaotic mess. For days, weeks, months, and even years after, many people have to make a change in lifestyle. Old habits are not easily broken: reading at night, cooking on an electric stove, getting cold drinks from the refrigerator, turning on the heat or air conditioning, just to name a few. Not having any power causes great hardships for many.*

There is a great feeling of dependency on others at times like these. Among the people who are able to help are those who work for the power company. They can fix the problem to restore the power. And once the power is restored again, every one feels grateful and has a new appreciation for the power they once took for granted.

This is also true in the spiritual realm of life. There are a variety of storms that come our way that can cut us off from our Source of spiritual power. Sometimes circumstances are at fault, but usually the blame for not having power to live the Christian life lies with us. Without God's power, we find ourselves severely disabled.

"Where were you when the lights went out?" You were probably standing there holding the plug.

This is a great passage covering a much needed subject—the power of God. If men ever needed anything, they need the power of God in their lives. If men have ever been gripped by evil and shame, bitterness and hate, lust and immorality, cursing and anger, robbery and assault, murder and war, selfishness and greed, division and strife, disappointment and emptiness, boredom and purposelessness, it is today. Men desperately need the power of God to help them in their daily lives and to right the wrongs of society.

The glorious news is that God offers His power to men—if they will only turn to His Son Jesus Christ. He promises His power to all believers. Note that this passage is a continuation of the prayer of Paul. He is praying that the Ephesian believers might know God personally and intimately, for God gives His power to those who truly come to know Him. Coming to know God is the key to receiving the power of God.

OUTLINE:

1. The power that is available to believers (v.19).
2. The power that raised Christ from the dead (v.20).
3. The power that took Christ to heaven and seated Him at God's right hand (v.20).
4. The power that exalted Christ above all creatures: in this age and in the next age (v.21).
5. The power that exalted Christ as the Supreme Head of the church (vv.22-23).

1. THE POWER THAT IS AVAILABLE TO BELIEVERS (v.19).

When a believer really knows God, he experiences power—the power of God Himself. Note how God's power is described:

⇒ It is "exceeding": surpassing, unlimited, immeasurable, beyond imagination.
⇒ It is "great": mighty, explosive, beyond measure. This is the word from which we get the English word *megathon* which measures atomic explosives. Imagine the great explosive power of God!

The thing to note is that God's power is given to us; that is, God takes His power and extends it, presents it, makes it available to the believer. How do we know this? Because of what God did for Christ. What God did for Christ He will do for us. God's power is demonstrated by what He did for Christ.

APPLICATION:
Have you ever experienced God's power? It is a very present reality for the Christian believer. God's power is available to the believer who has faith in God. His power extends through His willing vessels as Paul reminds us:

> **"For I am not ashamed of the gospel of Christ: for it is the power of God unto salvation to every one that believeth; to the Jew first, and also to the Greek" (Ro.1:16).**

QUESTIONS:
1. What is the connection between knowing God and the power of God?
2. Have you experienced the power of God in your life? When? When was the one time that stands out most in your mind?
3. Why do some people tend to think that God's power can be explained away as circumstantial and not supernatural?
4. Is there an area of your life that lacks God's power? Why isn't God's power at work in that area?

2. THE POWER THAT RAISED CHRIST FROM THE DEAD (v.20).

Believers are to experience the power of God—the same power that raised Jesus Christ from the dead. Imagine the enormous power needed to raise a person from the dead. God wrought such power when He raised Jesus Christ.

> **"Him, being delivered by the determinate counsel and foreknowledge of God, ye have taken, and by wicked hands have crucified and slain: whom God hath raised up, having loosed the pains of death: because it was not possible that he should be holden of it" (Ac.2:23-24).**

The point is this: when God raised Jesus Christ, He demonstrated three things for men.

1. The power to raise Christ shows that *God has the power to conquer all the trials and temptations of life*. When God exercised the power to raise Christ, He conquered the most powerful trial that faces man—death. And in conquering death, God demonstrated that He has the power to conquer any trial or temptation of man, no matter what it is.

> **"There hath no temptation [trial] taken you but such as is common to man: but God is faithful, who will not suffer you to be tempted above that ye are able; but will with the temptation also make a way to escape, that ye may be able to bear it" (1 Co.10:13).**

2. The resurrection of Jesus Christ shows that *God has the power to give man a new life and the power to live that new life before Him*. After Jesus Christ had been raised from the dead, He was not living His old life, the life He had before His death. He was a *new Man*; He had a new life. He had been raised from the dead to live a new life before God forever. He walked before God in newness of life.

> **"Therefore we are buried with him by baptism into death: that like as Christ was raised up from the dead by the glory [power] of the Father, even so we also should walk in newness of life" (Ro.6:4).**

3. The power to raise Christ from the dead shows that *God has the power to raise men from the dead*. The believer shall experience the great resurrection power of God when he is resurrected from the dead.

> **"Marvel not at this: for the hour is coming, in the which all that are in the graves shall hear his voice, and shall come forth; they that have done good, unto the resurrection of life; and they that have done evil, unto the resurrection of damnation" (Jn.5:28-29).**

ILLUSTRATION:
Does your Christianity work during a crisis? This true story is about a Christianity that works.

The phone call came to a pay phone at the end of the dormitory hall. In calm words that were cased in sadness, the voice on the other end said, "Linda has gone home to be with the Lord." My friend Linda: a faithful wife, a wonderful mother, and a trusted friend had gone ahead of the rest of us to be with the Lord forever.

When a loved one walks through the gate of death, the resurrection assures us of God's promise to raise the dead. After taking that phone call, the Lord immediately reminded me of this great promise:

"O death, where is thy sting? O grave, where is thy victory?...But thanks be to God, which giveth us the victory through our Lord Jesus Christ" (1 Co.15:54-56).

APPLICATION:
The promise of the resurrection is one the great doctrines of Christianity. Because of the resurrection, there is always hope, a hope the world can not give.

QUESTIONS:
1. Explain in your own words why the resurrection is important to the Christian.
2. Because of this Scripture, what words would you share with a family who had lost a loved one who was *not* saved?
3. What difference does God's resurrection power make when you are facing an enticing temptation?
4. Why do you think God wants you to have His power after He saves you?

3. THE POWER THAT TOOK CHRIST TO HEAVEN AND SEATED HIM AT GOD'S RIGHT HAND (v.20).

Believers are to experience the power of God—the same power that took Jesus Christ to heaven and set Him at God's right hand. God did not just have the power to resurrect Jesus Christ; He had the power to take Jesus Christ into another dimension of being—into the spiritual world, that is, the world of the Spirit. God brought Jesus Christ to Himself sitting Him at His own right hand. He is literally there; His body is in heaven—the spiritual world and dimension of being.

"So then after the Lord had spoken unto them, he was received up into heaven, and sat on the right hand of God" (Mk.16:19).

The point of God's power is clear: He took Christ into heaven and exalted Him in order to demonstrate that He has the power to take men to heaven and to exalt them.

"Knowing that he which raised up the Lord Jesus shall raise up us also by Jesus, and shall present us with you" (2 Co.4:14).

ILLUSTRATION:
Do you ever imagine what heaven will be like? If you are a Christian believer, there will be a special place waiting just for you.

Joe Thompson was a master at his trade. Time and time again people would marvel at his talents. Joe's job was to customize passenger vans. He would take a van with only four wheels and an engine to craft a beautiful vehicle for its proud owner.

Joe had a real gift of being able to see the potential while staring at the present. Where others saw only a shell, Joe saw a customized van. But even greater than that: he could build what he saw—a van especially customized for it's owner.

That is exactly what Jesus has done for us:

"In my Father's house are many mansions: if it were not so, I would have told you. I go to prepare a place for you. And if I go and prepare a place for you, I will come again, and receive you unto myself; that where I am, there ye may be also" (Jn.14:2-3).

The word prepare literally means to customize. Jesus has taken a shell and is building a place according to your heart's desire. It will be perfect. Just for you.

Need a customized job? Joe can help you with your van, but only Jesus can help you with eternity.

QUESTIONS:

1. Can and should a person look forward to dying and going to heaven? Why?
2. What guarantees do you have of Jesus' preparing a place for you in heaven?
3. Do you ever worry about eternity? Do you really believe that God's promise of heaven is true? If so, if you honestly believe His promise, are you living for Him like you should? If not, what kind of commitment do you need to make to live fully for Him?
4. Why do you think God wants to spend eternity with you?

4. THE POWER THAT EXALTED CHRIST ABOVE ALL CREATURES: IN THIS AGE AND IN THE NEXT AGE (v.21).

Believers are to experience the power of God—the same power that exalted Jesus Christ above all creatures, both in this world and in the next world. Being seated at the right hand of God simply means having the highest seat of honor and authority in the universe. What God did was exalt Jesus Christ to rule and reign over all authority, no matter how great or powerful. Christ has been exalted above "all principality, and power, and might, and dominion." And to make sure nothing is excluded—Jesus Christ has been exalted above "every name that is named, not only in this world, but in that [world] which is to come" (v.21). All things are placed in subjection under Him.

"Wherefore God also hath highly exalted him, and given him a name which is above every name: that at the name of Jesus every knee should bow, of things in heaven, and things in earth, and things under the earth" (Ph.2:9-10).

The point is this: God gave Jesus Christ the authority to rule and reign over all; He demonstrated that He has the power to exalt us to rule and reign with Christ. This God promises to do.

> **"His lord said unto him, Well done, good and faithful servant; thou hast been faithful over a few things, I will make thee ruler over many things: enter thou into the joy of thy lord" (Mt.25:23).**

QUESTIONS:
1. According to Scripture, where is Christ right now? Why is this important?
2. What do you think your role is in ruling and reigning with Christ?
3. What are some ways that you can prepare yourself to rule and reign with Christ?
4. Do you normally experience the power of God? Why or why not?
5. In what ways is His power seen in your life?
6. Is there anything above Christ? What kinds of things do men attempt to place above Him?

5. THE POWER THAT EXALTED CHRIST AS THE SUPREME HEAD OF THE CHURCH (vv.22-23).

Believers are to experience the power of God—the same power that made Jesus Christ the head of the church. Jesus Christ paid the supreme price to start and build the church: He died for it. Therefore, God has given Him the supreme position over the church. Note two points.

1. The church is called the *body of Christ*. This is one of the Bible's most descriptive pictures of Jesus Christ and the church: the picture of the *human body* with Christ being the Head and the church being His body. William Barclay points out that this picture says something of enormous value. Christ needs the church and the church needs Christ (Jn.20:21)[1] The head cannot function without the body, nor can the body function without the head. The head dreams dreams and plans plans. But a head, a mind by itself, is of no use. A head must have a body to carry out the plans so that the dream can be realized. Christ came to bring the dream and plan of peace and reconciliation to a world of lost men, men who were alienated from God and from one another. Now the body, the church, must carry out the dream and plan. The message of peace, in the power of Christ, must be taken to men by the church.

The point is this: if God had the power to create the church and to make Christ the head of the church, then He has the power to make the body *function and work* for Christ. God has the power to *get us busy* for the Lord—the power to help us in our witnessing—the power to stir us to proclaim the message of reconciliation and to minister to the desperate needs of a world lost and reeling under the weight of sin, darkness, starvation, disease, and suffering.

> **"And he gave some, apostles; and some, prophets; and some, evangelists; and some, pastors and teachers; for the perfecting of the saints, for the work of the ministry, for the edifying of the body of Christ" (Ep.4:11-12).**

2. The church completes all for Christ. Jesus Christ is working throughout the world and in human history to bring about God's eternal plan for the world. He is working and fitting everything into its proper place bit by bit, and He is doing it

---

1 William Barclay. *The Letters to the Galatians and Ephesians.* "The Daily Study Bible." (Philadelphia, PA: Westminster Press, Began in 1953), p.108.

through the church. The church is the instrument of God for bringing His will about on earth.[2]

Again, the point is that God has the power to use the church and its believers to work out His eternal plan for the world. Just think—the church is the body upon the earth that God is using to work out human history!

> **"Go ye therefore, and teach all nations, baptizing them in the name of the Father, and of the Son, and of the Holy Ghost: teaching them to observe all things whatsoever I have commanded you: and, lo, I am with you alway, even unto the end of the world" (Mt.28:19-20).**

APPLICATION:

It was Peter Lord, a Baptist minister from Florida, who said "*We practice daily what we believe. All the rest is religious froth.*" Do we really believe in the urgency of The Great Commission or are our lives filled with other passions?

If we really believe that men and women and boys and girls are lost without Christ and are bound for an eternity without God's presence, then we live differently.

⇒ Our prayers are fervent for the souls of the lost.
⇒ Our financial resources are committed to the spread of the gospel.
⇒ Our vocations are simply ways to fund His work around the world.
⇒ Our missionaries have a place of honor in our church.
⇒ Our lives are yearning to do His will.

QUESTIONS:

1. What institution has God ordained to work out His eternal plan on earth?
2. What steps can you begin to take in order to become a more active member of the church body?
3. What are you practicing daily? The Great Commission of reaching the world for Christ or self-fulfillment? What practices show that we are sold out to…
   - self-fulfillment?
   - the Great Commission?

SUMMARY:

The lack of spiritual power is always our doing and not God's. God never experiences a power-shortage.

Your choice is simple but life-determining: you either plug into God as a source of power or you do not. What you choose actually determines the way you live your life. A failure to plug into God's power is accepting a life of self-power that will soon die out. If you choose to plug into God's power, He will provide:

1. The power that is available to believers.
2. The power that raised Christ from the dead.
3. The power that took Christ to heaven & seated Him at God's right hand.
4. The power that exalted Christ above all creatures: In this age & in the next age.
5. The power that exalted Christ as the Supreme Head of the church.

---

2 William Barclay. *The Letters to the Galatians and Ephesians*. "The Daily Study Bible," p.109.

Ephesians 1:19-23

Personal Journal Notes
(Reflection & Response)

1. The most important thing that I learned from this lesson was:

2. The area that I need to work on the most is:

3. I can apply this lesson to my life by:

4. Closing Statement of Commitment:

1. **A life of the walking dead** 2. **A life of transgressions & sins** a. Following the ways of the world	**CHAPTER 2** **II. THE LIFE OF THE CHRISTIAN BELIEVER, 2:1-22** **A. The Believer's Life Before Conversion: Life Without Christ, 2:1-3** **A**nd you hath he quickened, who were dead in trespasses and sins; 2 Wherein in time past ye walked ac-	cording to the course of this world, according to the prince of the power of the air, the spirit that now worketh in the children of disobedience: 3 Among whom also we all had our conversation in times past in the lusts of our flesh, fulfilling the desires of the flesh and of the mind; and were by nature the children of wrath, even as others.	b. Following the ways of the devil c. Following the ways of the disobedient 3. **A life spent with the disobedient of the world** a. Spent gratifying one's flesh or sinful nature b. Spent following one's own mind—desires & thoughts 4. **A life under God's wrath**

Section II
THE LIFE OF THE CHRISTIAN BELIEVER, Ephesians 2:1-22

Study 1: **THE BELIEVER'S LIFE BEFORE CONVERSION: LIFE WITHOUT CHRIST**

Text: **Ephesians 2:1-3**

Aim: To flee from sin, from the kind of life you lived before Christ.

Memory Verse:

"And you hath he quickened [made alive], who were dead in trespasses and sins" (Ep.2:1).

SECTION OVERVIEW:

This chapter is one of the most important chapters in the Bible. It focuses upon the life of the Christian believer. It discusses his past, present, and future. It shows what life was like before Christ came and what it is like since He has come. It discusses what God has done for man in the *work of His mercy* and the *gift of His grace*. It also paints six pictures of the church. It is a chapter that should be lived in; it should be studied and taught time and again.

A. The Believer's Life Before Conversion: Life Without Christ (2:1-3).
B. The Believer's Conversion (Part 1): The Work of God's Mercy (2:4-7).
C. The Believer's Conversion (Part 2): The Work of God's Grace—Salvation (2:8-10).
D. Remember What Life Is Like Since Christ Came: Reconciliation and Peace (2:11-18).
E. Remember Who You Are: Six Pictures of the Church (2:19-22).

INTRODUCTION:

What was the believer's life like before he came to know Christ, before conversion? When God looks down upon a man who is unconverted, how does God see him? What is the picture in God's mind of a man who is unsaved? William Barclay descriptively titles this passage, "Life without Christ." Well, what is it like—this life without Christ? What kind of life did the believer live before conversion?

OUTLINE:

1. A life of the walking dead (v.1).
2. A life of transgressions and sins (vv.1-2).
3. A life spent with the disobedient of the world (v.3).
4. A life under God's wrath (v.3).

1. A LIFE OF THE WALKING DEAD (v.1).

Before conversion man lives a life of death. Note the words "you...were dead." How can a man be living and yet be dead? To answer this question, we must understand what death means. The basic meaning of death is *separation*. Death never means extinction, annihilation, non-existence, or inactivity. Death simply means that a person is separated, either separated from his body or from God or from both. H.S. Miller says, "Death is the separation of a person from the purpose or use for which he was intended."[1] Man was created to know, fellowship, worship, and serve God; but man does not do it. If he worships at all, he worships his *own ideas and concepts of God*, creating a god to suit his own notions—a god that will allow him to go ahead and live as he wishes.

The point is this: man does not fulfill his purpose on earth, not the purpose for which he was created. He has little if anything to do with God. He is *separated from and dead* to God. The Bible speaks of three deaths.

1. *Physical death*: the *separation* of a man's spirit from his body. This is what men commonly call death. It is when a person ceases to exist on this earth and is buried.

> **"For since by man came death, by man came also the resurrection of the dead. For as in Adam all die, even so in Christ shall all be made alive" (1 Co.15:21-22).**
>
> **"And as it is appointed unto men once to die, but after this the judgment" (He.9:27).**

2. *Spiritual death*: the separation of a man from God while he is still living and walking upon earth. This is the *natural state* of a man on earth without Jesus Christ. Man is seen as still in his sins and dead to God.

⇒ A person may walk in life *without God and Christ*, rejecting, rebelling and cursing God. The man is spiritually *separated* from God; he is *dead* to God.

⇒ person may walk in life as a religious person, worshipping a god of his own thoughts and notions, rejecting the only living and true God who was revealed by Jesus Christ. The religious person is spiritually separated from God; he is dead to God.

Spiritual death speaks of a person who is dead while he still lives (1 Ti.5:6). He is a natural man living in this present world, but he is said to be dead to the Lord Jesus Christ, to God, and to spiritual matters.

a. A person who wastes his life in riotous living is spiritually dead.

> **"It was meet that we should make merry, and be glad: for this thy brother was dead, and is alive again; and was lost, and is found" (Lu.15:32).**

b. A person who has not partaken of Christ is spiritually dead.

---

[1] Quoted by Lehman Strauss, *Devotional Studies in Galatians and Ephesians*, p.137.

"Then Jesus said unto them, Verily, verily, I say unto you, Except ye eat the flesh of the Son of man, and drink his blood, ye have no life in you" (Jn.6:53).

c. A person who does not have the Spirit of Christ is spiritually dead.

"But ye are not in the flesh, but in the Spirit, if so be that the Spirit of God dwell in you. Now if any man have not the Spirit of Christ, he is none of his" (Ro.8:9).

d. A person who lives in sin is spiritually dead.

"And you hath he quickened [made alive], who were dead in trespasses and sins" (Ep.2:1).

e. A person who is alienated from God is spiritually dead.

"Having the understanding darkened, being alienated from the life of God through the ignorance that is in them, because of the blindness of their heart: who being past feeling have given themselves over unto lasciviousness, to work all uncleanness with greediness" (Ep.4:18-19).

f. A person who sleeps in sin is spiritually dead.

"Wherefore he saith, Awake thou that sleepest, and arise from the dead, and Christ shall give thee light" (Ep.5:14).

g. A person who lives in sinful pleasure is dead while she lives.

"But she that liveth in pleasure is dead while she liveth" (1 Ti.5:6).

h. A person who does not have the Son of God is dead.

"He that hath the Son hath life; and he that hath not the Son of God hath not life" (1 Jn.5:12).

i. A person who does great religious works but does the wrong works is dead.

"And unto the angel of the church in Sardis write; These things saith he that hath the seven Spirits of God, and the seven stars; I know thy works, that thou hast a name that thou livest, and art dead" (Re.3:1).

3. *Eternal death*: the separation of man from God's presence forever. This is the second death, an eternal state of being *dead to God*. It is spiritual death, separation from God that is prolonged beyond the death of the body. It is called the "second death" or eternal death.

"For the wages of sin is death; but the gift of God is eternal life through Jesus Christ our Lord" (Ro.6:23).

"For to be carnally minded is death; but to be spiritually minded is life and peace" (Ro.8:6).

APPLICATION:
Everyone who has not trusted Christ is spiritually dead—dead to God, dead even while he lives upon this earth. This was the life of the believer before he was converted.

QUESTIONS:
1. Does Ephesians 2:1 mean that even good Christians were dead spiritually, dead before they came to know Christ?
2. What was your life like before Christ saved you? What has been the biggest change in your life since conversion?
3. In what three ways does a lost sinner die?
4. As you think about your life before Christ, what concerned you the most about how you lived? Why? How was this resolved after Christ saved you?

2. A LIFE OF TRANSGRESSIONS AND SINS (vv.1-2).

Before conversion, man lives a life of trespasses and sins. Note that it is trespasses and sins that separate men from God, that place him in a *state or process of death*. It is while men are living in trespasses and sins that they are dead (separated from God).

The word "trespass" means to fall, slip, blunder, deviate, turn aside, or wander away. It is a person who...

- falls from the right way
- slips from doing what he should
- blunders and fails
- deviates off the right road
- turns aside from what is right
- wanders away from God and righteousness

> **"[Christ] who was delivered for our offences [trespasses], and was raised again for our justification" (Ro.4:25).**

The word "sin" means to miss the mark, to err. Sin is the word most often used to describe man's wicked, fallen condition. It is what is meant by coming *short of the glory of God*. Man should live in a state of God's glory, but it is evident that he does not. There is no glory—no glow, splendor, brilliance, or light shining out from his body. And there is certainly no glory or light emanating from his behavior. Listening to any newscast on any given day is clear evidence of man's *inglorious behavior*.

The point is this: God is perfect but man is imperfect. And imperfection is as different from perfection as day is from night. Man is ever so short of God's perfect glory:

⇒ Man does not measure up to God.
⇒ Man is not on the same level as God.
⇒ Man does not reach up to God.

Man sins; he misses the mark of life. He does not live a perfect life. He may be respectable, but he is imperfect. He is never all he could be.

⇒ No husband or wife is free from selfishness and disturbance all the time—not perfectly.
⇒ No father or mother treats his child like they should all the time—not perfectly.
⇒ No child obeys his or her parent all the time—not perfectly.
⇒ No workman is diligent in his labor every minute of every day—not perfectly.
⇒ No neighbor is as good and kind and helpful as he should be all the time—not perfectly.

⇒ No person disciplines his body in eating, exercising, and sleeping all the time—not perfectly.
⇒ No person controls his mind from impure and selfish thoughts all the time—not perfectly.
⇒ No person uses his mind fully, to the maximum all the time—not perfectly.

Man is not perfect; he is short of perfection—short of God's glory—short of the purpose for which God created him. This is what is meant by sin. Sin separates man from God. Man is dead (separated) in trespasses and sins. He is dead because he blunders and comes short of God.

> **"For all have sinned, and come short of the glory of God" (Ro.3:23).**
>
> **"Wherefore, as by one man sin entered into the world, and death by sin; and so death passed upon all men, for that all have sinned" (Ro.5:12).**

Now, note a significant fact: the man who sins is said to be walking after three things.

1. *The sinner walks after the "course of this world."* This simply means he follows the world in its...

- opinions
- lifestyles
- speculations
- pleasures
- selfishness
- positions
- popularity
- honor
- religion
- values
- purposes
- technology
- possessions
- science
- standards

> **"For what is a man profited, if he shall gain the whole world, and lose his own soul? or what shall a man give in exchange for his soul?" (Mt.16:26).**

2. *The sinner walks under the power of Satan.* Note that Satan is called the "prince of the power of the air." Man was never created to be evil nor to do evil. Evil originated with an alien force that exists in another world, the spiritual world or dimension of being. The Bible calls that evil force a person, and he is named Satan or the devil. The spiritual world has access to this world and can influence the spirit of man. What has happened is that man, who has free will, has chosen to follow the evil way of Satan. When Satan tries to influence the spirit of man to sin, man often listens and sins. This is exactly what Scripture declares:

> **"Ye are of your father the devil and the lusts of your father ye will do. He was a murderer from the beginning, and abode not in the truth, because there is no truth in him. When he speaketh a lie, he speaketh of his own: for he is a liar, and the father of it" (Jn.8:44).**

3. *The sinner walks in disobedience.* Very simply, he refuses to obey God, refuses to do what God says. He chooses to do what he wants instead of what he should do. And note: he is classified by God as one of the "children of disobedience." He is a child of disobedience; that is, he is in the family of disobedience, not in the family of God.

> **"And every one that heareth these sayings of mine, and doeth them not, shall be likened unto a foolish man, which built his house upon the sand: and the rain descended, and the floods came, and the**

winds blew, and beat upon that house; and it fell: and great was the fall of it" (Mt.7:26-27).

ILLUSTRATION:
Do you know of anyone who has lived a life of trespasses and sins? A story is told of a 94-year-old man who had over the course of his life been charged with 46 crimes, convicted of five felonies, placed on probation three times and served eight prison sentences.

Facing the judge for his latest crime, he stated that he would rather go to jail than to be sentenced to a nursing home. He said, "If I go to a jail, I may be out in a couple of years, If I go to a nursing home, I may be there the rest of my life."

This is a vivid example of a man who chose to walk after the course of this world. His choice was open and defiant rebellion against the laws of the land. This is exactly the same for those who choose to openly rebel against God. This person is described as a child of disobedience: he is committed to a life of crime against God's law.

QUESTIONS:
1. What things are noticeable about someone who walks after the course of this world?
2. According to Scripture, what kind of relationship did we have with the world before Christ saved us?
3. What is the end result of a life of trespasses and sin?
4. How do these verses help you understand what separates men from God?
5. Do you worry about previous sins you committed before Christ came into your life and saved you?

3. A LIFE SPENT WITH THE DISOBEDIENT OF THE WORLD (v.3).

Before conversion, man lives a life with the disobedient of the world. Note the words "among whom." They refer to the children of disobedience mentioned in the previous verse. Note that the major stress of the disobedient is the desires of the flesh and of the mind. When most persons think of desire or lust, they think of the sins of the flesh such as:

⇒ illicit sex
⇒ overeating
⇒ intoxication
⇒ laziness
⇒ pornography

But note: the mind also desires and lusts. Some sinful lusts of the mind would be:

⇒ immoral thoughts
⇒ anger
⇒ unbelief
⇒ idolatry
⇒ envy
⇒ false beliefs

The point is this: the unconverted man lives to fulfill the desires of his flesh and mind. In reality, he has nothing else for which to live. He knows nothing but this world and its appeals; therefore, he seeks as much of the world as he can possess and enjoy. His life is self-centered, not God-centered; world-centered, not heaven-centered; selfish, not giving; banking and hoarding, not sacrificial—not meeting the needs of a world reeling in desperate need and death. The unconverted man spends his life with the disobedient of the world living after the desires of the flesh and of the mind.

"But I say unto you, That whosoever looketh on a woman to lust after her hath committed adultery with her already in his heart" (Mt.5:28).

"And the cares of this world, and the deceitfulness of riches, and the lusts of other things entering in, choke the word, and it becometh unfruitful" (Mk.4:19).

ILLUSTRATION:
Those who are on the path of disobedience are blinded to its destructive consequences. This point is illustrated graphically:

In 1982, "ABC Evening News" reported on an unusual work of modern art—a chair affixed to a shotgun. It was to be viewed by sitting in the chair and looking directly into the gunbarrel. The gun was loaded and set on a timer to fire at an undetermined moment within the next hundred years.

The amazing thing was that people waited in lines to sit and stare into the shell's path! They all knew that the gun could go off at point-blank range at any moment, but they were gambling that the fatal blast wouldn't happen during their minute in the chair.

Yes, it was foolhardy, yet many people who wouldn't dream of sitting in that chair live a lifetime gambling that they can get away with sin. Foolishly they ignore the risk until the inevitable self-destruction.[2]

APPLICATION:
A habit of sin dulls the spiritual senses. Habitual sin encases the heart and hardens it like concrete, freeing the person to fulfill the desires of the flesh and mind. Do not be fooled. The chains of sin that have men bound can only be undone by Jesus Christ. Every other solution will fail.

QUESTIONS:
1. What things fill the lives of the lost?
2. Do you ever worry about backsliding? What guards do you need—what kinds of things can you do—to keep from backsliding? To keep from returning to a worldly lifestyle?
3. What are some of the natural results of a life of disobedience?

4. A LIFE UNDER GOD'S WRATH (v.3).

Before conversion, man lives under the wrath of God. Note the wording of this statement: "[We] were by nature the children of wrath." The unconverted man...

- acts against God; he does not act for God
- rejects God; he does not receive God
- ignores God; he does not confess God
- denies God; he does not acknowledge God
- curses God; he does not praise God
- serves religion; he does not serve God
- honors a personal idea; he does not honor Christ, the very Son of God

Man acts in wrath against God: he is a child of wrath, not a child of God. Therefore, he shall reap what he has sown. What he has measured to God shall be measured to him. The wrath of God shall fall upon him.

---

2 Craig B. Larson, Editor. *Illustrations for Preaching & Teaching*, p.226.

"He that believeth on the Son hath everlasting life: and he that believeth not the Son shall not see life; but the wrath of God abideth on him" (Jn.3:36).

ILLUSTRATION:
Our choice of sin and rebellion smoothes the path for a nature of wrath to consume us. Children of wrath are their own worst enemy. For example:

Thomas Costain's history...describes the life of Raynald III, a fourteenth-century duke in what is now Belgium.

Grossly overweight, Raynald was commonly called by his Latin nickname, Crassus, which means "fat."

After a violent quarrel, Raynald's younger brother Edward led a successful revolt against him. Edward captured Raynald but did not kill him. Instead, he built a room around Raynald in the Nieuwkerk castle and promised him he could regain his title and property as soon as he was able to leave the room.

This would not have been difficult for most people since this room had several windows and a door of near-normal size, and none was locked or barred. The problem was Raynald's size. To regain his freedom, he needed to lose weight. But Edward knew his older brother, and each day he sent a variety of delicious foods. Instead of dieting his way out of prison, Raynald grew fatter.

When Duke Edward was accused of cruelty, he had a ready answer: "My brother is not a prisoner. He may leave when he so wills."

Raynald stayed in that room for ten years and wasn't released until after Edward died in battle. By then his health was so ruined he died within a year...a prisoner of his own appetite.[3]

APPLICATION:
Like it or not, all of us have family roots that link us to the other children of wrath. Our appetite for sin's pleasure kept us locked up until Christ came and set us free.

QUESTIONS:
1. What sin still "whets" (arouses) your appetite? Why?
2. Do you really believe that you were by nature, a child of wrath?
3. What does this verse teach you about the fall of man?
4. Why do some people tend to think that they were never sinners? How would you explain the truth to them?

SUMMARY:

It is never a pretty sight when we look back at our days before Christ saved us. But it is a very healthy thing when we examine our roots. It should give us an even greater appreciation of all that God has done for us. Remember, Jesus Christ saved us from:

1. A life of the walking dead.
2. A life of transgressions and sins.
3. A life spent with the disobedient of the world.
4. A life under God's wrath.

---

3 Craig B. Larson, Editor. *Illustrations for Preaching & Teaching*, p.229.

EPHESIANS 2:1-3

Personal Journal Notes
(Reflection & Response)

1. The most important thing that I learned from this lesson was:

2. The area that I need to work on the most is:

3. I can apply this lesson to my life by:

4. Closing Statement of Commitment:

Ephesians 2:4-7

1. **God has quickened, made us alive with Christ** a. Why: Because His very nature is mercy & love b. When: While we were dead in sins	**B. The Believer's Conversion (Part I): The Work of God's Mercy, 2:4-7** 4 But God, who is rich in mercy, for his great love wherewith he loved us, 5 Even when we were dead in sins, hath quickened us together with Christ,	(by grace ye are saved;) 6 And hath raised us up together, and made us sit together in heavenly places in Christ Jesus: 7 That in the ages to come he might show the exceeding riches of his grace in his kindness toward us through Christ Jesus.	c. How: By Christ's death 2. **God has raised us up with Christ** 3. **God has seated us in the heavenly realm—in Christ** 4. **God had one great purpose: To show us the riches of His grace—in the ages to come**

Section II
The Life of the Christian Believer,
Ephesians 2:1-22

Study 2: The Believer's Conversion (Part I): The Work of God's Mercy

Text: Ephesians 2:4-7

Aim: To strive to live worthy of God's mercy.

Memory Verse:

"God, who is rich in mercy, for His great love wherewith He loved us, even when we were dead in sins, hath quickened us together with Christ" (Ephesians 2:4-5).

Introduction:

Does the name Uwe Holmer mean anything to you? Perhaps not. How about the name of Erich Honecker? The lives of these two men crossed in 1990 and became a vivid example of God's mercy to the entire world.

> *Uwe Holmer is a pastor who served the Lord in what was formerly known as East Germany, a former communist nation. Like many other believers, he suffered from the 40 years of Erich Honecker's iron-fisted rule. But history has changed things. Honecker had been disposed of as leader and was facing trial on the charges of treason. While awaiting his trial, he was operated on for cancer and needed a place to recover. This beaten and sick man had no where to go: he was too sick to stay in prison and no one dared to open up his home to him because he was so hated.*
>
> *Pastor Holmer's church ran a convalescent center in the secluded village of Lobetal. Unfortunately, there was no room for Honecker. Pastor Holmer could have easily rationalized this situation and closed his heart, but instead, he opened up his own home to Honecker and his wife. The gospel compelled Uwe Holmer to reach out and minister to this man's needs. After all, that was the Christian thing to do…wasn't it?*
>
> *Torrents of rage were directed at Pastor Holmer: hate mail, bomb threats and threats to cut off funding to his ministry—all because Holmer had offered mercy to an enemy.*

Uwe Holmer explained to the nation (and to the world) why he had mercy on Erich Honecker in a letter to an East German newspaper, Neue Zeitung:

"In Lobetal" he wrote, "there is a sculpture of Jesus inviting people to Himself and crying out: 'Come unto Me all ye that labor and are heavy laden, and I will give you rest.' We have been commanded by our Lord Jesus to follow Him and to receive all those who are weary and heavy laden, in spirit and in body, but especially the homeless...What Jesus asked His disciples to do is equally binding on us."[1]

Pastor Holmer did not do the politically correct thing at all, which would have been to join the others in throwing stones at Honecker. Instead, Uwe Holmer did things the Jesus way: **"Love your enemies, do good to those who hate you, bless those who curse you, pray for those who mistreat you" (Lu.6:27-28).** Erich Honecker deserved to die a horrible death, alone. Pastor Holmer did not give him what he deserved. Instead, he gave him mercy.

Do you want to know more about this kind of mercy? This is the subject of this great passage of Scripture: the work of God's mercy.

The most astounding interruption in human history is the word "but" in this passage. Man is dead in trespasses and sins, but God is rich in mercy. He has intervened in the destiny of man; He has interrupted the doom of death and judgment. God has had mercy upon us!

OUTLINE:

1. God has quickened, made us alive with Christ (vv.4-5).
2. God has raised us up with Christ (v.6).
3. God has seated us in the heavenly realm—in Christ (v.6).
4. God had one great purpose: to show us the riches of His grace—in the ages to come (v.7).

1. GOD HAS QUICKENED, MADE US ALIVE WITH CHRIST (vv.4-5).

The work of God's mercy is to quicken us with Christ. The word "quickened" means to be made alive. We were dead in trespasses and sins, but God has made us alive. Note three significant points.

1. Why has God quickened us? Because of His very nature. God does not have a nature like most men picture: distant, disinterested, unconcerned, vengeful, and fearful.

   a. *God is full of mercy*: feelings of pity, compassion, affection, kindness. It is a desire to succor, to tenderly draw to oneself and to care for. Two things are essential in order to have mercy: seeing a need and being able to meet that need. God sees our need and feels for us (Ep.2:1-3). Therefore, He acts; He has mercy upon us...
      - God withholds His judgment
      - God provides a way for us to be saved

   b. *God is love*; He is full of love (agape): a selfless and sacrificial love; a love of the mind, of the reason, of the will as well as of the heart and affections. It is the love that goes so far...
      - that it loves a person even if he does not deserve to be loved
      - that it loves the person who is utterly unworthy of being loved
      - that it is compelled to sacrifice itself for its enemies (Ro.5:8, 10)

---

1 Reported by Bud Bultman. (Carol Stream, IL: *Christianity Today)*, 11/11/91, page 25.

"For God so loved the world, that he gave his only begotten Son, that whosoever believeth in him should not perish, but have everlasting life" (Jn.3:16).

"But God commendeth his love toward us, in that, while we were yet sinners, Christ died for us" (Ro.5:8).

2. When did God quicken and make us alive to Him? When we were dead in sins. This refers back to the former passage and outline (Ep.2:1-3).

3. How did God quicken us? By quickening and making us alive *together with Christ*. Christ is alive; He is in heaven face to face with God right now. God quickens or regenerates, making us alive with Christ. How does He do this? This is the discussion of the next two major points. As they are discussed, remember that it is by God's grace that we are saved. Salvation is all of Him; none of it is of us. We are saved by the act of God and God alone.

QUESTIONS:
1. Why has God quickened us or made us alive with Christ? When did God do this?
2. How is God able to identify with our desperate need for mercy?
3. Contrast "being dead" with "but God." What does this verse teach about God's mercy?

2. GOD HAS RAISED US UP WITH CHRIST (v.6).

The work of God's mercy is to raise us up with Christ. Note a crucial fact. Scripture plainly declares that God has raised up believers *together with Christ*. How is this possible when Christ was crucified and raised up thousands of years ago? What does Scripture mean? It means this: God raised Jesus Christ for three reasons.

1. *Jesus Christ lived a sinless and perfect life*. God loved man and wanted to save man, but He had a problem. Man had already sinned. Righteousness and perfection had already been lost, and only perfection can live in the presence of God. However, there was one hope. If a man could live a perfect and ideal life, that man could secure the perfect, ideal righteousness. And then the ideal man could stand for and cover all men who would trust Him. This is what Jesus Christ did. He came to earth as a Man and lived a perfect and sinless life. He never broke the law nor went against God's will—not even once. He was the Ideal and Perfect Man. Therefore, He did not deserve to die; He deserved to live eternally with God.

2. *Jesus Christ died for man*. God loved man and wanted to save man, but He had a problem. Man had *already sinned* and broken the law; he had already committed rebellion against God. Therefore, the penalty of death had *already been enacted and pronounced*. Man had to die. However, there was one way out of the dilemma. If the Perfect and Ideal Man would bear the penalty of sin for man, then His death could stand for and cover any man who really trusted Him. This is exactly what Jesus Christ did. He was the Ideal and Perfect Man who loved God with all His heart. Therefore, when God willed Christ to bear man's penalty and judgment for sin, He surrendered and sacrificed Himself. He died for man; He bore man's penalty and punishment for sin. He was perfectly obedient to God the Father *even in death*. Therefore, He did not deserve to die; He deserved to live forever with God.

3. *Jesus Christ was raised up from the dead*. He was the Ideal and Perfect Man; therefore, His resurrection can stand for and cover any person who truly trusts Him.

Now, how does God raise up the believer together with Christ? By belief—trust—faith. When a person truly believes in Jesus Christ, God loves His Son so much that He *counts* the person's faith as his identification with Christ. God sees the persons' faith and love for Christ, and He honors his faith and love by doing the very thing the person believes. The person believes and loves Christ for His righteousness, death, and resurrection; therefore, God counts the person as *being together* with Christ in His righteousness, death, and resurrection. God counts or credits the persons' faith...

- as his having already died and been raised with Christ
- as his having been bound together with the death and resurrection of Christ

> **"And he [Abraham] believed in the LORD; and he counted it to him for righteousness" (Ge.15:6).**
> **"For what saith the scripture? Abraham believed God, and it was counted unto him for righteousness" (Ro.4:3).**

ILLUSTRATION:
Have you ever gone somewhere for a special event, and you could not see because your vision was blocked? Do you remember how frustrating it was to be where you wanted to be but not have a good view? This little boy's story is for all of us who have experienced this:

> "*I can't see anything!*" cried the little boy. The circus had come to his town, and the parade was passing him by. He could hear the instruments playing with excitement. He could hear the *oohs* and *aahs* from the crowd as the circus passed by. All he could see was a sea of legs.
>
> Fortunately, the little boy's father took notice of his son's plight and immediately picked him up to place him high above the crowd on his shoulders.
>
> "*Wow! Look at all of those colorful costumes. The clowns are so funny to watch. Daddy, daddy, look at the elephants!*"
>
> The little boy's perspective had changed from only listening to what others were seeing; now he could also enter in, enjoying everything about the parade. His view of life was much richer upon his father's shoulders.

APPLICATION:
Where we sit is very important if we plan to see what God has done for us. Being raised up with Christ gives us a better view of God's grace. Instead of just hearing about His grace, we can view it for ourselves. Our view of life is much richer up on our Father's shoulders.

QUESTIONS:
1. Why did God raise up Jesus Christ?
2. Unless you have a good view to see God's grace at work in your life, circumstances can be very discouraging. Considering the situations in your life, where do you need to place yourself to have a better view of God's grace?
3. According to Scripture, how does God raise up the believer together with Christ?

3. GOD HAS SEATED US IN THE HEAVENLY REALM—IN CHRIST (v.6).

The work of God's mercy is to sit us in heavenly places in Christ. Note two facts.

1. "Heavenly places" should read "in the heavenlies." The believer is said to be *in Christ*. Christ is said to be "in the heavenlies." Therefore, the believer is in the heavenly realm of experience with Christ. True, the believer physically lives on earth, but spiritually he has already been placed "in the heavenlies." The believer is of both realms. He belongs to two worlds. He has two addresses: *in Ephesus* and *in Christ*. He maintains two relationships: one to earth and one to heaven (see He.3:1; 1 Pe.2:11).

2. The believer's salvation, his resurrection and exaltation, *is an accomplished fact*. In the word "together" or "with Him," a profound truth is unfolded.

a. God's unsurpassing power is said to have raised Christ from the dead and made Him sit at God's right hand in the heavenly places (Ep.1:20).
b. Believers are said to have been raised *with Christ* and are urged to "seek those things which are above, where Christ sits on the right hand of God...." (Co.2:12; 3:1, 3).
c. It is said that believers are already raised from the dead *with Christ* and already seated *with Christ* at the right hand of God. The words "quickened," "raised," and "made to sit" are all in the Greek aorist tense. They express what God has already done for His children in Christ. Christ has already died and been raised and exalted to live in heaven with God forever. God sees all things as they really are. Therefore, He sees believers as having already been raised and exalted to live eternally with Him—all because He sees them in Christ Jesus. He sees their faith and counts them as being in Christ.

"But if the Spirit of him that raised up Jesus from the dead dwell in you, he that raised up Christ from the dead shall also quicken your mortal bodies by his Spirit that dwelleth in you" (Ro.8:11).

APPLICATION:
In order to enjoy the great promises of God, we have to be *in Christ*. This is the wonderful truth of this verse and point. God has made us sit in heavenly places—in Christ. Surely, this is a work of God's mercy!

QUESTIONS:
1. Look closely at the text. Is it written in the past, present or future tense? Why is the tense in this verse significant?
2. At which "address" do you spend most of your time? What changes do you need to make to spend more and more time in your Father's presence, at your heavenly address?

4. GOD HAD ONE GREAT PURPOSE: TO SHOW US THE RICHES OF HIS GRACE—IN THE AGES TO COME (v.7).

The work of God's mercy has one great purpose—to show believers the riches of His grace throughout all the ages to come.

God has done so much for us through Christ Jesus that it will take an eternity to show it all off. "Ages" literally means in the ages that are coming one upon another; that roll in one upon another. It means an eternity of ages. Grasping this verse is easier if broken up like this...

- the exceeding riches
- of His grace in His kindness
- toward us
- through Christ Jesus

God is going to be eternally glorified for His grace and kindness toward us. All creatures will live in *stark amazement* at God's wondrous mercy shown toward men—all through Christ Jesus (see Ep.3:10).

"Then shall the righteous shine forth as the sun in the kingdom of their Father. Who hath ears to hear, let him hear" (Mt.13:43).

EPHESIANS 2:4-7

ILLUSTRATION:
Take a look at two trophy cases and what it takes to be a proud owner of one of the trophies.

> *A loser again. Satan thought for sure this time that he would add Martin to his trophy collection. He had his game plan outlined in sinister detail: blind him from seeing the gospel during his formative youthful years, offer him the lie that he could take care of his own problems, hook him with addictions, and destroy his marriage. "By the time I'm through with him, he will be all mine," Satan thought to himself. So confident was he, that he began his celebration early by giving a thumbs-up to his demon henchmen. "Boys, take some time off. Martin is going in our trophy case."*
>
> *Martin lived most of his adult life in the gutter. Over the years, his heart had become as hard as a rock. He would scoff with disdain whenever anyone would share the gospel with him.*
>
> *"I don't need any religion. I'm a man's man," was his rehearsed speech. Over the course of life, he became an alcoholic which ruined his career and marriage. By the time he was 50 years old, he was as good as dead, an accident waiting to happen.*
>
> *Unknown to Martin, God was at work in his life. Martin did not know that God also has a trophy case that is filled with trophies that resembled Martin. God takes personal pleasure in redeeming people just like Martin and in showing them off as trophies of His mercy.*
>
> *Thus God had a plan for Martin's life: replace his heart of stone with a heart of flesh, open his eyes to see his need for a Savior, and allow other believers to have a burden for him. God wanted to heal Martin from his addictions and provide a new Christian wife who would be a helpmate to him.*
>
> *The result: Martin became a trophy of God's mercy. He was saved. He was added to God's great trophy case of believers, of people who have experienced God's great mercy.*
>
> *Now, whose trophy are you?*

QUESTIONS:
1. Who are the Martin's in your circle of influence? What practical things can you do to help them become a trophy of God's mercy?
2. What is the purpose of the work of God's mercy?
3. On a scale of 1 (Need a lot of help) to 10 (Got it all together), rate yourself:
   ____ I'm very trusting of God
   ____ I'm consistently victorious over sin
   ____ I'm a guaranteed prize in God's trophy case
   Which one of these needs your immediate attention? What course of action must you take in order to raise your grade?

SUMMARY:

Do you now have a better understanding of the work of God's mercy? God does not give us what we deserve: PUNISHMENT. God gives us MERCY. Remember that:
1. God has quickened, made us alive with Christ.
2. God has raised us up with Christ.
3. God has made us sit in heavenly realm—in Christ.
4. God had one great purpose: To show us the riches of His grace—in the ages to come.

EPHESIANS 2:4-7

PERSONAL JOURNAL NOTES
(Reflection & Response)

1. The most important thing that I learned from this lesson was:

2. The area that I need to work on the most is:

3. I can apply this lesson to my life by:

4. Closing Statement of Commitment:

	C. The Believer's Conversion (Part II): The Work of God's Grace—Salvation, 2:8-10	9 Not of works, lest any man should boast.	not of works e. Reason: Lest you boast
1. You are saved a. By God's grace b. Through faith c. Not of yourself d. As a gift of God,	8 For by grace are ye saved through faith; and that not of yourselves: it is the gift of God:	10 For we are his workmanship, created in Christ Jesus unto good works, which God hath before ordained that we should walk in them.	**2. You are God's workmanship** a. Created in Christ Jesus b. Created to do good works

Section II
THE LIFE OF THE CHRISTIAN BELIEVER, Ephesians 2:1-22

Study 3: **THE BELIEVER'S CONVERSION (PART II): THE WORK OF GOD'S GRACE—SALVATION**

Text: **Ephesians 2:8-10**

Aim: To gain a perfect understanding and assurance of your salvation.

Memory Verse:

"For by grace are ye saved through faith; and that not of yourselves: it is the gift of God" (Ephesians 2:8).

INTRODUCTION:

As you browse through the employment section of a newspaper's classified ads, you will usually find a variety of entries to meet almost any need. Here is one you *will not* see, but any one of us might have placed at sometime in our lives:

> "WANTED: MASTER CRAFTSMAN NEEDED TO REMODEL DAMAGED LIFE. Current life has been damaged beyond normal repairs due to original sin. Owner has tried a variety of ways to correct the problem but has failed every time. The qualified applicant must have the following:
>
> 1. Must have own tools.
> 2. Must be willing to work .
> 3. Must have impeccable references.
> 4. Must have a previous successful track record with similar restorations.
> 5. Must be willing to work for nothing. Owner cannot pay anything.
>
> The owner will be willing to work for the Master Craftsman upon successful completion of his remodeled life.
>
> There is an immediate need to fill this position.
>
> Call 1-800-REMODEL for an appointment."

This classified ad closely resembles the cry of every Christian prior to salvation. Our damaged lives are beyond human repair, and all of our own efforts to correct the problem have failed.

Thankfully, the Master Craftsman, our Lord Jesus, was qualified to answer our ad. He had all of the tools needed to save us. He was willing to provide the work needed to save us. He was referred to us by His Father. His track record is all of the other saints that have gone before us. Finally, He would not accept any payment for our salvation. As the great hymn reminds us, "***Jesus paid it all. All to Him I owe. Sin had left a crimson stain. He washed it white as snow***" (*Jesus Paid it All.* Text by Elvina M. Hall).

This passage is one of the great evangelistic summaries of the Bible. If a man wants to be saved, these verses tell him how to be saved. Salvation is the work of God, of God's grace and of God's grace alone. It is not of man, not to any degree whatsoever.

⇒ *Salvation is a free gift of God.* It is by grace alone that man is saved. Man can do nothing whatsoever to save himself. He cannot earn, win, or merit salvation. All man can do is accept the fact that God says He will save him, accept as true the free offer of salvation (Ro.11:6).

⇒ *Salvation is received by faith* (Ro.3:27; 4:2, 5; 1 Co.1:31). Man must believe just what God says and accept His Word, accept His free offer of salvation. And when he accepts the fact that God says He will save him, God takes him and creates him into a "new man" (2 Co.5:17; Ep.4:24; 1 Pe.1:23; 2 Pe.1:4).

OUTLINE:

1. You are saved (vv.8-9).
2. You are God's workmanship (v.10).

1. YOU ARE SAVED (vv.8-9).

You are saved by God and by God alone. This is the major stress of this passage.

1. *You are saved by God's grace.* Grace means the favor and kindness of God, but there is a uniqueness about God's favor and kindness. His favor and kindness are given *despite the fact that it is undeserved and unmerited.* God has done a thing unheard of among men: God has given His grace to men despite their…

- cursing Him
- rejecting Him
- rebelling against Him
- hostility toward Him
- denial of Him
- neglect of Him
- half-hearted commitment to Him
- worship of religion instead of Him
- false worship
- idolatrous worship
- trespasses and sins

Grace is giving, but it is giving to people who do not deserve the gift. What is the gift that God has given? Jesus Christ. God has given His Son, Jesus Christ, to save men. He did not have to give His Son. God could have wiped man from the face of the earth. Man deserved it, but this is God's grace. God is full of mercy and love and kindness—by His very nature He is full of these glorious qualities. Therefore, God was *bound* to shower His grace upon man. God was bound to send His Son to save man.

God is not off someplace in the distance, far removed from man, disinterested and unconcerned with man's sufferings and death. God is gracious, full of mercy, love, and kindness for man; therefore, He has reached out through His Son Jesus Christ to help man. How?

⇒ By giving His Son to die *for man.* When Jesus Christ hung upon the cross, He was *taking our sins* upon Himself and bearing the punishment for our sins. We had committed high treason against God: rejected and rebelled against Him. The penalty for high treason is death; we are condemned to die. But Christ took our penalty and condemnation upon Himself. He died for us—in our place, in our stead, as our substitute. This is what Scripture means when it says that Christ died *for us*.

> **"But God commendeth his love toward us, in that, while we were yet sinners, Christ died for us" (Ro.5:8).**

Note that the people for whom Christ died did not deserve His sacrificial love. They were men who were…

- "without strength" (Ro.5:6)
- "ungodly" (Ro.5:6)
- "sinners" (Ro.5:8)
- "enemies" (Ro.5:10)

This is the grace of God—God's grace that showered itself upon sinful men who were lost and condemned—God's grace that gave the greatest gift possible to men—the gift of His Son to save the world.

> **"Being justified freely by his grace through the redemption that is in Christ Jesus" (Ro.3:24).**

APPLICATION:

Have you ever received a gift from someone unexpectedly, and then worried about not having a gift to give in return? If you turned down their gift because you did not have one to give in return, the giver may have been insulted—for the gift was just that—a gift. No strings attached, freely given with no expectations.

To a small degree, this expresses God's gift of grace to us. Not only is it free, with no strings attached, it is totally undeserved! What an insult to be offered such a great gift from God and not even accept it. But not only this, can you imagine giving a gift to an enemy? God did! To every one of us—while we were sinners. All He asks is that we accept His gift.

QUESTIONS:

1. What did you do to deserve God's grace? What kinds of things can anyone do to deserve God's grace?
2. Did you ever turn down God's gift before you were saved? Why?
3. Must we accept the gift of God's grace to receive salvation? Why?

2. *You are saved through faith*. What does it mean to be saved through faith? Simply this: Jesus Christ died *for us*. He bore our sin and punishment upon the cross. When we believe, really believe, that Jesus Christ died for us, God does a wonderful thing. God takes our faith and counts it as the death of Jesus Christ *for us*. That is, when we honor God's dear Son by believing in Him so much that we give all we are and have to Him, God takes the death of Jesus Christ and applies it to us.

The point is this: it is our faith that causes God to look upon us as having been in Christ when He died. It is our faith that causes God to credit us with salvation.

Jesus Christ is God's gift to us. Salvation through Christ has been wrapped up as a gift, and God hands it over to us. But note: a gift is not ours until we believe it is ours and we take and receive it. Suppose I hand you my Bible and say, "Here, this is yours. I give it to you as a gift. It is yours; take it." What is necessary for the Bible (the gift) to become yours? You have to believe it is yours and reach out to receive it. You could say, "No thank you…

⇒ I do not believe you.
⇒ I don't want it.
⇒ I deny its existence.
⇒ I don't have the time to use it."

If this is your attitude, what happens to the gift? It never becomes yours. In my mind I gave it to you, but you never received it. You either did not believe it or did not want it. This is what is meant by faith. If you really believe that Jesus Christ died *for you*, you will reach out and receive the gift of God's grace.

> **"For God so loved the world, that he gave his only begotten Son, that whosoever believeth in him should not perish, but have everlasting life" (Jn.3:16).**

QUESTIONS:
1. What does it mean to be saved through faith?
2. What is the relationship between grace and faith?
3. Could we be saved through faith without God's grace? Or could we be saved through God's grace without faith? Why?

3. *You are not saved of yourselves.* God is perfect, and to live in His presence, a person must be perfect. This is the great problem of man. Man is not perfect; therefore, he can never live in God's presence—not in and of himself. Even if man could be good enough and do enough good to become perfect (he cannot, but even if he could) he would not be acceptable to God. Why? Because he has already transgressed and become imperfect. He already stands imperfect, corruptible, aging, dying, and decaying. If man is ever to be acceptable to God—if he is ever to be perfected and have his past wiped clean—it will not be by his own hands. He cannot save himself. Salvation is not of man.

> **"For by grace are ye saved through faith; and that not of yourselves: it is the gift of God: not of works, lest any man should boast" (Ep.2:8-9).**

QUESTIONS:
1. Can anyone be good enough to be saved on his own merit?
2. If we cannot be good enough to save ourselves, why do we need to continue to try to be good and do good?

4. *You are saved as a gift of God, not of works.* There are at least seven reasons why salvation must be a free gift. (Note: some of these were stirred by thoughts from William Barclay.)[1]

a. *Man cannot make God owe him.* Man cannot put God in debt for work performed. A man who works puts his employer in debt for his services (Ro.4:4). God is completely independent. He cannot be put in debt to any man. God cannot be made to owe anything or to be obligated for anything. God does not save man because He is obligated to man or owes man but because He loves and wills to save man.

b. *Man cannot bring perfection to God.* God is perfect, incorruptible, and permanent. Man and everything about man is imperfect, corruptible, and decaying. Man cannot offer and cannot give anything to God that will satisfy His perfection. Any offer or gift from an imperfect man to a perfect God is short

1 William Barclay. *The Letters to the Galatians and Ephesians*, p.121f.

and inadequate. God accepts man's offer of himself not because man merits acceptance but simply because God loves and wills to accept man.

c. *Man cannot make God forgive him*. Man is the one who has done wrong, offended and hurt God. It is man who has broken off the friendship and relationship with God (Ro.3:23; 8:6-8). Therefore, man is the one who is to apologize and ask forgiveness, and God is the One who is to have mercy and do the forgiving. If God chooses to have mercy, it comes from a heart of grace not because man deserves it.

d. *Man cannot heal God's heart*. Man's sin breaks the heart of God (Ro.5:6, 8, 10). Therefore, man's offense is primarily against God's very nature of love, mercy, and peace. Since man's main offense is breaking the heart of God, he can only cast himself upon the love of God, apologize and ask forgiveness, trusting God to forgive. This is the glorious message of salvation. If man turns to God to ask forgiveness, God forgives and accepts man back into His glorious grace.

e. *Man cannot save himself* (Ep.2:8-9). No matter what law or work was chosen to be the channel for salvation, there would be some men who could never keep that particular law or perform that particular work. If salvation were by law and works, man could never be saved. There are always many who are totally unable to work and earn their way: the deformed, the poor, the sick, the weary, the underprivileged, the disadvantaged, the oppressed, and many, many others. However, the needy are always before God's keen eyes, and He counts them precious. Therefore, He has made provision for salvation by grace and by grace alone.

f. *Man cannot make God love him* (Tit.3:4-7). If salvation were by law and works, the love of God could never be known. God would be forced to save and bless us because He owes us not because He loves us. Our works would forever require Him to pay our wages. He would not be free to do something for us simply because He loved us. We would never know what it is to be loved by God. We would know only what it is to be paid by God for work done.

g. *Man cannot set himself free and bring about liberty of conscience*. If we were saved by law and works, liberty and freedom of spirit and conscience would never be experienced. We constantly fail and come short. This eats and gnaws away at us. If God does not forgive us simply because He loves us, then what can remove the guilt and aggravation of failure from our hearts? The law? No, for the law only points out our failure; and once we have failed, the gnawing away of conscience begins. The only way for the gnawing guilt of conscience to be removed is for God to forgive us for failing and to convince us of His forgiveness. This He has done by grace—His grace.

APPLICATION:
How small we are and how glorious God is! There is no perfection apart from God. There are no perfect gifts or even good gifts apart from God. Therefore, man must turn to God for the gift of salvation, the perfect gift for us all!

> **"Every good gift and every perfect gift is from above, and cometh down from the Father of lights, with whom is no variableness, neither shadow of turning" (Ja.1:17).**

5. *The reason salvation is by grace and not by works is to prevent men from ever boasting*. God is the Supreme and Majestic Being of the universe. He is the Creator of all that is in heaven and earth. God is the One who dwells in the ultimate light and holiness and who deserves all the worship and glory of eternity. The honor and glory due

His name are not to be shared with anyone. If man were saved by some effort of his own, he would be due some credit, some honor. This God cannot allow. His very nature forbids it. As God, He is the Supreme Glory of the universe, and as the Supreme Being, He is to receive all the glory, praise, and honor. His Supremacy—His being God—demands it.

> **"They that trust in their wealth, and boast themselves in the multitude of their riches; none of them can by any means redeem his brother, nor give to God a ransom for him" (Ps.49:6-7).**

QUESTIONS:
1. What percentage of what you own was created by you? Your possessions? Your time? Your abilities? Your environment?
2. To whom should you give praise and thanks for what you call yours?
3. Can you take credit for any good thing that you have—apart from God?
4. Why will God not tolerate men's boasting in themselves, their accomplishments, their possessions?
5. Who or what other than God can give you salvation?

2. YOU ARE GOD'S WORKMANSHIP (v.10).

You are God's workmanship. Note two points.

1. *We are God's workmanship, created in Christ Jesus.* The believer experiences two creations, both a natural birth and a spiritual birth. The spiritual birth is the point of this verse. When a man believes in Jesus Christ, God *creates him in Christ.* What does this mean?

⇒ It means that God *quickens the spirit* of the believer and makes his spirit alive. Whereas the believer's spirit was dead to God, God creates it anew and makes it alive to God.

> **"And you hath he quickened, who were dead in trespasses and sins" (Ep.2:1).**
>
> **"Even when we were dead in sins, [God] hath quickened us together with Christ, (by grace ye are saved)" (Ep.2:5).**

⇒ It means that God causes the believer to be *born again spiritually.*

> **"Jesus answered and said unto him, Verily, verily, I say unto thee, Except a man be born again, he cannot see the kingdom of God....Jesus answered, Verily, verily, I say unto thee, Except a man be born of water and of the Spirit, he cannot enter into the kingdom of God. That which is born of the flesh is flesh; and that which is born of the Spirit is spirit" (Jn.3:3, 5-6).**

⇒ It means that God actually places His *divine nature* into the heart of the believer.

> **"Whereby are given unto us exceeding great and precious promises: that by these ye might be partakers of the divine nature, having escaped the corruption that is in the world through lust" (2 Pe.1:4).**

⇒ It means that God actually makes a *new creature* of the believer.

"Therefore if any man be in Christ, he is a new creature: old things are passed away; behold, all things are become new" (2 Co.5:17).

⇒ It means that God actually creates a *new man* out of the believer.

"And that ye put on the new man, which after God is created in righteousness and true holiness" (Ep.4:24).

⇒ It means that God *renews the believer* by the Holy Spirit.

"Not by works of righteousness which we have done, but according to his mercy he saved us, by the washing of regeneration, and renewing of the Holy Ghost" (Tit.3:5).

2. *We are created to do good works*. God saves man *for good works* not by good works. God fashions man and creates a masterpiece, a work of art. The believer does not create the beauty, the art that shows in the canvas of his life. The believer just shows that he is God's workmanship by the life he lives and displays. Works are an evidence of salvation. Those who walk in trespasses and sins show that they are not God's workmanship no matter what profession they make (Ep.2:1-2). God's people give ample evidence of the *power of a new life* which operates in them.

Note that God has *ordained* us to walk in good works. Doing good works is not an option for the believer; it is the very nature of the believer. If a man has been created in Christ—if God has truly worked in him—the man does good works. His very nature dictates it. He cannot do otherwise. He is not perfect, and he fails; but he keeps coming back to God and falling upon his knees, believing and asking forgiveness, and getting back up and going forth once again to do all the good he can. As stated, it is his nature. He is a new creature created to do good works. Therefore, he does them. Just like a tree, he bears the fruit of his nature.

"Let your light so shine before men, that they may see your good works, and glorify your Father which is in heaven" (Mt.5:16).

ILLUSTRATION:

God not only created you physically, He also created you spiritually when you were born again. As a Christian believer, God's creative power continues as you do good works. Look closely at this story:

A sculptor had been hired to build a statue for the city square of a small eastern town. The subject of his statue was to be just an ordinary man who had no noticeable attractions. The artist had been hired because he had an eye that would bring out the details of the subject that only a master sculptor could. From the first, the artist had been determined to add the details that are unseen by the natural eye. He knew that the detail would take time but he had made a promise to himself that he would do his very best—no matter what circumstances or criticism came his way. And criticism did come, for the project had drug on and on. The city leaders had grown more and more impatient as month after month had passed without the statue being finished.

But finally, the seasoned sculptor completed his most excellent work. And now the great day of presentation had arrived. The response was just what he had planned: phenomenal.

"What a wonderful work of art!"

"Who is the subject?"

EPHESIANS 2:8-10

"There is no one here who looks like this statue!"
"Look at the attention given to detail."
"How do you describe something so magnificent?"
The sculptor smiled and thought to himself, "The subject, the ordinary man, is me."

The Seasoned Sculptor is also at work in our lives. Like the above illustration, we are His most excellent work that He is unveiling to the world. The Lord Jesus makes us suitable. He gives attention to the small details in our lives that need to come out, and His finished work in us leaves us speechless. Remember His promise to the believer:

> **"Being confident of this very thing, that He which hath begun a good work in you will perform it [or complete it] until the day of Jesus Christ" (Ph.1:6).**

What a great blessing for the Christian—We are His workmanship!

QUESTIONS:
1. What "good works" has God ordained for you to do?
2. Has God saved you because of your good works? Why has He saved you?
3. Why do some people think that doing good works will get them into heaven?
4. Knowing that God wants you to do good works, what practical difference should this make in your life?

SUMMARY:

Have you sent in a classified ad for the Master Craftsman? Jesus Christ is the only One who is up to the task of rebuilding broken lives. We have learned from this session two wonderful truths for the believer:
1. You are saved: by grace, through faith in God's Son, the Lord Jesus Christ.
2. You are God's workmanship, created to do good works.

PERSONAL JOURNAL NOTES
(Reflection & Response)

1. The most important thing that I learned from this lesson was:

2. The area that I need to work on the most is:

3. I can apply this lesson to my life by:

4. Closing Statement of Commitment:

	D. Remember What Life Is Like Since Christ Came: Reconciliation & Peace, 2:11-18	14 For he is our peace, who hath made both one, and hath broken down the middle wall of partition between us;	**3. Christ brings us peace** a. He made all men as one b. He broke down all barriers between Jew & Gentile
1. We were far off & separated from God a. We were barricaded from God: Were Gentiles & uncircumcised	11 Wherefore remember, that ye being in time past Gentiles in the flesh, who are called Uncircumcision by that which is called the Circumcision in the flesh made by hands;	15 Having abolished in his flesh the enmity, even the law of commandments contained in ordinances; for to make in himself of twain one new man, so making peace;	c. He wiped out all rules, the whole system of laws that divided people d. He is creating a "new man," a "new person," a "new race" of believers
b. We were cut off from Christ c. We were excluded from God's people (Israel) d. We were excluded from God's covenant & promises e. We were without hope & without God	12 That at that time ye were without Christ, being aliens from the commonwealth of Israel, and strangers from the covenants of promise, having no hope, and without God in the world:	16 And that he might reconcile both unto God in one body by the cross, having slain the enmity thereby: 17 And came and preached peace to you which were afar off, and to them that were nigh.	**4. Christ brings us reconciliation** a. By the cross b. By the preaching of peace
2. Christ brings us near to God—through His blood	13 But now in Christ Jesus ye who sometimes were far off are made nigh by the blood of Christ.	18 For through him we both have access by one Spirit unto the Father.	**5. Christ brings us access to God**

Section II
THE LIFE OF THE CHRISTIAN BELIEVER, Ephesians 2:1-22

Study 4: REMEMBER WHAT LIFE IS LIKE SINCE CHRIST CAME: RECONCILIATION AND PEACE

Text: **Ephesians 2:11-18**

Aim: To live victoriously in the peace of Christ, the peace which only Christ can bring.

Memory Verse:

"For He is our peace, who has made both one, and hath broken down the middle wall of partition between us" (Ephesians 2:14).

INTRODUCTION:

Have you ever felt like you were cut off from everyone, like you were free-falling through space with no chance for a soft landing?

James Lovell, John Swigert, and Fred Haise had this feeling also. These men served as the crew for Apollo 13 of the US space program. On Monday, April 13, 1970, their space craft became disabled on their way to the moon. A supply tank of oxygen exploded and left the crew with little provisions and plenty of worry.

There they were: three mortal men floating in space, piloting a disabled ship and sinking fast. They were helpless men who needed help. Their present reality was very sobering; chances were they would either float through the black space forever or burn in the earth's atmosphere in a blazing inferno. There was one glimmer of hope. The men at Mission Control were trying to find a way to keep them alive while salvaging what was left of the ship. For the next several days, every effort was made to rescue these astronauts from their captivity in space.

Miraculously, their lives were spared, and they returned to earth safe and sound.

This illustration reminds us of what Jesus Christ has done for us. For we, too, were "lost in space." We were separated by a gulf of space from God's presence, and our landing was bound for an eternity in hell away from His presence.

The Apollo 13 astronauts had a Mission Control to count on for help. The Christian can improve on that because it is Jesus Christ who controls the mission, and He has rescued us with reconciliation and peace. Let's look to Him and His Word, rejoicing for what He has done for us.

In verses 11-22, Paul wants the reader to grasp what God has done for man from three points of view.

1. From an *historical view*. Before Christ, God dealt with man through the Jewish nation. Since Christ, God has been moving on a world-wide scale to include both Jews and Gentiles who are willing to follow Christ. God takes both Jew and Gentile believers, and He makes them the citizens of His *new race*, His *new nation*, His *new creation*.

2. From an *individual view*. The Jewish nation was made up of individual Jews, and the Gentile nations were made up of individual Gentiles. Therefore, God deals with each single person even as He deals with the Jewish nation and with the corporate nations of the Gentile world.

3. From a *new creation* view. God is no longer dealing with earthly divisions of nations. He is dealing with a new nationality of people, a *new body* of people who make up the true citizens of His Kingdom. These citizens are individuals from all the nations of the world who now approach God through the Lord Jesus Christ. God promises to *spiritually recreate* any person who approaches Him through Christ. God causes that person to be *born again*; He makes a *new man* out of him. God further promises the *new man* that he will become a member of God's *new body* and *new nation* of people—His true church (1 Co.10:32). It is these believers—those who believe in Christ—who are to constitute the true *family of God* and to inhabit the *new heavens and earth* which God is to create in the future (2 Pe.3:10-13; Re.21:1f).

The present passage is one of the most wonderful passages in all of Scripture. Remember what life is like since Christ came: reconciliation and peace.

OUTLINE:

1. We were far off and separated from God (vv.11-12).
2. Christ brings us near to God—through His blood (v.13).
3. Christ brings us peace (vv.14-15).
4. Christ brings us reconciliation (vv.16-17).
5. Christ brings us access to God (v.18).

1. WE WERE FAR OFF AND SEPARATED FROM GOD (vv.11-12).

Note that Paul addresses the second person here, "you." He is referring to Gentiles, that is, to everyone who was not a Jew. Glance at the words "far off" in verse 13. There was a time when all of us who are Gentiles were "far off" and separated from God, a time when great division separated us from heaven. When? Before Christ.

Before Christ there was a great gulf, a great distance that separated most of the world from God. This is the discussion of these two verses. Six things kept us from God.

1. *We were barricaded from God by the Jews.* God Himself had caused the Jewish nation to be born of Abraham. He had challenged the Jews to be the missionary force to the world, proclaiming that He and He alone was the true and living God, that He was going to send the Messiah to save the world. But the Jews failed in their mission. They became exclusive, super-spiritual, prideful, and boastful in their religion, failing to reach out to the other people of the world.

⇒ They took their own name, Jews, and called themselves by that name, but they classified everyone else in a package by the name of Gentile.

⇒ They took the major ritual of their religion, circumcision, and called themselves by that name, but they classified everyone else as *the uncircumcised.*

The point is this: we as Gentiles were barricaded from God by religion, a religion that had known the truth but had allowed itself to become corrupted.

APPLICATION:
Religion can keep a man from God—a corrupted religion. We must be on guard to protect the truth of Jesus Christ from corruption.

2. *We were "without Christ."* This means that we as Gentiles neither knew nor expected the Messiah, that is, the anointed One of God. As Gentiles we had no hope of the coming Saviour for the world.

3. *We were "aliens" from God's people, that is, from Israel.* This means that we as Gentiles were not citizens of God's people—the nation of people being built by God for Himself. As Gentiles we had no destiny.

4. *We were "strangers from the covenant and promises of God."* This means that we as Gentiles were not the covenant people of God. God did not approach the Gentiles directly with the covenant relationship. The Jews alone had a covenant relationship with God.

5. *We had "no hope."* This means that we as Gentiles lived in all the fears and the anxieties of life and in constant expectancy of death. We had no hope of a life beyond this world, beyond human history.

6. *We were "without God in the world."* This means that we as Gentiles stood alone in this world. We had no source of strength or hope beyond that which we ourselves could muster or which others like us could provide. There was nothing to which we could look beyond ourselves. We had "gods many, and lords many" (1 Co.8:5), but we were alienated from the only living and true God.

APPLICATION:
Since Christ has come, we now have no excuse for being separated from God. And yet many people are still *lost,* still without God. What a tragedy and waste when God has provided the means to be rescued!

"This people draweth nigh unto me with their mouth, and honoureth me with their lips; but their heart is far from me" (Mt.15:8).

QUESTIONS:
1. What kinds of things keep men away from God today?
2. If you are not saved, what barriers keep you away from God? If you are saved, what keeps you from experiencing a close relationship with God?
3. Do you ever experience feelings of hopelessness? Do you think God can bring you hope in every situation you face? Why or why not?
4. Why do you think God wants your source of strength to come from Him? What happens to you if your strength is your sole source?

2. CHRIST BRINGS US NEAR TO GOD—THROUGH HIS BLOOD (v.13).

The words "but now" are a forceful contrast. Christ Jesus has now come into the world. There was a time when He had not entered the world, a time when men were divided and separated from God and from each other, *but now* Christ has come to bring all men to God as well as to each other. How does Christ bring us near God? Note how clearly and unmistakably Scripture declares: "By the blood." It is by the blood of Christ that men are brought near God. But why blood? Why was it necessary for Christ to die in order to bring us near God? There are at least two reasons.

1. *Man was estranged from God*: he had rejected and rebelled against God, committing high treason against Him. Man was working all kinds of evil and injustice in the world—all against the will and law of God. And, even as the case is among men, the penalty for high treason and insurrection is exile and separation or death.

Now note: there was only one way man could ever be brought back to God—if God loved him enough to forgive his transgression and rebellion. The glorious gospel is that God did love man that much. God was willing to forgive man. However, there was one problem. The judgment of exile or death had already been pronounced, and the Lord's Word could not be revoked. What could God do? Only one thing: God had to provide a Perfect, Ideal Man for men, a Man who could stand as the Pattern for all men. If He could provide the Ideal Man, then He could die *for man,* and His death would stand for the death of all men.

This God has done. God has loved man with a perfect love—a love so strong that He was willing to substitute His Son for man. Only God and God's Son could love that much. This is the first reason Christ had to die, to shed His blood for man.

> **"For he hath made him to be sin for us, who knew no sin; that we might be made the righteousness of God in him" (2 Co.5:21).**

APPLICATION:
In the Old Testament days, blood was used to "cover" the sins of God's people. But now, Jesus Christ's blood "cleanses" us from our sins. He actually washes them away, completely cleanses us from sin. Only Christ can do this!

2. *God wanted to show just how much He loves the world.* No "greater love can a man give than this, that a man lay down his life for his friends" (Jn.15:13). However, God has gone much farther than just giving His life for His friends; He has given His life for enemies. Note the point: we were not friends of God. We were enemies, in rebellion against Him, rejecting Him and every righteous law of His. Therefore, when Christ died, He died for men who were...

- "without strength" (Ro.5:6)
- "ungodly" (Ro.5:6)
- "sinners" (Ro.5:8)
- "enemies" (Ro.5:10)

> **"For when we were yet without strength, in due time Christ died for the ungodly" (Ro.5:6).**
>
> **"But God commendeth his love toward us, in that, while we were yet sinners, Christ died for us. Much more then, being now justified by his blood, we shall be saved from wrath through him. For if, when we were enemies, we were reconciled to God by the death of his Son, much more, being reconciled, we shall be saved by his life" (Ro.5:8-10).**

QUESTIONS:
1. Why was it necessary for Christ to die in order to bring you near God?
2. How do you think God wants you to respond as He draws you near?
3. What does this verse tell you about God's promise to the Christian believer?

3. CHRIST BRINGS US PEACE (vv.14-15).

Note that Jesus Christ Himself is our peace.

⇒ Christ brings us peace when we realize that He died for us, offering us deliverance from the bondage of sin and death and a life of eternity with God.

⇒ Christ brings a deeper sense of peace when we realize that He gives the daily power to overcome the aggravating and terrible weight of anguish, guilt, loneliness, emptiness, and fear.

⇒ Christ brings a still deeper sense of peace when we realize that He has brought perfect love and unity to the world—that He has eliminated all divisions and barriers and differences between God and man and between men.

Christ is *man's peace* because He does four things for man.

1. Christ brings peace by bringing men together as "one" (v.14). Note that He has made "both one," that is, Jew and Gentile. There are two ways that Christ makes men as one.

a. All men now approach God on the same basis, on an equal footing: by the blood of Jesus Christ. There is no other way. Therefore, when a man comes to the cross, he comes with everyone else who is standing at the feet of Jesus. He stands as one with them—all on an equal basis: sinners who need a Savior. Standing there, he is not accepted by God because he is better, healthier, wealthier, more intelligent, more capable, or more religious than anyone else. He is acceptable to God because he acknowledges his unworthiness and nothingness—his desperate need—to be saved by the blood of Christ. He is acceptable to God because he acknowledges that he is as all other men—lost and needful—and he comes as one with all other men to confess Christ as his Savior.

"Peace I leave with you, my peace I give unto you: not as the world giveth, give I unto you. Let not your heart be troubled, neither let it be afraid" (Jn.14:27).

b. All men who come to Christ for salvation receive a common love and purpose and work.

⇒ First, there is the common love. Every believer who comes to Jesus Christ loves Him, and that common love *among* believers stirs a common love between believers. Love for Jesus Christ stirs love for all those whom Christ loves—which is everyone. Christ leads men to love one another.

⇒ Second, there is the common purpose and work: that of living righteously and bearing testimony to the glorious message of salvation and to life eternal.

"But if we walk in the light, as he is in the light, we have fellowship one with another, and the blood of Jesus Christ his Son cleanseth us from all sin" (1 Jn.1:7).

2. Christ brings peace by breaking down all barriers (v.14). This is a picture taken from the temple. The temple was surrounded by a series of courts. Each court had a high wall separating it from the preceding court.

⇒ As one approached the temple, he entered first of all the outer Court of the Gentiles. This is where the buying and selling of animals as well as the exchanging of money for foreign worshippers took place.

⇒ Then there was the Court of the Women. A Jewish woman was limited to this court unless she had come to make a sacrifice.

⇒ The next court was the Court of the Israelites. This is where the whole congregation gathered on the great feast days to hand over sacrifices to the priests.

⇒ The Court of the Priests was next. This court was in the temple proper where the temple itself stood. This area was considered sacred and was accessible only to the services of the priests.

⇒ Finally, within the very heart of the temple stood the Holy of Holies or the Most Holy Place where the very presence of God was to dwell. Only the High Priest could enter the Holy Place, and he could enter only once a year—at the great Passover Feast.

Partition after partition separated people from the presence of God. Tablets hung around the wall of the Gentile Court announcing that if any Gentile walked into any other court, he was to be put to death. The picture is that of Jesus Christ breaking down all barriers and walls that separate man from God. All men can now approach God equally through the death of Jesus Christ. Men build all kinds of barriers and prejudices against other men. Society is plagued with barriers and prejudices built around such things as...

- race
- color
- religion
- position
- wealth
- organizations
- morality
- dress
- appearance
- health
- commitment
- ability

But Christ has now done away with all barriers and prejudices. He has broken them all down by the blood of His cross. All men now approach God and become worthy on the same basis: by bowing before the cross and surrendering their lives to God's Son, the Lord Jesus Christ.

"But be not ye called Rabbi: for one is your Master, even Christ and all ye are brethren" (Mt.23:8).

3. Christ brings peace by wiping out the enmity of the law against us. Before Christ, man had to approach God through law. However, man discovered something: the law did not make him acceptable to God: it condemned him and showed him how far away from God be really was—totally depraved. Every time he broke the law, the law cried out "guilty" and pronounced the penalty of being imperfect, unworthy, and unacceptable to God. Man discovered that the law was against him—at enmity with him. But now, Christ has done away with the enmity and condemnation of the law.

⇒ He has lived a sinless life, fulfilling the law perfectly; and thereby He has secured the Perfect and Ideal Righteousness.

⇒ He has also paid the penalty for man's having broken the law. As the Ideal and Perfect Man, He could do this. When He died on the cross, He bore our condemnation and punishment.

The point is this: Christ fulfilled all the law. He is now the Way for man to approach God—through Christ not through the law. Therefore, there are no laws, no rules, and no decrees to keep men from God. There is only one thing that keeps a man away from God: refusing to come to God through His Son Jesus Christ.

> **"Think not that I am come to destroy the law, or the prophets: I am not come to destroy, but to fulfill" (Mt.5:17).**

4. Christ brings peace by creating a "new man." God planned and promised a "new creation"—the creation of a *new man* individually and corporately, a new man in whom Jesus Christ dwells (Co.1:27).

Individually when a man turns to Christ, Christ causes the man to be *born again*. He recreates the man. The man has a new life; he begins life all over again. He has a new beginning, and this new beginning brings peace—peace of heart and mind.

Corporately in Jesus Christ all men who believe, both Jew and Gentile, make up *one new body* (Ep.2:16), *one new family* (Ep.2:19), *one new building* (Ep.2:20-22), *one new temple* (Ep.2:21), *one new fellowship* (Ep.1:22).

QUESTIONS:
1. Who is the believer's source for peace?
2. What area of your life is in need of peace right now?
3. What example can you remember when you experienced God's peace?
4. What keeps men from experiencing the peace of God? Do these same barriers frustrate you also? What steps need to be taken in order to overcome these barriers?

4. CHRIST BRINGS US RECONCILIATION (vv.16-17).

The word "reconcile" means to change thoroughly, to exchange, to change from enmity to friendship, to bring together, to restore. The idea is that two persons who should have been together all along are brought together; two persons who had something between them are restored and reunited.

Five points should be noted about reconciliation.

1. The thing that broke the relationship between God and man was sin. Men are said to be enemies of God (Ro.5:10), and the word "enemies" refers back to the sinners and the ungodly (Ro.5:6, 8). The "enemies" of God are the sinners and ungodly of this world. This simply means that every man is an enemy of God, for every man is a sinner and ungodly. This may seem unkind and harsh, but it is exactly what Scripture is saying. The fact is clearly seen by thinking about the matter for a moment.

The sinner cannot be said to be a friend of God's. He is antagonistic toward God, opposing what God stands for. The sinner is...

- rebelling against God
- rejecting God
- cursing God
- ignoring God
- disobeying God
- fighting against God
- denying God
- refusing to live for God

When any of us sin, we work against God and promote evil by word and example.

⇒ When the sinner lives for himself, he becomes an enemy of God. Why? Because God does not live for Himself. God gave Himself up in the most supreme way possible: He gave His only Son to die *for* us.

⇒ When the sinner lives for the world and worldly things, he becomes an enemy of God. Why? Because he chooses the temporal things which pass away over God. Man chooses temporal things when God has provided eternal life for him through the death of His Son.

This is the point of God's great love or reconciliation. He did not reconcile and save us when we were righteous and good. He reconciled and saved us when we were enemies, ignoring and rejecting Him. As stated above, it is because we are sinners and enemies that we need to be reconciled.

2. The way men are reconciled to God is by the death of His Son, Jesus Christ. Very simply stated, when a man believes that Jesus Christ died for him...

- God accepts the death of Jesus Christ *for* the death of the man
- God accepts the sins borne by Christ as the sins committed by the man
- God accepts the condemnation borne by Christ as the condemnation due to the man

Therefore, the man is freed from his sins and the punishment due his sins. Christ bore both the sins and the punishment for the man. The man who truly believes that God loves that much—enough to give His only begotten Son—becomes acceptable to God, reconciled forever and ever.

3. God is the One who reconciles, not men. Men do not reconcile themselves to God. They cannot do enough work nor enough good to become acceptable to God. Reconciliation is entirely the act of God. God is the One who reaches out to men and reconciles them unto Himself. Men *receive* the reconciliation of God.

4. All men can be reconciled to one another, can be brought together, if they look up to God "through the Lord Jesus Christ." Men who look up to Jesus Christ for reconciliation and peace with God are linked arm in arm under the same Lord.

5. Men learn about reconciliation by the preaching of Jesus Christ. Christ was the first to preach the message. His followers are to follow in His trail, for there is no other way men can know that they *can* be reconciled to God apart from preaching.

> **"And all things are of God, who hath reconciled us to himself by Jesus Christ, and hath given to us the ministry of reconciliation" (2 Co.5:18; see v.19-21).**

QUESTIONS:
1. How do men try to reconcile themselves to God? Why do they fail?
2. Why doesn't God just overlook your sin?
3. What is the ultimate goal between people—what is the very thing God is after among people—after we confess our sin to God?

5. CHRIST BRINGS US ACCESS TO GOD (v.18).

The word access means to bring to, to move to, to introduce, to present. The thought is that of being in a royal court to be presented and introduced to the King of kings. Jesus Christ is the One who throws open the door into God's presence. He is the One who presents us to God, the Sovereign Majesty of the universe.

Note that it is the Holy Spirit who escorts us into God's presence. The idea is that of daily access—hour by hour, moment by moment. The Holy Spirit keeps us in the presence of God.

⇒ The Holy Spirit is the Divine Nature of God within us that gives us permanent access into God's presence. (Jn.3:5; Ro.8:11; 2 Pe.1:4).

⇒ The Holy Spirit is the One who works in us and stirs us to move more and more into God's presence (Ro.8:14; Ga.4:6-7).

⇒ The Holy Spirit is the constant companion with us, teaching us to live in God's presence (Jn.14:26; 1 Co.2:12-13).

⇒ The Holy Spirit is the One within us who bears witness that we are children of God and should approach God continually (Ro.8:15-16; Ga.4:4-6).

"I am the door: by me if any man enter in, he shall be saved, and shall go in and out, and find pasture" (Jn.10:9).

"Having therefore, brethren, boldness to enter into the holiest by the blood of Jesus" (He.10:19).

ILLUSTRATION:

Do you picture your heavenly Father as too busy running His Kingdom for you to interrupt Him? Do your needs really matter to Him?

Kay Arthur, the founder of Precept Ministries, shared this insight with a group of Bible college students concerning access to God by the believer.

> *A little boy bruised his knee and needed his Daddy to fix it up. With tears streaming down his face, he ran to see his Daddy. Seeing him coming, the [secretary] quickly opened the massive doors and let him into his Daddy's office.*
>
> *His father was busy managing his business and was surrounded by his assistants. But in the midst of all of this, the little boy ran up to his father and climbed onto his waiting lap.*
>
> *What do you think his Daddy did? Push his son aside and have him removed from the room? No! Daddy's first response was "where does it hurt and how can I make it better?"*

And so it is with our Heavenly Father and us, His children. When we need our Father, we have direct access to Him through Jesus Christ. And in the middle of His managing the Kingdom, He invites us to sit in His lap to tell Him where it hurts.

QUESTIONS:

1. Our Father invites you to come and sit in His lap. Where does it hurt? How can He make it better?
2. Who is the Person who gives you access to the Father?
3. Share a time when you especially needed to enter God's presence. When were you most aware of His presence?
4. What are you told to do in order to come into God's presence?

SUMMARY:

We remembered what life was like *before* Christ came into our lives: we were lost, without God in this present world. We also remembered what life is like *since* Christ came into our lives. He has brought us reconciliation and peace:

1. We were far off and separated from God.
2. Christ brings us near to God—through His blood.
3. Christ brings us peace.
4. Christ brings us reconciliation.
5. Christ brings us access to God.

Ephesians 2:11-18

Personal Journal Notes
(Reflection & Response)

1. The most important thing that I learned from this lesson was:

2. The area that I need to work on the most is:

3. I can apply this lesson to my life by:

4. Closing Statement of Commitment:

	F. Remember Who You Are: Six Pictures of the Church, 2:19-22	of the apostles and prophets, Jesus Christ himself being the chief corner stone;	
		21 In whom all the building fitly framed	**4. Picture 4: A growing organism**
1. Picture 1: A new nation	19 Now therefore ye are no more strangers and foreigners, but	together groweth unto an holy temple in the Lord:	**5. Picture 5: A worldwide temple—the universal or worldwide church**
2. Picture 2: God's family	fellowcitizens with the saints, and of the household of God;	22 In whom ye also are builded together for an habitation of	**6. Picture 6: A local temple—the local church**
3. Picture 3: God's building	20 And are built upon the foundation	God through the Spirit.	

Section II
THE LIFE OF THE CHRISTIAN BELIEVER, Ephesians 2:1-22

Study 5: REMEMBER WHO YOU ARE: SIX PICTURES OF THE CHURCH

Text: **Ephesians 2:19-22**

Aim: To understand your vital role in God's church.

Memory Verse:

"Take heed therefore unto yourselves, and to all the flock, over the which the Holy Ghost hath made you overseers, to feed the church of God, which he hath purchased with his own blood" (Acts 20:28).

INTRODUCTION:

Have you ever wondered how the film in your camera is developed into pictures? The principle is very simple: point your camera at your subject, press the shutter button, and the light will burn an impression of your subject on the film. After your film is processed by a lab, pictures appear. If everything worked (such as adjusting all the settings, holding the camera still, using the proper lighting), you have in your possession a record of your memories.

As you will learn in this session, God has taken six pictures of the church in order to help you better understand how you relate to each "picture." God has pointed His camera at the church, pressed the shutter, and His light has burned an impression on the film. The fruit of His labor is a photo album of six pictures of the church.

In order for you to have a better view of these pictures, a type of picture is assigned to each of the outline points:

OUTLINE:

1. Picture 1: a new nation (v.19).
2. Picture 2: God's family (v.19).
3. Picture 3: God's building (v.20).
4. Picture 4: a growing organism (v.21).
5. Picture 5: a worldwide temple—the universal church or worldwide church (v.21).
6. Picture 6: a local temple—the local church (v.22).

Now gather around God's photo album to share the joy of His labor!

Ephesians 2:19-22

1. PICTURE 1: A NEW NATION (v.19).

Note the word "fellowcitizens." We, the Gentiles, are no longer strangers and foreigners to God; we are now fellowcitizens with all the saints of God.

1. We were strangers and foreigners. The word "stranger" means an outsider, an unknown person, a person who does not belong. The word "foreigner" means sojourner, alien, a migrant, an exile. There was a time when we...

- were outside God and His kingdom
- were unknown to God and His kingdom
- did not belong to God and His kingdom
- were sojourners, living outside God and outside His kingdom
- were alien to God and to His kingdom
- were migrants, not belonging to God nor to His kingdom
- were exiles to God and to His kingdom

There was a time when we were as a stranger and a foreigner to God, when we were not citizens of God's kingdom. We had no relationship and no fellowship with God and no home and no rights to citizenship in His kingdom.

But note the glorious news: we are no longer strangers and foreigners to God. Jesus Christ has brought us to God. We are now *fellowcitizens* with all of God's people. We now have a home and all the rights of citizenship in God's kingdom.

2. Note the word "saints." It means those who are set apart or separated to God. The picture is that of a people who are *fellowcitizens* in a nation being created by God. The people are called...

- *Saints*: a people set apart to God
- *Fellowcitizens*: a people being built into a new nation under God

> **"By faith he sojourned in the land of promise, as in a strange country, dwelling in tabernacles with Isaac and Jacob, the heirs with him of the same promise: for he looked for a city which hath foundations, whose builder and maker is God" (He.11:9-10).**

ILLUSTRATION:

Have you ever wondered what emotions entered the mind of Columbus when he discovered a new world? After finally finding land (the island of San Salvador), we pick up his story:

> *They reached the southern tip of the island, just as the sun rose above the blue horizon on their larboard beam. A new day was dawning, a new era for mankind. The fears and aches of weeks at sea seemed like nothing at all now. In every heart was dawning an awareness of the enormity of what they had accomplished—and the awe of it was overwhelming! Whereas, at the time of the first sighting, there had been laughing and dancing, now they were silent, as every eye followed the coastline slowly unfolding before them, glowing in the morning sun...Columbus was the first to set foot on dry land...Their eyes filled with tears, as they knelt and bowed their heads... Columbus prayed: "O Lord, Almighty and everlasting God, by Thy holy Word Thou hast created the heaven and the earth, and the sea; blessed and glorified be Thy Name, and praised be Thy Majesty, which hath deigned to use us, Thy humble servants, that Thy holy Name may be proclaimed in this second part of the earth."*[1]

---

[1] Peter Marshall & David Manuel. *The Light and the Glory*. (Old Tappan, NJ: Fleming H. Revell Co., 1977), p.41.

Historians have called the United States a "melting pot." Ever since there has been an America to come to, people from all over the world have come to this land looking for a new start in a new land. Many families came to America with only the clothes upon their backs. Others came to America bringing with them great wealth. But no matter what their economic status or what part of the world they came from, once in America, they became part of a new nation. America became a picture of men, women, boys, and girls from every part of the earth—a spectacular blending of cultures and races.

There was a time when we were as strangers and foreigners to God, when we were not citizens of God's kingdom. We had no relationship and no fellowship with God and no home and no rights to citizenship in His kingdom.

But note the glorious news: we are no longer strangers and foreigners to God. Jesus Christ has brought us to God. We are now fellowcitizens with all of God's people. We now have a home and all the rights of citizenship in God's kingdom.

QUESTIONS:

1. Imagine yourself in a writing contest. Your assignment is to share in one sentence what your citizenship in God's Kingdom means to you. What would you say?
2. Are you comfortable with the fact that the church is a "melting pot" of people with differences? What are some differences which are readily seen?
3. Why is it that some Christians treat each other like strangers and foreigners?

2. PICTURE 2: GOD'S FAMILY (v.19).

Note the phrase "household of God." Jesus Christ has brought us into the family of God. This involves two glorious privileges.

1. *The privilege of adoption.* We have been adopted as children of God, sons and daughters of His. We now live in the same house with God and His family, and all the experiences of God's family are now ours:

⇒ love	⇒ provision	⇒ clothing (Mt.6:25f)	⇒ direction
⇒ care	⇒ protection		⇒ fellowship
⇒ help	⇒ food	⇒ training	⇒ interest
⇒ concern	⇒ shelter (Mt.6:25f)	⇒ discipline	⇒ intimacy
⇒ companionship			

"For ye have not received the spirit of bondage again to fear; but ye have received the Spirit of adoption, whereby we cry, Abba, Father. The Spirit itself beareth witness with our spirit, that we are the children of God: and if children, then heirs; heirs of God, and joint-heirs with Christ; if so be that we suffer with him, that we may be also glorified together" (Ro.8:15-17).

2. *The privilege of responsibility and service.* Again, note the term household. Every person of the household has duties to perform, some service to render for the sake of the family. We are responsible to love and care, provide and teach each other—do all the things mentioned in the previous point as well as everything else that will build up and strengthen the family of God.

"As we have therefore opportunity, let us do good unto all men, especially unto them who are of the household of faith" (Ga.6:10).

APPLICATION:
Every family should have a list of chores that are divided up and shared. As a child, you may have done your chores willingly, grudgingly, or only after many reminders and threats. But as a parent or adult, you hope that your children will be responsible and caring enough to do their chores with a good spirit, without having to be asked or told what to do.

How different is this from what our heavenly Father desires of us? Willing service with a good spirit—without having to be asked. He's already told us what to do and provided the tools, the strength, and all the resources we need to serve Him. Now it's up to us to obediently serve!

QUESTIONS:
1. What are your chores in your spiritual family?
2. Should we offer to serve or wait to be asked to serve in our church family?
3. Is it easier for you to serve or to be served? Why? What should our attitude be toward other family members in the church?

3. PICTURE 3: GOD'S BUILDING (v.20).

Believers are pictured as being the building stones which are being used to construct a building for God. Note two significant points.

1. Jesus Christ Himself is the *chief cornerstone*. The symbolism of the chief cornerstone says three significant things to us.

a. *The cornerstone is the first stone laid.* All other stones are placed after it. It is the preeminent stone in time. So it is with Christ. He is *the first* of God's new movement.

⇒ Christ is the captain of our salvation. All others are crew members who follow Him.

> **"For it became him, for whom are all things, and by whom are all things, in bringing many sons unto glory, to make the captain of their salvation perfect through sufferings" (He.2:10).**

⇒ Christ is the author of eternal salvation and of our faith. All others are the readers of the story.

> **"Looking unto Jesus the author and finisher of our faith; who for the joy that was set before him endured the cross, despising the shame, and is set down at the right hand of the throne of God" (He.12:2).**

⇒ Christ is the beginning and the end. All others come after Him.

> **"I am the Alpha and Omega, the beginning and the ending, saith the Lord, which is, and which was, and which is to come, the Almighty" (Re.1:8; see 21:6; 22:13).**

⇒ Christ is the forerunner into the very presence of God. All others enter God's presence after Him.

> **"Which hope we have as an anchor of the soul, both sure and stedfast, and which entereth into that within the veil; whither the**

forerunner is for us entered, even Jesus, made an high priest for ever after the order of Melchisedec" (He.6:19-20).

b. *The cornerstone is the supportive stone.* All other stones are placed upon it and held up by it. They all rest upon it. The cornerstone is the preeminent stone in position and power. So it is with Christ. He is the support and power, the Foundation of God's new movement.

⇒ Christ is *the head cornerstone*, the only true foundation upon which man can build. All crumble who are not laid upon Him.

"For other foundation can no man lay than that is laid, which is Jesus Christ" (1 Co.3:11).

⇒ Christ is *the chief cornerstone* upon which all others are fitly formed together. All who wish to be fitly formed together have to be laid upon Him.

"And are built upon the foundation of the apostles and prophets, Jesus Christ himself being the chief corner stone; in whom all the building fitly framed together groweth unto an holy temple in the Lord: in whom ye also are builded together for an habitation of God through the Spirit" (Ep.2:20-22).

c. *The cornerstone is the directional stone.* It is used to line up the whole building and all the other stones. It can be called the *instructional stone*—upon it all the lines and instructions of the building are based. So it is with Christ. He is the Person who gave and gives the directions and instructions to God's people. We—the church—are to build our lives upon His instructions and His instructions only. If we follow any other instructions or directions, we will be out of line; and when we are noticed, we will have to be removed, cast aside, and replaced with a stone that can be set in line. Jesus Christ is the chief cornerstone. God used Him to give direction to all the other stones.

"Wherefore also it is contained in the scripture, Behold, I lay in Sion a chief corner stone, elect, precious: and he that believeth on him shall not be confounded. Unto you therefore which believe he is precious: but unto them which be disobedient, the stone which the builders disallowed, the same is made the head of the corner, and a stone of stumbling, and a rock of offence, even to them which stumble at the word, being disobedient: whereunto also they were appointed" (1 Pe.2:6-8).

APPLICATION:
Jesus Christ is the chief cornerstone. If He is removed, the church will collapse: no Christ, no church. Christ holds everything within the church together. Therefore, it is an absolute necessity that He and He alone be preached, taught, and lived.

"Therefore whosoever heareth these sayings of mine, and doeth them, I will liken him unto a wise man, which built his house upon a rock: and the rain descended, and the floods came, and the winds blew, and beat upon that house; and it fell not: for it was founded upon a rock. And every one that heareth these sayings of mine, and doeth them not, shall be likened unto a foolish man, which built his

> **house upon the sand: and the rain descended, and the floods came, and the winds blew, and beat upon that house; and it fell: and great was the fall of it" (Mt.7:24-27).**

2. We, the church, are built upon the foundation laid by the testimonies of the apostles and prophets. They surrounded the Lord Jesus Christ Himself. Their record and testimony of the Word of God itself is the foundation upon which the church is to be laid.

> **"And he gave some, apostles; and some, prophets; and some, evangelists; and some, pastors and teachers; for the perfecting of the saints, for the work of the ministry, for the edifying of the body of Christ" (Ep.4:11-12).**

ILLUSTRATION:

How many of us would hire a contractor to build our dream house if he did not use blueprints? If he used your money to build your house without instructions? You can imagine the results: he poured the foundation in the wrong place. He put the electrical wires where the hot water pipes should go. He made your bedroom the size of a phone booth and your fireplace wound up in a closet!

You would never entrust your house to a contractor without some plan or blueprint. In the same sense, God would not build His church without a blueprint. Unlike the contractor above, God made certain that His foundation was sure by making Jesus Christ the chief cornerstone. Because the Cornerstone is in place, every other stone will be in line, and the church will be built the right way. This is one building project that is very important to God. His investment cost Him a lot—His own Son, the Lord Jesus Christ.

QUESTIONS:

1. Name some things you have tried to do that failed because of a poorly laid foundation?
2. Scripture says that we are God's building. What things can you do in order to be sure your are staying 'in line' with Christ and His church?
3. What happens to a church that does not have a solid foundation built upon Christ?

4. PICTURE 4: A GROWING ORGANISM (v.21).

The word "grows" is a biological word, the idea of a living organism. The church is pictured as a living organism—the union of various parts of a living being, of a dynamic body. This may seem strange to speak of a building in biological terms—a building that grows. The point is that more and more parts, more and more believers are brought and fitted into the building as each day passes. The building grows and grows and shall continue to grow until the Lord Jesus Christ returns.

Note another fact as well. Peter calls Jesus Christ the *living stone*. Christ is the *living stone* upon whom all others are built. All others have to be built upon Him if they wish to live and have their spiritual sacrifice accepted by God.

> **"To whom coming, as unto a living stone, disallowed indeed of men, but chosen of God, and precious, ye also, as lively stones, are built up a spiritual house, an holy priesthood, to offer up spiritual sacrifices, acceptable to God by Jesus Christ" (1 Pe.2:4-5).**

Note that it is all of God; it is all due to God's work. He is the One who raises up the Savior. Note also that the Savior is the object of marvel and wonder.

APPLICATION:
The church and its believers have two dynamic challenges in this point.
1. The church must grow. It must be bringing new stones (believers) and fitting them into the building of God. The church must be adding on to the building. Its structure is not yet finished.
2. Every believer within the building is a part of the building and expected to fulfill its function within the building; that is, every believer is a laborer, a laborer who is expected to be busy adding on to the building of the church. We are all to be bringing new stones and fitting them into the great building of God, the church.

> **"Go ye therefore, and teach all nations, baptizing them in the name of the Father, and of the Son, and of the Holy Ghost: teaching them to observe all things whatsoever I have commanded you: and, lo, I am with you alway, even unto the end of the world" (Mt.28:19-20).**

ILLUSTRATION:
The church of Jesus Christ has a destiny to grow. Satan has opposed this growth throughout the ages. History has proven that he will stop at nothing to achieve his goal (which will ultimately fail).

Anyone who has seen a picture produced by a fetal *ultrasound* has seen one of God's greatest miracles: a growing organism; a little child who has hands and feet and a heart that beats. Today, there is a literal war that rages around the world, and the innocent children in their mothers' wombs are caught in the crossfire. There are many who desire to solve the problem of pregnancy by claiming that life begins after the fetus is born. But the fetal *ultrasound* allows us to see for ourselves that life begins before birth.

Look closely at the ultrasound and rejoice. The church is alive and growing!

Throughout the history of the church, Satan has also tried to abort or destroy the body of Christ, the church. He has, in a sense, seen God's spiritual *ultrasound* and fears a church that is a growing organism. In spite of his opposition, the church will be triumphant. Jesus reminded us of this when He said "**...upon this rock I will build my church; and the gates of hell shall not prevail against it**" (Mt.16:18b).

QUESTIONS:
1. What would God have you do to protect the 'growing' church, the church that is not yet fully formed?
2. Is your church growing?
3. What do you think builds a better foundation: a church that grows by adding church members only or a church that grows because of new converts to Christ?
4. How does trusting God help a church grow with new converts?

5. PICTURE 5: A WORLDWIDE TEMPLE—THE UNIVERSAL CHURCH OR WORLDWIDE CHURCH (v.21).

Note the word "all"—all believers make up the holy temple of God. All believers are pictured as a building, a universal church being structured for God's presence. Each new believer and each generation of believers are seen as being placed and fitted into

God's universal structure. As the little chorus says, "Red and yellow, black and white—they are precious in His sight." All believers of every generation who are being called from all across the world are being fitted into God's universal building which will literally be the new heavens and earth. We, the church—the believers of the earth from all generations—shall be a part, a building stone, of the new universe when God makes the new heavens and earth. However, note that each person is placed into the structure *only by Christ*. Only the person and the body of people who come to Christ as the chief cornerstone are fitted into the building. A man must build upon the foundation laid by the apostles and prophets, which is the foundation of Christ Himself. Any other cornerstone or any other foundation constructs some other kind of building, not God's building. People may follow their own thought structure or some man's profound philosophy or even their own life-style, but it is not God's building that they structure. In Christ alone, and upon the foundation laid by the apostles, is God's building being structured.

APPLICATION:
The gospel of Jesus Christ is open to all people everywhere. There is no place for division and prejudice, privilege and partiality, classes and caste systems in the temple or church of God. Every nation, even the uttermost part of the earth, is to be brought into the universal temple or church of God.

> **"And I saw another angel fly in the midst of heaven, having the everlasting gospel to preach unto them that dwell on the earth, and to every nation, and kindred, and tongue, and people" (Re.14:6).**

QUESTIONS:
1. Are you comfortable with the fact that people from every nation, tribe and tongue will be in heaven with you? Why or why not?
2. Do you pray for other nations?
3. Are you burdened for the lost souls in a particular part of the world? Are your praying that God's Kingdom will grow in that area?
4. Are you willing to serve to bring about the building of God's universal, international church?

6. PICTURE 6: A LOCAL TEMPLE—THE LOCAL CHURCH (v.22).

Note that Paul now uses the word "you," referring to the Ephesian church in particular. Each local church is pictured as a building structured for God's presence (v.22). And each member is seen as an integral, essential stone being placed and fitted into the building (Ep.4:16; 1 Pe.2:5). The church's stability lies in each stone's being placed, fitted and cemented by the same Lord, and by each stone's holding up its load, fulfilling its purpose in the structure. Note that the local church exists for the purpose of providing a habitation, a home for the presence of God—through His Spirit. The church is to allow the Spirit of God to live out His life through the church. The Holy Spirit dwells within the church to help its believers when they are…

- troubled, distressed, or confused
- suffering or dying
- slothful and inactive
- preaching and ministering
- discouraged or dispirited
- joyful and excited
- witnessing and teaching

The Spirit of God dwells within the church to conform the church to the image of God's will. The effectiveness of any local church depends upon how much it allows the Holy Spirit to dwell within and to control its body of members.

EPHESIANS 2:19-22

"Know ye not that ye are the temple of God, and that the Spirit of God dwelleth in you?" (1 Co.3:16).

QUESTIONS:
1. Why is it important for you to be involved in your local church?
2. What events led you to join your church? Which people influenced your decision? Why?
3. Are you in a church that is built upon Jesus Christ? If not, why not? Are you praying for God to lead you to the right church?
4. What can you personally do to improve the spiritual life in your church?
5. Are you committed to pray for your church? What will happen to your church if God answers your prayers?

SUMMARY:

You have now had the opportunity to closely examine God's photo album of the church. You saw the church from six different perspectives. They were:
1. Picture 1: A New Nation
2. Picture 2: God's Family
3. Picture 3: God's Building
4. Picture 4: A Growing Organism
5. Picture 5: A Worldwide Temple—The Universal church or worldwide church
6. Picture 6: A Local Temple—The Local church

If you look closely enough, you should be able to see yourself in each of these pictures. You have a vital role in the development of the church. Are you doing your part in developing the church, in making the church everything it should be?

PERSONAL JOURNAL NOTES
(Reflection & Response)

1. The most important thing that I learned from this lesson was:

2. The area that I need to work on the most is:

3. I can apply this lesson to my life by:

4. Closing Statement of Commitment:

CHAPTER 3

III. THE ETERNAL PURPOSE OF GOD FOR THE CHRISTIAN BELIEVER, 3:1-21

A. A New Body of People: The Great Mystery of Christ, 3:1-13

1. The mystery gave Paul a purpose for existing
   a. He existed to be a prisoner for Christ
   b. He existed to be a steward of God's grace

2. The mystery required a special revelation to become known
   a. Revealed to Paul
   b. Revealed to the other New Testament apostles & prophets

3. The mystery was a threefold revelation
   a. All are fellowheirs
   b. All are of one body
   c. All share in God's promise: The new creation

4. The mystery affected Paul—profoundly
   a. Caused him to become a minister—by the power of God
   b. Caused him to become a preacher—unworthy as he was
   c. Caused him to become an evangelist—to reach every person

5. The mystery affects heavenly beings even now, profoundly so: Causes them to stand in stark amazement
   a. At what God is doing in the church
   b. At God's eternal purpose—in Christ
   c. At the believer's access into God's presence—by faith

6. The mystery stirs a willingness within to serve & to suffer

For this cause I Paul, the prisoner of Jesus Christ for you Gentiles,
2 If ye have heard of the dispensation of the grace of God which is given me to you-ward:
3 How that by revelation he made known unto me the mystery; (as I wrote afore in few words,
4 Whereby, when ye read, ye may understand my knowledge in the mystery of Christ)
5 Which in other ages was not made known unto the sons of men, as it is now revealed unto his holy apostles and prophets by the Spirit;
6 That the Gentiles should be fellowheirs, and of the same body, and partakers of his promise in Christ by the gospel:
7 Whereof I was made a minister, according to the gift of the grace of God given unto me by the effectual working of his power.
8 Unto me, who am less than the least of all saints, is this grace given, that I should preach among the Gentiles the unsearchable riches of Christ;
9 And to make all men see what is the fellowship of the mystery, which from the beginning of the world hath been hid in God, who created all things by Jesus Christ:
10 To the intent that now unto the principalities and powers in heavenly places might be known by the church the manifold wisdom of God,
11 According to the eternal purpose which he purposed in Christ Jesus our Lord:
12 In whom we have boldness and access with confidence by the faith of him.
13 Wherefore I desire that ye faint not at my tribulations for you, which is your glory.

Section III
THE ETERNAL PURPOSE OF GOD FOR THE CHRISTIAN BELIEVER
Ephesians 3:1-21

Study 1: **A NEW BODY OF PEOPLE: THE GREAT MYSTERY OF CHRIST**

Text: **Ephesians 3:1-13**

EPHESIANS 3:1-13

Aim: This study has a twofold aim: 1) To understand the great mystery of Christ, that He is creating a new body of people upon earth; 2) to serve Christ more diligently than ever before—all because of what He has done for you.

Memory Verse:

"In whom we have boldness and access with confidence by the faith of him" (Ephesians 3:12).

SECTION OVERVIEW:

Chapter three begins a new division in Ephesians, "The Purpose of God for Christian Believers." But note: the passage discusses "The *Eternal* Purpose of God." God's purpose for believers involves much more than life on this earth. God has planned an eternal purpose for believers.

1. First, His purpose is to make a new body of people on earth who will love Him supremely. This is what is called the *mystery of Christ* (Ep.3:1-13).
2. Second, His purpose is to make the believer into a *mature person* filled with all the fullness of God (Ep.3:14-21).

INTRODUCTION:

Prejudice, bitterness, segregation, hatred, disturbance, hurt, anger, and division rage between people. They rage in the hearts of husbands and wives, children and parents, students and teachers, neighbors and workmen, races and religions, denominations and organizations, neighborhoods and nations. Division in all its various forms is one of the greatest problems confronting the world. It is the most serious problem confronting men, for as long as men are divided from God and from each other, there is no hope of man's ever being reconciled to God. God's eternal purpose has been to create a new body of people, a people who will love Him and each other supremely. Note that this is what is known as the great mystery of Christ.

OUTLINE:

1. The mystery gave Paul a purpose for existing (vv.1-2).
2. The mystery required a special revelation to become known (vv.3-5).
3. The mystery was a threefold revelation (v.6).
4. The mystery affected Paul—profoundly (vv.7-9).
5. The mystery affects heavenly beings even now, profoundly so: causes them to stand in stark amazement (vv.10-12).
6. The mystery stirs a willingness within to serve and to suffer (v.13).

1. THE MYSTERY GAVE PAUL A PURPOSE FOR EXISTING (vv.1-2).

These two verses give a glimpse into the very purpose for Paul's existence.

1. *Paul existed to serve Christ, no matter the cost.* Note: he says that he was a prisoner of Jesus Christ. He was speaking literally; he was a prisoner in Rome when he was writing these words. He was there because he was enslaved to Christ, enslaved to the point that he would bear any suffering to share the glorious news of Christ even if it meant imprisonment and death.
2. *Paul existed to be a steward of God.* The word "dispensation" means stewardship, management, administration, ownership. Paul was given the duty to oversee and administer the grace of God to the world.

APPLICATION:
What an enormous responsibility laid upon believers and the servants of God upon earth!

1. Every believer is a servant of God. As a servant, the believer is a slave of the Lord Jesus Christ. He is to serve Christ no matter the cost—even if it means imprisonment.

   "Even as the Son of man came not to be ministered unto, but to minister, and to give his life a ransom for many" (Mt.20:28).

2. Every servant of God is a steward of God's grace. He is responsible for ministering the grace of God to men.

   "Let a man so account of us, as of the ministers of Christ, and stewards of the mysteries of God. Moreover it is required in stewards, that a man be found faithful" (1 Co.4:1-2).

QUESTIONS:
1. What is your purpose for existing? Are you existing to serve Christ? Or to serve yourself?
2. How can a person tell what he is living for?
3. In very practical ways, how does a believer minister the grace of God to men?
4. What do these two verses teach about the price you must pay to follow Christ? What has following Christ cost you?
5. Have you ever regretted following Christ? Why or why not?

2. THE MYSTERY REQUIRED A SPECIAL REVELATION TO BECOME KNOWN (vv.3-5).

Note two points.

1. The mystery is called the mystery *of Christ* (v.4). Just what the mystery involves is discussed in the next verse (v.6).

2. The word mystery is defined in these verses: it was some truth that had to be revealed by God for man to know the truth. As verse five says: "in other ages it was not made known to the sons of men." Glance at verse nine where it is said to be "the mystery, which from the beginning of the world has been hid in God." All this simply means that the mystery of Christ was…

- a truth that was not known before the apostles and prophets
- a truth that could not be discovered by human reason
- a truth that had to be revealed by God if it were to ever be known

Note a striking point: the mystery of Christ was not a creation of man's mind, of his rationalizations, concepts, thoughts, and ideas. Man could never have figured out the mystery. No man in this physical world could ever penetrate the spiritual world to discover the truth, no matter what some have claimed. Jesus said so:

"And no man hath ascended up to heaven, but he that came down from heaven, even the Son of man which is in heaven" (Jn.3:13).

The spiritual world and the mystery of Christ had always been a mystery, and they would have remained a mystery if God had not acted to reveal them to Paul and the other apostles and prophets of his day.

ILLUSTRATION:
Natural man does not have a clue about solving the mystery of Christ. His attempt to figure out God's mind by using his own reason is futile. Use your imagination for a moment if you will:

Imagine a family of mice who lived all their lives in a large piano. To them in their piano-world came the music of the instrument, filling all the dark spaces with sound and harmony. At first the mice were impressed by it. They drew comfort and wonder from the thought that there was Someone who made the music—though invisible to them—above, yet close to them. They loved to think of the Great Player whom they could not see.

Then one day a daring mouse climbed up part of the piano and returned very thoughtful. He had found out how music was made. Wires were the secret; tightly stretched wires of graduated lengths which trembled and vibrated. They must revise all their old beliefs: none but the most conservative could any longer believe in the Unseen Player.

Later, another explorer carried the explanation further. Hammers were now the secret, numbers of hammers dancing and leaping on the wires. This was a more complicated theory, but it all went to show that they lived in a purely mechanical and mathematical world. The Unseen Player came to be thought of as a myth.

But the pianist continued to play.[1]

QUESTIONS:
1. In your search for the truth, have you ever reached the kinds of conclusions that these imaginary mice did? How did that affect your faith?
2. Are there still areas about your faith that you do not fully understand?
3. What does man have to have in order to figure out this great mystery of Christ?
4. What sort of attitude are you to have when you study God's Word?

3. THE MYSTERY WAS A THREEFOLD REVELATION (v.6)

The mystery of Christ was a threefold revelation.

1. *We, the Gentiles—all true believers—are fellowheirs of God with the Jews.* All of us are heirs of God. We are to share in the inheritance of all that God has.

Scripture declares that "salvation is of the Jews" (Jn.4:22). Before Jesus Christ, if a person wished to be saved, he had to approach God through the Jewish religion. The Jews who really believed the promises of God were the heirs of God. However, since Christ, Gentile believers—all peoples of the earth—no longer have to approach God through any other people or religion. No matter who we are, we are now to approach God face to face through His Son, the Lord Jesus Christ. Every person now has the glorious privilege of approaching God no matter…

- who he is
- what he has done
- where he is or has been
- when he comes
- how he comes
- why he comes

If a person is genuine in seeking after God, he can now approach God through Jesus Christ. There are no barriers—none whatsoever—to prevent his coming to God and being adopted by God as an heir of God with all other believers.

---

1 Reprinted from *The London Observer.* Craig B. Larson, Editor. *Illustrations for Preaching & Teaching,* p.81.

> **"For ye have not received the spirit of bondage again to fear; but ye have received the Spirit of adoption, whereby we cry, Abba, Father. The Spirit itself beareth witness with our spirit, that we are the children of God: and if children, then heirs; heirs of God, and joint-heirs with Christ; if so be that we suffer with him, that we may be also glorified together" (Ro.8:15-17).**

2. *We, the Gentiles, are of the same body with the Jews.* No longer does man have to approach God through one body or nation of people. God's love is universal. God is now allowing all men to approach him through the Lord Jesus Christ. God is now creating a new body of people made up of people from all nations and races—all centered around His Son, the Lord Jesus Christ. Believers now form what is called *the body of Christ*. But note: this means far more than just an organizational body. The body of Christ (believers in Christ) *is actually a living organism.* How is this possible?

⇒ By the Spirit of God. Believers are actually indwelt by the Spirit of God who energizes and empowers the spirit of believers. He creates a spiritual union by melting and molding the heart of the Christian believer to the hearts of other believers. Through the Spirit of God, believers become one in life and purpose. They have a joint life sharing their blessings and needs and gifts together.

> **"Neither pray I for these alone, but for them also which shall believe on me through their word; that they all may be one; as thou, Father, art in me, and I in thee, that they also may be one in us: that the world may believe that thou hast sent me" (Jn.17:20-21).**

3. *We, the Gentiles, receive the same promise of Christ as the Jews did.* The promise in Christ, of course, involves all the promises of God. But note: God had promised Abraham that he would inherit the promised land and have a great nation born of his loins. That great nation was the Jewish nation. This is the reason the Jews, even today, consider Palestine their land. However, there was a spiritual meaning to God's promise: Canaan is a type of heaven and of the new heavens and earth God is going to recreate. Therefore, the primary promise in Christ has to do with the glorious privilege of being saved, that of living with God and Christ for eternity in the new heavens and earth.

> **"But after that the kindness and love of God our Saviour toward man appeared, not by works of righteousness which we have done, but according to his mercy he saved us, by the washing of regeneration, and renewing of the Holy Ghost; which he shed on us abundantly through Jesus Christ our Saviour; that being justified by his grace, we should be made heirs according to the hope of eternal life" (Tit.3:4-7).**

ILLUSTRATION:

The Christian has the great blessing of being able to approach God through Jesus Christ. Those who serve other gods do not have it so good.

Oswana lives with her tribe in Africa. Her god is not approachable at all. Being an animist (one who believes that god is in everything), she spends the majority of her time appeasing the good and bad spirits. She fails most of the time.

Prima is a good Hindu. Her access to her god is framed by three ways to salvation:

1) the way of works, 2) the way of knowledge, and 3) the way of devotion. Just in case one god is unapproachable, there are a million others from which to choose. And if she does not like the way this life is going, she can always come back as a cow.

If you are a Buddhist, your goal is not access to god but to a place called Nirvana to become a god. Your goal of life is the end of existence. The only "catch" to Nirvana is that it is impossible to get there from here. Ask Dali. He was convinced that "the eightfold path" would get him to Nirvana: simple for a god; impossible for a mortal man. In order to get to Nirvana and have access to the gods and become a god, he had to: 1) have right views, 2) have right aspirations, 3) have right speech, 4) have right conduct, 5) have the right livelihood, 6) have the right effort or endeavor, 7) have the right mindfulness, and 8) have the right meditation or concentration.

What a glorious privilege Christians have, for our goal in life is to live in the presence of our Heavenly Father both now and forever! That guarantee does not depend on how effectively we can work out the details, nor does it depend upon our becoming gods. We have access to the Father as a result of one thing and one thing only: the shed blood of Jesus Christ.

QUESTIONS:

1. As a Christian who has access to God, how would you explain this to a person who was from another religion?
2. What barriers do non-Christians set up in their relationship with their gods?
3. Do Christians embrace any of those same barriers? Which ones come to mind?
4. What role does Jesus Christ play in your being able to approach God?

4. THE MYSTERY AFFECTED PAUL—PROFOUNDLY (vv.7-9).

William Barclay points out that *Paul's greatest glory was God's call and God's work.*[2] Paul saw the dignity of the ministry, the dignity of being especially chosen by God. The ministry was a radiant privilege for Paul. God did not have to persuade Paul to be a minister. No one had to persuade Paul to teach (Ep.4:1); to sing (Ep.5:19); to speak for God (Ep.4:17); to visit (2 Co.13:1f); to administer the affairs of the church (1 Co.7:1f); to give his money (2 Co.8:1f; 9:1f). Paul did not have to be coerced. He saw his call to be a minister of God as the greatest of all privileges.

Note another fact of primary importance: Paul's call to be a minister and a preacher was a gift, a free gift of God's grace. God had the right to call him simply because God has all rights. God is God. There was no merit, no worth, no value within Paul that caused God to choose him as a minister and as a preacher. Paul simply exclaims, "What a privilege! What a responsibility! the less of the least called of God to minister and to preach!"

1. Salvation in Christ caused Paul to become a minister or servant (v.7).

> **"Therefore seeing we have this ministry, as we have received mercy, we faint not; but have renounced the hidden things of dishonesty, not walking in craftiness, nor handling the word of God deceitfully; but by manifestation of the truth commending ourselves to every man's conscience in the sight of God" (2 Co.4:1-2).**

2. Salvation in Christ caused Paul to become a preacher. Note Paul's utter humility. He had what we all need: a deep, intense sense of unworthiness before God.

---

2 William Barclay. *The Letters to the Galatians and Ephesians*, p.145.

"For I determined not to know any thing among you, save Jesus Christ, and him crucified. And I was with you in weakness, and in fear, and in much trembling. And my speech and my preaching was not with enticing words of man's wisdom, but in demonstration of the Spirit and of power" (1 Co.2:2-4).

3. Salvation in Christ caused Paul to become a dynamic witness or evangelist. Note the statement "to make *all* men see...the mystery [salvation]."

"Then spake the Lord to Paul in the night by a vision, Be not afraid, but speak, and hold not thy peace: for I am with thee, and no man shall set on thee to hurt thee: for I have much people in this city" (Ac.18:9-10).

APPLICATION:
As Christians, we are all called by Christ to serve. Whether it be to preach, teach, sing, console, or whatever, it does not matter. Our greatest glory is the call to serve God. Does answering God's call and serving Him carry its proper weight in your life?

QUESTIONS:
1. What motivates you to serve Christ?
2. What motivates you to share Christ?
3. What is the hardest part for you when you share your faith with an unbeliever?
4. List some practical things that you can try in order to share your witness more effectively.
5. Paul was so affected by God's mystery that he was compelled to minister, preach, and witness for Christ. What sort of things has this mystery of Christ's caused you to do?

5. THE MYSTERY AFFECTS HEAVENLY BEINGS EVEN NOW, PROFOUNDLY SO: CAUSES THEM TO STAND IN STARK AMAZEMENT (vv.10-12).

The mystery of Christ profoundly affects heavenly beings. It causes them to stand in stark amazement at three things.

1. Heavenly beings stand in stark amazement at what God is doing in the church. God is saving people all over the earth, changing their lives and delivering them from the most terrible bondages imaginable. He is exalting them to be perfect beings who will live in His presence and serve Him forever. This is the meaning of verse ten. Looking at several different translations will show this.

"In order that the manifold wisdom of God might now be made known through the church to the rulers and the authorities in the heavenly places" (NAS).

"So that the many phases of God's wisdom may now through the church be made known to the rulers and authorities in heaven" (Williams).

"So that through the church God's many-sided wisdom would now be shown to the rulers and authorities in heaven" (Beck).

God's glorious purpose in salvation and in the church is to show His love and wisdom to the whole universe—to stir every creature in heaven to stand in stark amazement at what He is doing. Note that the heavenly beings see what is happening right now.

> **"O the depth of the riches both of the wisdom and knowledge of God! how unsearchable are his judgments, and his ways past finding out!" (Ro.11:33).**

2. Heavenly beings stand in stark amazement at God's eternal purpose in Christ Jesus.

> **"Who hath saved us, and called us with an holy calling, not according to our works, but according to his own purpose and grace, which was given us in Christ Jesus before the world began" (2 Ti.1:9).**

3. Heavenly beings stand in stark amazement at the believer's access into God's presence—at the fact that access is granted to us by *faith in Christ*.

> **"For through him we both have access by one Spirit unto the Father" (Ep.2:18).**

QUESTIONS:
1. The Scriptures say that heavenly beings are amazed at what God is doing. What is God doing in your life right now that would amaze these heavenly beings?
2. What is there about the church that causes heavenly beings to stand in amazement?

6. THE MYSTERY STIRS A WILLINGNESS WITHIN TO SERVE AND TO SUFFER (v.13).

Paul was willing to suffer for the church. The glory of all that lies ahead for the believer is so glorious that any suffering is worth the reward. Therefore, no believer should ever *faint* in suffering or in seeing other believers suffer. It is all worth the price of whatever suffering we are called to bear, even martyrdom.

QUESTIONS:
1. Has there ever been a time that you suffered for the church?
2. What do you think it was that made Paul willing to suffer for the church? Are those qualities in you, too?
3. What thoughts come to your mind when you hear the words "suffering for the church?"
4. Why do you suppose that God allows this kind of suffering to happen to His children?

Ephesians 3:1-13

Summary:

The great mystery of Christ is the new body of people God is creating. That new body is the church, the family and fellowship of believers, the people who truly believe and trust Jesus Christ to make them acceptable to God. In review:

1. The mystery gave Paul purpose for existing.
2. The mystery required a special revelation to become known.
3. The mystery was a threefold revelation.
4. The mystery affected Paul—profoundly.
5. The mystery affects heavenly beings even now, profoundly so: causes them to stand in stark amazement.
6. The mystery stirs a willingness within Paul to serve and to suffer for the church.

What is your purpose for existing? You, too, should be profoundly amazed and affected by what God has done for you and willing to serve and even suffer for the cause of Christ.

Personal Journal Notes:
(Reflection & Response)

1. The most important thing that I learned from this lesson was:

2. The area that I need to work on the most is:

3. I can apply this lesson to my life by:

4. Closing Statement of Commitment:

	B. A Mature Person in Christ: The Great Prayer for the Church & the Believer, 3:14-21	grounded in love, 18 May be able to comprehend with all saints what is the breadth, and length, and depth, and height;	**4. Request 3: For love** **5. Request 4: For understanding—a full understanding of spiritual things**
1. The prayer a. Was on bended knees b. Was addressed to the Father of all believers in both heaven & earth	14 For this cause I bow my knees unto the Father of our Lord Jesus Christ, 15 Of whom the whole family in heaven and earth is named,	19 And to know the love of Christ, which passeth knowledge, that ye might be filled with all the fulness of God.	**6. Request 5: To know the love of Christ** **7. Request 6: For the fullness of God**
2. Request 1: For strength, power within—by God's Spirit	16 That he would grant you, according to the riches of his glory, to be strengthened with might by his Spirit in the inner man;	20 Now unto him that is able to do exceeding abundantly above all that we ask or think, according to the power that worketh in us,	**8. Conclusion: The encouragement to pray & trust God for the answer** a. The fact: God is able b. The source: God's power in us
3. Request 2: For Christ to rule & reign within, take complete control—by faith	17 That Christ may dwell in your hearts by faith; that ye, being rooted and	21 Unto him be glory in the church by Christ Jesus throughout all ages, world without end. Amen.	c. The purpose: That God might be glorified in the church through Jesus Christ

Section III
THE ETERNAL PURPOSE OF GOD FOR THE CHRISTIAN BELIEVER
Ephesians 3:1-21

Study 2: **A MATURE PERSON IN CHRIST: THE GREAT PRAYER FOR THE CHURCH AND THE BELIEVER**

Text: **Ephesians 3:14-21**

Aim: To make a bold commitment to pray for the church, to pray as never before.

Memory Verse:

"Now unto Him that is able to do exceeding abundantly above all that we ask or think, according to the power that worketh in us" (Ephesians 3:20).

INTRODUCTION:

I have never met a person who took a test without wanting to know what to study. Nor have I met a soldier who was willing to go into battle without his gun. Also, I have never met a pilot who wanted to lose power while still in the air.

But I have met Christians who were perfectly willing to live their lives without God's power. Why is this so? Possibly, there are some who are ignorant of how to tap into God's vast resource of power. Others know about God's power but would rather supply their own source of strength.

If we as Christians fail to plug into God's power, the results spill out in how we live: The fruit within us spoils. We take our relationship with God and turn it into just a religion. Without the power of God, Christianity becomes an empty form (or as Paul told Timothy, **"having a form of godliness, but denying the power"—2 Tim. 3:5).**

EPHESIANS 3:14-21

Without the power of God, the joy of salvation is gone. The power of sin overwhelms us, and life becomes an endurance, not something to be enjoyed.

Do you want the power of God in your life, the power to conquer sin and to become victorious in life? God's power will come only when we learn to pray—to pray consistently and fervently.

Do you want the power of God in your life, the power to conquer sin and to become victorious in life? God's power will come only when we learn to pray—to pray consistently and fervently.

This is the great prayer of Paul for the church and the believer. It is probably the second most important prayer in all the Bible, ranking second only to the Lord's model prayer (Mt.6:9-13). Because of its importance, it should be prayed by believers every day. Certainly, this is the reason God had it included in Holy Scripture. Note the detail as it is read and studied. Its focus is a mature believer in Christ.

OUTLINE:

1. The prayer (vv.14-15).
2. Request 1: for strength and power within—by God's Spirit (v.16).
3. Request 2: for Christ to rule and reign within, take complete control—by faith (v.17).
4. Request 3: for love (v.17).
5. Request 4: for understanding—a full understanding of all spiritual things (v.18).
6. Request 5: to know the love of Christ (v.19).
7. Request 6: for the fullness of God (v.19).
8. Conclusion: the encouragement to pray and trust God for the answer (vv.20-21).

1. THE PRAYER (vv.14-15).

Note four things about this prayer.

1. The prayer was for a specific cause, a specific purpose. The words "for this cause" refer back to the eternal plan of God and the life of the Christian believer (Ep.2:1-3:13). That is, Paul is referring back to the great salvation and birth of the church which God has brought about through Christ. No greater thing has ever been done than what God has done through Christ. Through Christ…

- God has brought about salvation (Ep.2:1-10)
- God has given birth to the church, the new body of believers which He is building (Ep.2:11f)

Therefore, it is of utmost necessity that the work of salvation be completed, and the building of the body of believers (the church) must be completed. This is the *great cause* for which Paul prays.

2. The prayer was so important that it drove Paul to his knees. Bowing is a sign of desperate need and dependency. It shows that a person…

- is utterly dependent upon God
- is earnest
- is reverencing God
- is humble before God

3. The prayer addresses God as the Father of our Lord Jesus Christ. Jesus Christ came into the world to reveal God, to show men just what God is like. Before Christ, men had thought of God as far away, distant, and unconcerned with man and his world. But Christ revealed that this is just not true; it is a false picture of God. God is near and vitally interested in man and his world. In fact, "God so loved the world that he gave his only begotten Son, that whosoever believeth in him should not perish, but have everlasting life" (Jn.3:16).

The point is this: when Paul prayed to God, He prayed to the Father of the Lord Jesus Christ. It was He who would listen and answer Paul's prayer. Paul was not praying to the ceiling, nor into thin air, nor to some lifeless concept or idea in his mind. He was praying to the Father of the Lord Jesus Christ. He and He alone is the only living and true God; He is the very God who heard Paul's prayer. And He is the God who will hear our prayer.

4. The prayer was also addressed to the Father of the whole family of God. That is, God is the Father of all believers who have ever believed and trusted His promise, both past and present.

APPLICATION:
What images come to mind when you hear the word "Father"? All of us have had earthly fathers who have failed us at one time or the other. For some of us, Dad was never there when needed. For others, Dad was always there putting unbearable pressure on his kids. There is no escaping the fact that our view of our Heavenly Father must go through the grid of our experience with our earthly father. Because of sin, our view of God is warped.

Only God's Holy Spirit can heal that warped image. Once the healing process begins, our prayer life undergoes a radical change: our Father in Heaven becomes *accessible, intimate, caring and bigger than all of our problems*.

QUESTIONS:
1. Is it sufficient to be vague and talk in general terms when you pray? What are some things that you can do to bring a sharper focus to your prayers?
2. Do you tend to pray more intensely during times of personal crisis? How do you sense when it is time for you to pray?
3. How do these Scriptures drive home the point of whom we address when we pray?
4. Briefly express how you usually address God when you pray. What does it tell you about your relationship with the Father?

2. REQUEST 1: FOR STRENGTH AND POWER WITHIN—BY GOD'S SPIRIT (v.16).

Note several facts.

1. The word "strengthen" means to be made strong, tough, enduring. It means to have energy or force; to act, endure, or resist.

2. The word "power" means force, energy, might.

3. The believer needs to be strengthened with power in the "inner man," that is, in the deepest part of his being, in his soul, in his heart, in his spirit—in the spirit that God has renewed. It is there that the believer must be *strengthened with power*. Why?

a. *Because it is the only way he can overcome the flesh with all its weakness*. It is the only way he can conquer…

- temptation and sin
- trouble and trials
- disease and suffering
- grief and death
- selfishness and worldliness
- problems and circumstances

b. *Because it is the only way the believer can ever lay claim to all the blessings of God and fulfill God's eternal purpose for his life* (Chapter 1-3). The believer must be strengthened with power in order to break loose from the flesh and focus upon the eternal promises and call of God. Simply stated, his spirit must be strong and powerful…

- to be everything God wants him to be
- to do everything God wants him to do

4. Note the source of such conquering strength and power: the Holy Spirit of God. And note that He dwells within the *inner man* of the believer. There is no other source that has enough power to conquer the severe trials and corruptions of this world, all of which result in death and decay. No group of men—not even all the men in the world with all their science and technology—possesses the power to control the evil and death of man. We do not even have the power to make one single person perfect nor to stop one single person from dying. If there is a Power strong enough to conquer the evil and corruption of this world, it is in the Spirit of God and in Him alone. Therefore, the great prayer of the believer is that God would grant to His church…

- "that you might be strengthened with might by His Spirit in the inner man."

5. Note one other thing: How do we know God will hear and answer our prayer? How do we know that God will give us this strength and power? Because of what this verse says: "…according to the riches of his glory." The "riches of God's glory" is seen in Jesus Christ. It is God's glorious grace and salvation revealed in Christ. God loves us! This is the reason He will strengthen us with might by His Spirit. (See Ep.2:4-10.)

> **"And he said unto me, My grace is sufficient for thee: for my strength is made perfect in weakness. Most gladly therefore will I rather glory in my infirmities, that the power of Christ may rest upon me. Therefore I take pleasure in infirmities, in reproaches, in necessities, in persecutions, in distresses for Christ's sake: for when I am weak, then am I strong" (2 Co.12:9-10).**

QUESTIONS:

1. What, in simple terms, does "inner man" mean?
2. When do you notice God's power the most?
3. How can you continue improving the strength of your inner man?
4. Do you think it is possible to overcome the weakness of your flesh with your own strength? Why or why not?

3. REQUEST 2: FOR CHRIST TO RULE AND REIGN WITHIN, TAKE COMPLETE CONTROL—BY FAITH (v.17).

The word "dwell" means to live in a permanent not a temporary dwelling. It means to take up permanent residence; to live in a home; to enter, settle down, and be at home. When a person believes in Jesus Christ for the first time, Christ enters his life. Therefore, the believer is not praying for Christ to enter the hearts and lives of believers; Christ is already in their hearts and lives. What then does this request mean? Just what the verse says:

⇒ that Christ would be at home and live in a permanent sense within the believer.

⇒ that the believer would be aware and conscious of Christ within his heart—always aware and conscious that Christ has taken up residence within him.

⇒ that the believer would let Christ control and guide his life—permanently and constantly—because Christ is at home in his heart.

It is the presence of Christ within that motivates the believer to follow Christ. The more the believer is aware and conscious of Christ within him, the more he will *walk and live* in Christ.

Note that Christ dwells within the believer by faith. But note that Biblical faith is not a wish or hope that something is true. It is not *"perhaps* something is true or *perhaps* it is not." Biblical faith always means the belief and commitment of a person's life to truth and reality; it is a belief and commitment to fact.

> **"I am crucified with Christ: nevertheless I live; yet not I, but Christ liveth in me: and the life which I now live in the flesh I live by the faith of the Son of God, who loved me, and gave himself for me" (Ga.2:20).**

ILLUSTRATION:
Spiritual maturity takes time to grow deep roots. The temptation for many of us is just to put on the appearance of being mature. Of course, the danger in this is when the first good wind of tribulation blows our way, we fall over because our roots in the Lord are not deep and developed. Listen closely to this testimony:

> *I'll never forget a lesson the Lord taught me some time ago. I was walking beside a pond of water that was lined with towering pine trees on the opposite bank. Looking at the pond, I saw a reflection of the trees. I saw the tops of the trees, the branches, and the trunk. But the roots remained unseen for obvious reasons—they were hidden in the ground. In that still, small voice, the Lord impressed this great truth upon my heart: "the key to maturity is not the height of the trunk but the depth of the roots. If your roots fail to hold, the whole tree will fall."*

APPLICATION:
Faith is the anchor that roots and grounds us in love. To be rooted and grounded is a choice of our will that we must make: to allow the Lord to plant us in His will. To be "grounded" is an act of God's grace that keeps us from falling away. This grounding comes when the roots begin to spread out and anchor us firmly in God's love.

QUESTIONS:
1. If you are a believer, Jesus Christ has made His home in your heart. Do you have any "rooms" or parts of your life that are off-limits to Him? If so, why?
2. What can you do in order to make Jesus Christ feel welcome?
3. Give an example of a time recently when your faith was real to other people.
4. Do you believe that biblical faith is based upon feelings? Why or why not?

4. REQUEST 3: FOR LOVE (v.17).

This is *agape love*, the very same love God has for us. We have already studied this topic a few sessions ago (Ephesians 2:4-5), but we can add another thought to Paul's specific prayer and be able to answer the questions *where* and *how* and *why*.

APPLICATION:
1. Love is *where* the believer needs to be rooted and grounded.
2. Faith is *how* the believer is rooted and grounded in love.
3. Power to live the Christian life is *why* the believer must be rooted and grounded in love.
4. In a very real sense, love is the only outlet that we can plug our spiritual power cords into and live a victorious Christian life.

"Beloved, let us love one another: for love is of God; and every one that loveth is born of God, and knoweth God. He that loveth not knoweth not God; for God is love" (1 Jn.4:7-8).

QUESTIONS:

1. For those who are not rooted and grounded in love, they have chosen to plug into something else. What are some other things that replace love?
2. Was there a time when you faced tribulation and found that your roots were not grounded in God's love? What can you do to make sure that you are rooted and grounded in God's love in the future?
3. According to this verse, what is the source of the Christian's power?

5. REQUEST 4: FOR UNDERSTANDING—A FULL UNDERSTANDING OF SPIRITUAL THINGS (v.18).

It is crucial that the believer grasp God's eternal plan and glorious salvation—all that has been covered in chapters one through three:

⇒ the great blessings of God (Ep.1:3-14).
⇒ the knowledge and power of God (Ep.1:15-23).
⇒ the mercy and grace of God (Ep.2:1-10).
⇒ the reconciliation and peace wrought by Christ (Ep.2:11-18).
⇒ the church: who and what it is (Ep.2:19-22).
⇒ the new body of people God is forming, that is, the great mystery of Christ (Ep.3:1-13).

God has done so much for the believer that it cannot be measured. Therefore, believers must pray and seek God to increase their understanding and the understanding of all saints. All believers must comprehend the breadth and length and depth and height of what God has done for them and the church. The more believers comprehend, the more they will surrender their lives to Christ and serve Him.

APPLICATION:
The more we understand what God has done for us, the more we will reach out to take the love and salvation of God to a world reeling under the plight of evil, poverty, and death.

"But as it is written, Eye hath not seen, nor ear heard, neither have entered into the heart of man, the things which God hath prepared for them that love him. But God hath revealed them unto us by his Spirit: for the Spirit searcheth all things, yea, the deep things of God. For what man knoweth the things of a man, save the spirit of man which is in him? even so the things of God knoweth no man, but the Spirit of God. Now we have received, not the spirit of the world, but the spirit which is of God; that we might know the things that are freely given to us of God" (1 Co.2:9-12).

Where do we begin in our journey to comprehend spiritual things? The journey must begin at the cross. Perhaps Paul is describing the cross with this word picture, "what is the *breadth*, and *length*, and *depth*, and *height* (v.18[b]).

QUESTIONS:

1. What do you think your role is in understanding spiritual things? What is God's role in this process?
2. What are some spiritual things that you struggle to understand?
3. Take your answer above and submit it to God in prayer and share it with a trusted Christian friend.

6. REQUEST 5: TO KNOW THE LOVE OF CHRIST (v.19).

It is utterly impossible to grasp and experience the love of Christ anywhere close to its full measure. We must pray for God to help us learn more and more of His love—and we must make the request often every day. There has never been penned a greater description of the unsurpassing love of Christ than that of F.M. Lehman in the song, The Love of God:

Could we with ink the ocean fill,
And were the skies of parchment made;
Were every stalk on earth a quill,
And every man a scribe by trade,

To write the love of God above
Would drain the ocean dry.
Nor could the scroll contain the whole,
Though stretched from sky to sky.

O love of God, how rich and pure!
How measureless and strong!
It shall forever more endure.
The saints and angels song. [1]

"But God commendeth his love toward us, in that, while we were yet sinners, Christ died for us. Much more then, being now justified by his blood, we shall be saved from wrath through him. For if, when we were enemies, we were reconciled to God by the death of his Son, much more, being reconciled, we shall be saved by his life" (Ro.5:8-10).

ILLUSTRATION:
Are you satisfied with the depth of your love for Jesus Christ? Hopefully not! Believers should never become satisfied with the status quo. God has something much better for you to pursue: a passion for Christ!

As Gustave Dore' was putting the finishing touches on the face of Christ in one of his paintings, an admiring friend stepped quietly into the studio. She looked with bated breath upon the painting. Dore' sensed her presence and said graciously, "Pardon, madam, I did not know you were here." She answered, "Monsieur Dore', you must love Him very much to be able to paint Him thus!" "Love Him, madam?" exclaimed Dore', "I do love Him, but if I loved Him better I could paint Him better!"

If we loved Him better, we could serve Him better. [2]

---

1 Words by F.M. Lehman. (Nazarene Publishing House, 1945).

2 *W.B.K.* Walter B. Knight. *Knight's Treasury of 2,000 Illustrations.* (Grand Rapids, MI: Eerdmans Publishing Co., 1963), p.212.

QUESTIONS:
1. How do we actually come to know the love of Christ?
2. How does an understanding of the love of Christ make a difference in your life?
3. Do you think it is possible to fully know the love of Christ?

7. REQUEST 6: FOR THE FULLNESS OF GOD (v.19).

The Amplified New Testament is excellent in describing the meaning of this request:

> **"That you may be filled (through all your being) unto all the fullness of God...[that is] may have the richest measure of the divine Presence, and become a body wholly filled and flooded with God Himself!" (Ep.3:19, *The Amplified New Testament*).**

The believer possesses the indwelling presence of the Spirit, Christ, and God. When Jesus Christ was promising to send the Holy Spirit to believers, He promised that the trinity—the Father, Son, and Holy Spirit—would all three come and indwell believers:

> **"And I will pray the Father, and he shall give you another Comforter, that he may abide with you for ever....If a man love me, he will keep my words: and my Father will love him, and we will come unto him, and make our abode with him" (Jn.14:16, 23).**

The point is this: each Person of the Godhead has a different function within the believer. Therefore, the believer is to ask specific things concerning each. He has already prayed to be strengthened by the Spirit and to have Christ dwell within and control his heart. Now the believer is to pray for "all the fullness of God Himself"—for God and His presence in all its fullness to fill and flood him, ruling and reigning and having His perfect way in the life of the believer.

Note one other point stressed by F.F. Bruce. The preposition "unto" suggests a progressive experience. The believer is to pray for God to constantly fill him, to constantly flood him with all the fullness of God.[3]

> **"O the depth of the riches both of the wisdom and knowledge of God! how unsearchable are his judgments, and his ways past finding out! For who hath known the mind of the Lord! or who hath been his counsellor! or who hath first given to him, and it shall be recompensed unto him again! For of him, and through him, and to him, are all things: to whom be glory for ever" (Ro.11:33-36).**

ILLUSTRATION:

Picture a glass filled half way with water. Is the glass of water half full or half empty? Some people would say half full; others half empty. Full is a matter of perspective in this case. Some Christians are content with either condition of being half full or half empty.

But the praying believer is not content with a partial filling of God. His heart's cry is "fill me up!" Prayer gives the Christian the passion needed to seek the fullness of God. **"O taste and see that the Lord is good" (Ps. 34:8).**

---

3 F.F. Bruce. *The Epistle to the Ephesians.* (Westwood, NJ: Fleming H. Revell Co., 1968), p.69.

APPLICATION:
1. To be filled with all the fullness of God should be the goal of the Christian believer.
2. The Christian believer needs to get "under the spout where the glory pours out." And where is this "spout"? It comes from spending time with the Lord in prayer and in the Word of God. There is no suitable substitute for spending time with Him.

"Thou wilt show me the path of life: in Thy presence is fulness of joy; at Thy right hand there are pleasures for evermore" (Ps.16:11).

QUESTIONS:
1. With what does God fill the believer? How does God's fullness fill the believer?
2. Give some examples when you sensed God's fullness in your life.
3. What does this verse tell you about God's promise of the Holy Spirit for the Christian believer?

8. CONCLUSION: THE ENCOURAGEMENT TO PRAY AND TRUST GOD FOR THE ANSWER (vv.20-21).

There is the encouragement to pray and to trust God for the answer. Note two points.

1. God is able to do what we ask. Note just how strong and powerful God is. He is able to do…

- "exceeding": to surpass; to go beyond any request; to overcome and do anything
- "abundantly": to overflow and to do more than enough
- "above": to go over and above, beyond any need
- "all that we ask or think": imagine going beyond anything we can think! What is the greatest answer or deliverance we can think? God is able to do exceedingly, abundantly, above all that we can think

APPLICATION:
1. The Thompson Chain Reference Bible points out what Scripture says about God's power:

⇒ God is able to raise up children from stones.

"Bring forth therefore fruits worthy of repentance, and begin not to say within yourselves, We have Abraham to our father: for I say unto you, That God is able of these stones to raise up children unto Abraham" (Lu.3:8).

⇒ God is able to fulfill promises even if they are humanly impossible.

"And being fully persuaded that, what he had promised, he was able also to perform" (Ro.4:21).

⇒ God is able to make grace abound.

"And God is able to make all grace abound toward you; that ye, always having all sufficiency in all things, may abound to every good work" (2 Co.9:8).

⇒ God is able to do exceeding abundantly.

"Now unto him that is able to do exceeding abundantly above all that we ask or think, according to the power that worketh in us" (Ep.3:20).

⇒ God is able to subdue all things.

"Who shall change our vile body, that it may be fashioned like unto his glorious body, according to the working whereby he is able even to subdue all things unto himself" (Ph.3:21).

⇒ God is able to guard the soul's treasure.

"For the which cause I also suffer these things: nevertheless I am not ashamed: for I know whom I have believed, and am persuaded that he is able to keep that [the soul] which I have committed unto him against that day" (2 Ti.1:12).

⇒ God is able to save us to the uttermost.

"Wherefore he is able also to save them to the uttermost that come unto God by him, seeing he ever liveth to make intercession for them" (He.7:25).

⇒ God is able to keep us from falling.

"Now unto him that is able to keep you from falling, and to present you faultless before the presence of his glory with exceeding joy" (Jude 24).

2. Note the source of answered prayer: it is the power that works in us. What is that power within us? It is the combined power of all that God has put within us, all that for which we are praying:

⇒ the power of the Spirit strengthening us.
⇒ the power of Christ indwelling us.
⇒ the power of love working in us.
⇒ the power of understanding all that God does.
⇒ the power of the fullness of God Himself.

"But Jesus beheld them, and said unto them, With men this is impossible; but with God all things are possible" (Mt.19:26).

3. Note the purpose of God in answering prayer and in doing all this for us: that He might be glorified in the church through Christ Jesus. And note how long He is to be glorified: throughout all ages, world without end.

QUESTIONS:

1. According to Scripture, why does God answer prayer?
2. What "impossible" situations are you facing now? Write them down and turn them over to the Lord.
3. What is the source of answered prayer?

Ephesians 3:14-21

Summary:

As we strive to grow and mature in our Christian life, we must go to God in prayer for His special presence:

1. The prayer
2. Request 1: For strength, power within—by God's Spirit
3. Request 2: For Christ to rule & reign within—by faith
4. Request 3: For love
5. Request 4: For understanding—a full understanding of all spiritual things
6. Request 5: To know the love of Christ
7. Request 6: For the fullness of God
8. Conclusion: The encouragement to pray & trust God for the answer

Personal Journal Notes:
(Reflection & Response)

1. The most important thing that I learned from this lesson was:

2. The area that I need to work on the most is:

3. I can apply this lesson to my life by:

4. Closing Statement of Commitment:

             1. The way to walk worthy a. With humility &	**CHAPTER 4** **IV. THE WALK OF THE CHRISTIAN BELIEVER, 4:1–6:9** **A. The Believer is to Walk Worthy of His Calling, 4:1-6** I therefore, the pris- oner of the Lord, be- seech you that ye walk worthy of the vocation wherewith ye are called, 2 With all lowliness	and meekness, with longsuffering, for- bearing one another in love; 3 Endeavouring to keep the unity of the Spirit in the bond of peace. 4 There is one body, and one Spirit, even as ye are called in one hope of your calling; 5 One Lord, one faith, one baptism, 6 One God and Fa- ther of all, who is above all, and through all, and in you all.	gentleness b. With patience c. With love **2. The purpose for walking worthy: To keep the unity, the peace** **3. The seven basic reasons** a. Only one body b. Only one Spirit c. Only one hope d. Only one Lord e. Only one faith f. Only one baptism, v. 5 g. Only one God & Father of all

Section IV
THE WALK OF THE CHRISTIAN BELIEVER
Ephesians 4:1–6:9

Study 1: **THE BELIEVER IS TO WALK WORTHY OF HIS CALLING**

Text: **Ephesians 4:1-6**

Aim: To stir yourself to walk worthy of the Lord.

Memory Verse:

"I therefore, the prisoner of the Lord, beseech you that ye walk worthy of the vocation wherewith ye are called" (Ephesians 4:1).

SECTION OVERVIEW:

How is the believer to live as he walks day by day throughout life? This chapter begins a discussion on the walk of the Christian believer. The instructions are very practical. Up until now the instructions have dealt with doctrine:

- the eternal plan of God for Christian believers
- the great blessings of God
- the knowledge and power of God
- the work of God's mercy and the gift of God's grace: our great salvation
- reconciliation and peace
- the church—the true church—the new body of people God is creating to be the citizens of the new heavens and earth

We have seen great theological truths revealing the *believer's position in Christ*—truths that show the believer soaring in the heavenlies! But now, coming down to earth and dealing with where we are: How are we to live day by day? How does our *position in Christ* work itself out in our lives? How does Christ help us deal with the trials, problems, difficulties, and sufferings of day to day living? The believer's walk is the subject of Ephesians from this point on.

EPHESIANS 4:1-6

A. The Believer is to Walk Worthy of His Calling, Ep.4:1-6.
B. The Believer is to Walk by Using His Gifts, Ep.4:7-16.
C. The Believer is to Walk Differently From the Gentiles, Ep.4:17-24.
D. The Believer is to Walk Putting Off the Garments of the Old Man, Ep.4:25-32.
E. The Believer is to Walk Following God, Ep.5:1-7.
F. The Believer is to Walk as a Child of Light, Ep.5:8-14.
G. The Believer is to Walk Carefully and Strictly, Ep.5:15-21.
H. The Believing Wife and Husband are to Walk in a Spirit of Submission and Love, Ep.5:22-33.
I. Believing Children and Parents are to Walk Under God's Authority, Ep.6:1-4.
J. Believing Slaves and Masters (Employers-Employees) are to Walk Under God's Authority, Ep.6:5-9.

We owe God more than we could ever pay. God has taken His own dear Son and...

- provided the Ideal and Perfect righteousness for us
- provided a Substitute to die for us—to actually bear our punishment for having rejected, rebelled, and cursed God, and for having broken God's law
- provided deliverance from death for us through the reconciliation of Christ
- provided a new life for us—a life of love, joy, peace, and power through the Holy Spirit living within us
- provided the absolute assurance of living eternally with God forever and ever
- provided so much more that even an eternity could not describe it

God has honored us as much as a creature can be honored—and more. He has seated us with Christ in the heavenlies to rule and reign with Christ forever and ever. God has done so much for us that He could do no more than what He has done. We do not see it all yet, for we are still on this earth—left here to be witnesses to the great and glorious salvation that is in Christ Jesus. But the day is soon coming when we will experience it all. God is going to make a new heavens and earth that will be perfect, in which there will be no suffering and no death, and we shall live eternally, ruling and reigning with Christ.

As stated, we owe God; we owe God so much that we could never even begin to pay Him back. What then can we do? Very little, but there is one thing that we must do: we must walk worthy of our calling. We must walk worthy of the honored position to which God has exalted us.

INTRODUCTION:

It was Vance Havner who said, "*Walking is a lost art. Any pedestrian along a country road these days is presumed to be either out of his head or out of gas.*"[1]

This philosophy is clearly seen in the language of our culture today:
1) "Life in the fast lane"
2) "I'm going to run to the store"
3) "Why walk, when we can ride?"

What is it about walking?
1) "Walking is too boring"
2) "Walking is too slow"
3) "Walking just wears me out"

---

1 Dennis J. Hester, Editor. *The Vance Havner Quote Book.* (Grand Rapids, MI: Baker Book House, 1986), p.241.

Excuses, excuses, excuses. But walking is:
1) A good way to slow down the pace of life and enjoy God's creation
2) Good for your health
3) Meant to be done left...right...left...right....

Walking requires us to be consistent. When we were born, walking was not an immediate skill we performed. It was something that had to be learned. The same is true in the spiritual realm. Walking with God is a practical skill that takes time to learn.

And once you learn to walk as a Christian, you have a lifetime to practice and keep in top form.

OUTLINE:

1. The way to walk worthy (vv.1-2).
2. The purpose for walking worthy: to keep the unity, the peace (v.3).
3. The seven basic reasons (vv.4-6).

1. THE WAY TO WALK WORTHY (vv.1-2).

How can the believer walk worthy? What must the believer do to please God as he lives day by day...

- at work?
- at play?
- at school?
- at church?
- at home?
- with neighbors?
- with fellow believers?
- with family?
- with friends?

Once a person believes in Jesus Christ and becomes a member of God's people and of God's church, what must he do to walk worthy of God's great calling—to bring honor to the name of Christ and His church?

1. The believer must walk with all lowliness: modest, humble.
2. The believer must walk with all meekness: without resentment; submissive.
3. The believer must walk with longsuffering: patient, enduring.
4. The believer must walk forbearing others in love: compassionate, lenient, controlled.

APPLICATION:
The attributes in verse 2 will never be ours unless we make the choice to *yield* to the Holy Spirit. These attributes or *attitudes* become ours when we give Him permission to work in our hearts.

ILLUSTRATION:
Those who decide to walk in a worthy manner have also made the choice to walk with integrity. Donald Barnhouse shares this story:

> *A man was going with a girl who, some of us thought, was not worthy of him. Some breathed a sigh of relief when he went into the army and was gone for...years. The girl drifted around with other fellows, and the worthy young man met a worthy girl in a distant city, fell in love with her, and married her. When the war was over, he returned to his home with his bride; one evening the first girl drove by the house and dropped in to see her old flame and to meet his wife. But the wife was not there. The first girl made no attempt to hide her affection; the man realized that he had but to reach out his hand and she would be his...There was within him something that goes with male desire, but there was something more within him also, and he began to talk about the wonderful girl he had married. He showed pictures of his wife...and praised his wife to the skies, acting as though he did not understand the obvious advances of the girl.*

It was not long before she left, saying as she went, "Yes, she must be quite a girl if she can keep you from reaching." The young man was never more joyful in his life. He said that in that moment all of the love between him and his wife was greater and more wonderful than ever...A philanderer might have scoffed at him, derided him for "sacrificing" his pleasure...There was...every sacrifice in the sense of Romans 12:1, ***"I beseech you therefore, brethren, by the mercies of God, that ye present your bodies a living sacrifice, holy, acceptable unto God which is your reasonable service."***

A man was going with a girl who, some of us thought, was not worthy of him. Some breathed a sigh of relief when he went into the army and was gone for...years. The girl drifted around with other fellows, and the worthy young man met a worthy girl in a distant city, fell in love with her, and married her. When the war was over, he returned to his home with his bride; one evening the first girl drove by the house and dropped in to see her old flame and to meet his wife. But the wife was not there. The first girl made no attempt to hide her affection; the man realized that he had but to reach out his hand and she would be his...There was within him something that goes with male desire, but there was something more within him also, and he began to talk about the wonderful girl he had married. He showed pictures of his wife ...and praised his wife to the skies, acting as though he did not understand the obvious advances of the girl.

It was not long before she left, saying as she went, "Yes, she must be quite a girl if she can keep you from reaching." The young man was never more joyful in his life. He said that in that moment all of the love between him and his wife was greater and more wonderful than ever...A philanderer might have scoffed at him, derided him for "sacrificing" his pleasure...There was...every sacrifice in the sense of Romans 12:1, ***"I beseech you therefore, brethren, by the mercies of God, that ye present your bodies a living sacrifice, holy, acceptable unto God which is your reasonable service."***[2]

QUESTIONS:

1. What must a believer be willing to do in order to walk worthy?
2. Why do some Christians tend to think that their faith is only for church on Sunday mornings?
3. In which area(s) do you need a change of attitude in order to improve your walk?

2. THE PURPOSE FOR WALKING WORTHY: TO KEEP THE UNITY AND THE PEACE (v.3).

The purpose for walking worthy is onefold—unity. Believers are to work at keeping the peace so that they can stay bound together in the unity of God's Spirit. Jesus Christ has broken down all walls and barriers existing between men. Everyone can now be saved:

⇒ all nationalities ⇒ the poor ⇒ the white
⇒ all peoples ⇒ the rich ⇒ the red
⇒ all languages ⇒ the black ⇒ the yellow

Every person is precious in the sight of God. When a person approaches God through Jesus Christ, he comes like everyone else: on the same ground and on the same level. He is no better and no worse than anyone else: he is a man who stands in need of God's forgiveness; and he, along with everyone else, is bowing before Christ and ac-

2 Donald Grey Barnhouse. *Let Me Illustrate*, pp.365-366.

cepting Him as his Lord and Master. The man, just like everyone else, is subjecting himself to become the servant of Christ. Wealth, position, social status—it is all forgotten. The only thing that matters is the salvation and life which Christ offers.

The point is this: when a person comes to Christ in such a spirit, the Spirit of God enters his life and binds the person to all other believers. There is a great spiritual *bond of peace* wrought by the Spirit of God between all believers. All divisiveness, differences, and prejudices are set aside; and a spirit of love, peace, and unity exist.

Within the church there is a *prevailing spirit of peace* wrought by God's Spirit. However, note a tragic fact: not every believer walks in the Spirit—not all the time. Too often, believers allow self and the *old life* to re-enter the picture—their old...

- prejudices
- differences
- hurts
- jealousies
- complaints
- criticisms
- grumblings
- gripes
- pride
- arrogance
- comparisons
- dislikes

The result is catastrophic for the church: divisiveness and a disturbance of the peace and spirit of unity. This is the reason for this charge. Note the word "endeavor." It means being diligent, working to take care, doing one's very best, and making haste to do it. The only way to walk worthy of God's great calling is to work at keeping the peace and unity which God has given us. Nothing cuts the heart of God like divisiveness between His people, divisiveness which tears apart His church. The very thing God is doing is creating a new body of people to live together in the love and unity of His Son. He is going to create a new heaven and earth in which there will be no other spirit. Therefore, He expects us to live in the love and unity of His Spirit now.

> **"Now I beseech you, brethren, by the name of our Lord Jesus Christ, that ye all speak the same thing, and that there be no divisions among you; but that ye be perfectly joined together in the same mind and in the same judgment" (1 Co.1:10).**

ILLUSTRATION:

Simply said, division is a wall between two sides. In the 1960's the Berlin Wall was erected by the Communists of East Germany to prevent East Germans from uniting with West Germans. History tells us that this was no innocent barrier: many were killed trying to scale the wall that divided the East from the West. This wall of division separated friends from friends and family from family. The result of this division brought death and despair. At times, it seemed that the wall would stay up forever.

But God had another plan. The Communist world was turned upside down as the people in Communist countries were swept up in a global wave of nationalism and the desire for freedom. The Berlin Wall had no power against the forces of unity and freedom—and it fell, becoming prize souvenirs for collectors.

Types of Berlin Walls are built every day in churches and between believers. There is no wall worth the cost of division. The only way to keep the unity of the Spirit in the church and between believers is to remain in the Spirit.

APPLICATION:

1. How hard do you work at preserving the unity of the Spirit? You can be called by God and yet ruin everything by being an instrument of division.
2. What causes the division of the Spirit?
   a. Instead of lowliness (*humility*), there is pride.
   b. Instead of meekness (*gentleness),* there is arrogance.
   c. Instead of longsuffering (*patience),* there is impatience.
   d. Instead of *forbearance,* there is a critical spirit.

3. Because we all have to battle with the old nature in us, a "working walk" is required of the believer. Humility, gentleness, patience, and forbearance do not come naturally…they come *supernaturally*.

QUESTIONS:
1. In your opinion, what is the greatest cause of division in the church?
2. What kinds of things happen when there is divisiveness within the church?
3. What can you do to bring unity to your church?
4. What kinds of things does unity produce in a church?

3. THE SEVEN BASIC REASONS (vv.4-6).

There are seven basic reasons why we should walk worthy and strive to keep the peace and unity of God's Spirit *in the church*. Note what has just been said, for the point needs to be stressed: there is great need to keep the peace and unity *within the church*. Far too often the church is the place where the peace and unity of believers fly apart. Again, there are seven reasons why this should never happen—seven reasons why believers should always walk in the peace and unity of the Spirit.

1. There is only "*one body*." There are not two bodies nor several bodies of believers. However, in this imperfect world, there are many different denominations and churches. But note what God is doing: God is *creating only one body of people* who trust and follow His dear Son. When a person places his trust in Jesus Christ, God does six things to the believer that place him into the body of Christ:

⇒ God gives a *new birth* to the believer—quickens him spiritually—causes him to be born again (Jn.1:12-13; 3:3-6; Tit.3:5; 1 Pe.1:23; 1 Jn.5:1).
⇒ God makes a new creature, a *new man* out of the believer (2 Co.5:17; Ep.4:24; Co.3:10).
⇒ God places His divine nature into the believer (2 Pe.1:4).
⇒ God puts His Holy Spirit into the believer, actually has His Spirit enter the believer's body. The believer's body becomes a temple for the presence of God's Spirit (Jn.14:16-17; 1 Co.3:16; 6:19-20).
⇒ God causes the believer to bear the fruit of the Holy Spirit which is love, joy, peace, longsuffering, gentleness, goodness, faith, meekness, control (Ga.5:22-23).
⇒ God places the believer into the *new body of people* He is creating, that is, into the body of Christ, His church.

> **"For by one Spirit are we all baptized into one body, whether we be Jews or Gentiles, whether we be bond or free; and have been all made to drink into one Spirit" (1 Co.12:13).**

Note the last two experiences in particular. There is no way a believer can be in conflict with another believer unless he is walking after the flesh and is in a backslidden condition. There are just some things that are contrary to love and joy and peace that hurt and damage the body…

- an ill spirit
- struggling for position
- self-centered differences
- reactions
- feeling superior
- seeking our own way
- forming cliques
- selfishness
- envy
- anger

Such things have no place in the church, not in the *new body* which God is creating. There is only one body of true believers. This is the reason we are to strive to keep the peace and the unity of the Spirit. Only as we keep the peace and unity of the body can we walk worthy of God's great calling.

> **"So we, being many, are one body in Christ, and every one members one of another" (Ro.12:5).**

2. There is only "*one Spirit.*" The *same Spirit* that dwells within one member of the body dwells in all members of the body.

⇒ It is God's Spirit that causes a man to be born again.

> **"Jesus answered, Verily, verily, I say unto thee, Except a man be born of water and of the Spirit, he cannot enter into the kingdom of God. That which is born of the flesh is flesh; and that which is born of the Spirit is spirit" (Jn.3:5-6).**

⇒ It is God's Spirit that calls and gifts and directs each member to fit in and work within the body.

> **"As they ministered to the Lord, and fasted, the Holy Ghost said, Separate me Barnabas and Saul for the work whereunto I have called them" (Ac.13:2).**

The point is this: each member is to do his part in carrying out the mission of the body—for Christ. Acting independent of the body is of another spirit, for there is only One Spirit creating the body of Christ.

3. There is only "*one hope.*" Every genuine believer has the same hope: the great day of redemption. It is to be a new world created perfectly for Christ Jesus and His people. Life in the new heavens and earth will be a life of love and joy and peace—a life of oneness and unity and brotherhood—all perfected. What God is after is for us to live as we shall live in the future. Our future lives in the new heavens and earth are to be the pattern for the way we live together now. We shall be redeemed and reconciled to God and to each other—all living together in a perfect world of love and joy and peace for ever and ever. The hope for eternity—the hope that fills our hearts for such a world—is to be the driving force that stirs us to live together in peace and unity.

> **"For whatsoever things were written aforetime were written for our learning, that we through patience and comfort of the scriptures might have hope" (Ro.15:4).**

4. There is only "*one Lord.*" There is only one Master and King. Every believer has bowed before the same Lord to become His subject and to receive His orders. As His subjects, believers are unequivocally instructed...

- to live as He said: holy and righteous and pure, bearing the fruit of His Spirit (Ga.5:19-21).
- to carry out His orders as one body (Mt.7:21-23; 1 Co.12:5; Ph.2:9-11).

> **"Not every one that saith unto me, Lord, Lord, shall enter into the kingdom of heaven; but he that doeth the will of my Father which is in heaven. Many will say to me in that day, Lord, Lord, have we not prophesied in thy name? and in thy name have cast out devils? and in thy name done many wonderful works? And then will I profess unto them, I never knew you: depart from me, ye that work iniquity" (Mt.7:21-23).**

5. There is only "*one faith.*" There are not two faiths nor several faiths. There is only one faith that leads into God's presence, and that is the faith founded by the Lord Jesus Christ. There is no other approach to God. If a person wishes to live with God—to be approved and accepted by Him—that person has to approach God through the faith of the Lord Jesus Christ.

The point is this: every believer has come to God in the very same way—by believing in the Lord Jesus Christ. Faith in Him is the only way, the only true faith. Therefore, standing before God and having come to Him through the same faith, there is no room for any differences. We all stand on the same ground, on the same level.

> **"But they had heard only, That he which persecuted us in times past now preacheth the faith which once he destroyed" (Ga.1:23).**
>
> **"Jesus saith unto him, I am the way, the truth, and the life: no man cometh unto the Father, but by me" (Jn.14:6).**

6. There is only "*one baptism.*" By being publicly baptized, all believers have given public witness to their faith. Each has been identified as being a member of *the same body*. How? By being initiated through the *same ritual*. Therefore, having entered the church through the same ordinance, we should not become divisive. Divisiveness denies and brings shame to the meaning of baptism. Divisiveness shows that our commitment is shallow. It shows that our sincerity in being baptized was greatly lacking. It shows that we care little for Christ and for our baptism experience, for the great ordinance which initiated us into the church.

> **"Know ye not, that so many of us as were baptized into Jesus Christ were baptized into his death?" (Ro.6:3).**

7. There is only "one God and Father of all." This is probably a primitive confession of faith.

- ⇒ "One God": God is creator of all and as such is supreme over all.
- ⇒ "One Father of all": as Father, God loves all. The Christian belief begins with God as love.
- ⇒ "Above all": God controls all.

The point is striking: If there is only one God and Father of all believers, how then could He be leading two believers to stand toe to toe against each other? The answer is obvious: He could not. One or both believers are following their own fleshly, carnal ways. Someone is not following the only God and Father.

> **"And Jesus answered him, The first of all the commandments is, Hear, O Israel; The Lord our God is one Lord" (Mk.12:29).**

ILLUSTRATION:

When we have become one with each other, all of us who are Christian believers will become nourished and will grow.

> *The article "What Good Is a Tree?" in Reader's Digest explained that when the roots of trees touch, there is a substance present that reduces competition. In fact, this unknown fungus helps link roots of different trees—even of dissimilar species. A whole forest may be linked together. If one tree has access to water, another to nutrients, and a third to sunlight, the trees have the means to share with one another.*
>
> *Like trees in a forest, Christians in the church need and support one another.*[3]

---

3 Craig B. Larson, Editor. *Illustrations for Preaching & Teaching*, p.32.

EPHESIANS 4:1-6

QUESTIONS:

1. The key word here is "One." Which one of these seven basic reasons do you struggle with the most? Why?
2. How does your great *hope*, the hope of redemption, help you in your daily walk with God?
3. Why doesn't God allow more than one way to heaven? Do you think that God is being narrow-minded?

SUMMARY:

The believer is to walk worthy of his calling.

1. The way to walk worthy:
   a. with lowliness
   b. with meekness
   c. with longsuffering
   d. with love
2. The purpose for walking worthy: to keep the unity & peace
3. The seven basic reasons to walk worthy:
   a. only one body
   b. only one Spirit
   c. only one hope
   d. only one Lord
   e. only one faith
   f. only one baptism
   g. only one God and Father of all

PERSONAL JOURNAL NOTES:
(Reflection & Response)

1. The most important thing that I learned from this lesson was:

2. The area that I need to work on the most is:

3. I can apply this lesson to my life by:

4. Closing Statement of Commitment:

	B. The Believer is to Walk by Using His Gifts, 4:7-16	of Christ:	others
1. Every believer is gifted	7 But unto every one of us is given grace according to the measure of the gift of Christ.	13 Till we all come in the unity of the faith, and of the knowledge of the Son of God, unto a perfect man, unto the measure of the stature of the fulness of Christ:	b. An eternal purpose: To become a mature person like Christ
2. Every believer's gift has cost the greatest possible price a. The picture	8 Wherefore he saith, When he ascended up on high, he led captivity captive, and gave gifts unto men.	14 That we henceforth be no more children, tossed to and fro, and carried about with every wind of doctrine, by the sleight of men, and cunning craftiness, whereby they lie in wait to deceive;	c. A personal purpose 1) To no longer be as children—immature
b. The great cost: The death of Christ, His descending into the lower parts of the earth	9 (Now that he ascended, what is it but that he also descended first into the lower parts of the earth?		
c. The great value: That Christ might fill the whole universe with His presence	10 He that descended is the same also that ascended up far above all heavens, that he might fill all things.)	15 But speaking the truth in love, may grow up into him in all things, which is the head, even Christ:	2) To grow up in all things—mature
3. Every believer's gift is Christ-centered	11 And he gave some, apostles; and some, prophets; and some, evangelists; and some, pastors and teachers;	16 From whom the whole body fitly joined together and compacted by that which every joint supplieth, according to the effectual working in the measure of every part, maketh increase of the body unto the edifying of itself in love.	3) To do one's part in building up the church
4. Every believer's gift has a threefold purpose a. An immediate purpose: To equip	12 For the perfecting of the saints, for the work of the ministry, for the edifying of the body		

Section IV
THE WALK OF THE CHRISTIAN BELIEVER
Ephesians 4:1–6:9

(Note: Because of the length of this outline and commentary, you may wish to split this passage into two or three studies).

Study 2: **THE BELIEVER IS TO WALK BY USING HIS GIFTS**

Text: **Ephesians 4:7-16**

Aim: To discover and share your spiritual gifts.

Memory Verse:

> **"Wherefore He saith, When He ascended up on high, He led captivity captive, and gave gifts to men" (Ephesians 4:8).**

Ephesians 4:7-16

Introduction:

Think about it for a moment: Do you know your purpose in life? There are many people who struggle through the day-to-day rigors of life never fulfilling their God-given purpose. These people invest a lot of time and energy expending natural gifts and abilities, but what they do fails to have any lasting significance.

There is a much better way to make a difference in the world in which we live. God has given each one of us a wonderful opportunity to join with Him in His work using His gifts. One of the greatest things we can do is to make a passionate search for significance as we put into practice the spiritual gifts God has entrusted to us. The reward of finding your spiritual gift or gifts is a personal blessing. But as important as it is, your spiritual gift has no value unless you are willing to use it, to give it away. Do you know what your spiritual gift is? Are you willing to share it?

As studied in the previous passage, the church is one body, and every member is to strive to keep the oneness and unity of the Spirit. But believers are not only unified, they are diversified. There are differences between believers. What are those differences? They are gifts, special abilities given by God that are to be used to strengthen believers, to reach the world, and to minister to the people of the world. Spiritual gifts given by God are the subject of the present passage. The believer is to walk through life using the gifts God has given him.

Outline:

1. Every believer is gifted (v.7).
2. Every believer's gift has cost the greatest possible price (vv.8-10).
3. Every believer's gift is Christ-centered (v.11).
4. Every believer's gift has a threefold purpose (vv.12-16).

1. EVERY BELIEVER IS GIFTED (v.7).

Note the words, "But unto every one of us is given...the gift of Christ." There is not a single believer exempted or left out; Christ has given every believer some spiritual gift. It is important to note what is meant by spiritual gifts. A spiritual gift does not mean the natural ability or talent of a person. God, of course, keeps natural abilities and talents in mind when He gifts a person, but spiritual gifts are special gifts given to believers. They are highly specialized gifts—gifts that are given to build up believers in the church and in witnessing and ministering to the world. The point to note is that every genuine believer has received a spiritual gift, a highly specialized gift. He has received his gift to carry out the ministry of the Lord upon the earth.

Note another significant point. Jesus Christ gives us the grace to use our gifts. Grace means the strength, wisdom, courage, motivation, love, concern, care, and power—all the favor and blessings of Christ. Whatever is needed to use the gift, Christ gives us. He measures out the exact amount of grace needed for the maximum use of a gift.

> **Application:**
>
> What a glorious truth! What a spark of encouragement! Everyone of us is gifted by Christ—gifted with a highly specialized gift. And we have the measure of grace—whatever measure is needed—to use our gifts. Christ pours out His grace upon us, equipping us to carry out our task upon earth. This is significant, for it means that our gift is the gift of Christ. It is the very best gift *for us*. We should not be displeased with our gift, nor covet to be like someone else and have his gift. Christ has placed us and given us the very best gift for us—if we are truly His, yielded and committed to serve Him.
>
> **"God hath dealt to every man the measure of faith" (Ro.12:3).**

ILLUSTRATION:
The story is told of a simple man who prayed every day for a gift that he could share with his church family. Routinely, he would pray this simple prayer: "Lord, please give me at least one gift that I can share with my church family." After he prayed this prayer, he would go outside to sit by his mail box, waiting for the gift to come. Always being the friendly fellow he was, he made a point to share an encouraging word with the mailman.

Andy had been a mailman for years; and, like most folks, he had his share of problems both at home and at work. Trouble seemed to follow him like a cloud, and it showed on his face. On this particular day, as he had so many other times, he saw this man sitting down by his mail box. Andy really liked this fellow because every time he visited with him, he always went away feeling better about himself. The simple man greeted him again with a smile and said, "*Have you got a package for me today? I really prayed double-hard that God would send me a gift that I could share with my church family.*" Andy looked long and hard inside his mail bag but could find no such thing for this man. "*I'm sorry friend. I have nothing for you today.*" Dejected, the simple man walked back to his house with slow, plodding steps. "*I'll never get my gift to share with my Christian family,*" he sobbed out loud.

Suddenly, a light flashed in Andy's mind, and he rushed to embrace the simple man. "*Friend! God has sent you a gift. I've seen it with my very own eyes,*" said Andy as he looked the man in the face. Feeling confused, the simple man asked, "*You have...you mean He has...where?*"

"*For all of these months you have asked God for a gift that you already had with you. There have been days when I was as down and discouraged as I could be. But you were always there to cheer me up. You exhorted me to press on and not to give up. God has given you a great gift, the gift of encouragement to share with your Christian family. Your gift has enriched my life.*"

The simple man thanked Andy for his time and then went back to his house. "*Lord, I've had it all wrong. Now I'm going to use all I have to help others:*

⇒ *my voice to encourage them*
⇒ *my hand to help them*
⇒ *my feet to walk and fellowship with them*

And, Lord, I'm trusting you to gift me more and more so that I can help Your people more and more."

QUESTIONS:
1. Do you know what your spiritual gift(s) is?
2. If your answer is yes, how is it being used in the body of Christ? If your answer is no or not sure, now is the time to find out what your spiritual gift(s) is.
3. Have you ever failed to share your gifts when an opportunity was provided?
4. What difference does knowing what your gifts are make as you fellowship with other believers?

2. EVERY BELIEVER'S GIFT HAS COST THE GREATEST POSSIBLE PRICE (vv.8-10).

1. Note the picture. The picture of Christ giving gifts to men is dramatic. It is the picture of an ancient king who has conquered his enemies. The king is sitting astride his white stallion, riding under the arch of triumph as he enters the city. Teeming thousands shout their adoration and praise. Following in his train is his army. And then

following his army they come, the enemy stumbling along on foot in chains, looking like the defeated foe they are. They had initially come to fight tooth and nail to subject the people of the great king to their tyranny. But now they come to offer gifts to the great conqueror. The conqueror receives the gifts and in turn bestows the gifts upon his own people (see Ps.68:18).

⇒ There are great enemies of man—enemies that attack time and time again—enemies that try to make man aimless and meaningless. There is the great enemy of alienation and separation. Alienation is the energy and tendency that tries to shut God and others out of a person's life. Tragically, alienation results in a sense of emptiness, uselessness, and loneliness.

⇒ There are two great enemies that snap away all meaning for man—sin and death.

However, Christ has gone to war in behalf of man. Christ has conquered all enemies that make life useless and meaningless. Now He gives the greatest gift of all—the gift of meaning, purpose, and significance in life. He fills life with all that a man could possibly desire and use. He gives the greatest gifts, gifts that keep a person busy with the most meaningful and purposeful life imaginable.

APPLICATION:
If Christ has really given such meaning and purpose to life, why then are so many people bored with their work and life? Why are so many (even believers) dissatisfied, empty, without purpose, and wanting a change? Scripture tells us, and it tells us plainly.

1. A person has not committed his life to Christ—not fully, not totally. He does not really deny himself and follow Christ.

"And he said to them all, If any man will come after me, let him deny himself, and take up his cross daily, and follow me" (Lu.9:23).

2. A person has not sacrificed himself, all he is and has, to serve Christ and mankind. A person has not committed himself to a life of service. Real life is found *only* in service. God has ordained it so.

"For whosoever will save his life shall lose it: and whosoever will lose his life for my sake shall find it" (Mt.16:25).

3. A person lives and sows to his flesh instead of the Spirit.

"For he that soweth to his flesh shall of the flesh reap corruption; but he that soweth to the Spirit shall of the Spirit reap life everlasting [meaning, purpose, significance]" (Ga.6:8).

2. Note the great cost Christ paid to gain the right to gift believers. He had to die and descend into the lower parts of the earth.

The point is this: Jesus Christ had to die and experience hell for men in order to gain the right to gift men. That is the enormous price our gifts cost. If He had not died, then we could not be saved or gifted with spiritual gifts. There would be no purpose or significance to life—not beyond a few short years upon this earth. All we would have to look forward to would be death. But Christ has died, and He has conquered all the enemies of man—conquered them in order to gain the right to save and gift us.

"And having spoiled principalities and powers, he made a show of them openly, triumphing over them in it" (Co.2:15).

3. The great value of what Christ did is glorious. He died that He might ascend above the heavens and fill all things, that is, fill the whole universe with His presence. Jesus Christ is the Sovereign Majesty of the universe. He is seated at the right hand of God the Father, and He rules and reigns over all. He is now able to save and gift men. But remember: it is because He paid the greatest price possible. He died for us—died to gain the right to pour His grace and gifts out upon us.

> **"And what is the exceeding greatness of his power to us-ward who believe, according to the working of his mighty power, which he wrought in Christ, when he raised him from the dead, and set him at his own right hand in the heavenly places" (Ep.1:19-20).**

QUESTIONS:
1. What did Jesus Christ have to do in order to give us spiritual gifts?
2. Knowing how costly spiritual gifts were to Christ, how should a Christian care for their gifts?
3. How do you think God feels when Christians refuse to share the gifts that He has given them? How does God feel about you?

3. EVERY BELIEVER'S GIFT IS CHRIST-CENTERED (v.11).

Note the words, "He gave." It is Christ and Christ alone who gives spiritual gifts to men. Men cannot work up the gifts, nor give the gifts to other men. Christ alone possesses the spiritual gifts to give to men. Five gifts are mentioned here.

1. The gift of an *apostle*. The word "apostle" means to send out. An apostle is a representative, an ambassador, a person who is sent out into one country to represent another country. Three things are true of the apostle.

⇒ He belongs to the One who has sent him out.
⇒ He is commissioned to be sent out.
⇒ He possesses all the authority and power of the One who sends him out.

The word "apostle" has both a narrow and a broad usage in the New Testament.

a. The narrow sense. It refers to the twelve apostles and to Paul as an apostle (Ac.1:21-22; 1 Co.9:1). In this narrow sense there were at least two basic qualifications.
   1) The apostle was a man chosen directly by the Lord Himself or by the Holy Spirit (see Mt.10:1-2; Mk.3:13-14; Lu.6:13; Ac.9:6, 15; 13:2; 22:10, 14-15; Ro.1:1). He was a man who had either seen or been a companion of the Lord Jesus.
   2) The apostle was a man who had been an eyewitness of the resurrected Lord (Ac.1:21-22; 1 Co.9:1).
b. The broad sense. The word "apostle" refers to other men who preached the gospel. It is used of two missionaries, Barnabas (Ac.14:4, 14, 17) and Silas (1 Th.2:6); and two messengers, Titus (2 Co.8:23) and Epaphroditus (Ph.2:25). There is also a possibility that James, the Lord's brother (Ga.1:19) and Andronicus and Junia (Ro.16:7) are referred to as apostles.

In the narrow sense, the gift of an apostle was bound to die out because of the unique qualifications to receive the gift. It would have died out when the apostles of the Lord Jesus died. But historically, in the broad sense, there is perhaps a sense in which the qualifications and gift itself are still given and used by the Lord. The Lord's servant of any generation must *see* the Lord through the eyes of faith and know Him intimately. Similarly, the servant must personally *see and experience* the power of the resurrection through faith. Certainly there are some in every generation who have *seen* the Lord Jesus through the eyes of faith and who *know* and *experience* the power of the

Lord's resurrection. Perhaps the Lord Jesus endues them with the very special gift of an apostle to be used throughout His most precious domain—the church.

2. The gift of a *prophet*. This is the gift of speaking under the inspiration of God's Spirit. It includes both prediction and proclamation, and neither one should be minimized despite the abuse of the gift.

There is no question, the gift to predict events has been abused to the point of the ridiculous. However, the abuse of a gift does not eliminate the fact that the Spirit of God sometimes gives believers a glimpse into coming events in order to prepare and strengthen them to face the events.

However, the major function of prophecy is clearly stated by Scripture, and the fact should be heeded by all believers:

> **"But he that prophesieth speaketh unto men to edification, and exhortation, and comfort" (1 Co.14:3).**

3. The gift of an *evangelist*. This is the gift of carrying the gospel all over the world. It is the gift that specializes in proclaiming the gospel to the lost of the world. It would include both what we call the evangelist and the missionary.

> **"But watch thou in all things, endure afflictions, do the work of an evangelist, make full proof of thy ministry" (2 Ti.4:5).**

4. The gift of a *pastor*. This word means shepherd. The Greek scholar A.T. Robertson points out that the Lord Jesus told Peter to shepherd His sheep (Jn.21:16), that Peter told other ministers to shepherd the flock of God (1 Pe.5:2), and that Paul told the elders (ministers) of Ephesus to shepherd the church of God for which Christ had died (Ac.20:28).[1] The traits of a shepherd can be seen by looking at the references to Christ as the shepherd of believers. The pastor is an under-shepherd to the Chief Shepherd, Christ Jesus our Lord.

a. The shepherd knows the sheep; He knows each one by name. This is said to have been a fact among shepherds and their sheep in Jesus' day. Shepherds actually knew each sheep individually, even in large herds. The fact is certainly true with Christ and His sheep.

> **"I am the good shepherd, and know my sheep, and am known of mine" (Jn.10:14).**

b. The shepherd feeds the sheep even if He has to gather them in His arms and carry them to the feasting pasture.

> **"He shall feed the flock like a shepherd: he shall gather the lambs with his arm, and carry them in his bosom, and shall gently lead those that are with young" (Is.40:11).**

c. The shepherd guides the sheep to the pasture and away from the rough places and precipices.

> **"The LORD is my shepherd; I shall not want. He maketh me to lie down in green pastures: he leadeth me beside the still waters. He restoreth my soul: he leadeth me in the paths of righteousness for his name's sake. Yea, though I walk through the valley of the shadow of**

1 A.T. Robertson. *Word Pictures in the New Testament*, Vol.4, p.53.

death, I will fear no evil: for thou art with me; thy rod and thy staff they comfort me" (Ps.23:1-4).

d. The shepherd seeks and saves the sheep who get lost.

"I will seek that which was lost, and bring again that which was driven away, and will bind up that which was broken, and will strengthen that which was sick" (Ezk.34:16).

e. The shepherd protects the sheep. He even sacrifices His life for the sheep.

"I am the good shepherd: the good shepherd giveth his life for the sheep" (Jn.10:11).

f. The shepherd restores the sheep who go astray and return.

"For ye were as sheep going astray; but are now returned unto the Shepherd and Bishop of your souls" (1 Pe.2:25).

g. The shepherd rewards the sheep for obedience and faithfulness.

"And when the chief Shepherd shall appear, ye shall receive a crown of glory that fadeth not away" (1 Pe.5:4).

h. The shepherd shall keep the sheep separate from the goats.

"And before him shall be gathered all nations: and he shall separate them one from another, as a shepherd divideth his sheep from the goats: and he shall set the sheep on his right hand, but the goats on the left" (Mt.25:32-33).

5. The gift of a *teacher*. The function of the teacher is the gift to instruct believers in the truth of God and His Word. It is the gift to root and ground people in doctrine, reproof, correction, and righteousness. Teaching is a high calling, one of the greatest of callings. Teaching is ranked second only to the spiritual gifts of apostle and prophet (Ac.13:1;1 Co.12:28; Ep.4:11). Every apostle, prophet and pastor has the gift of teaching, but every teacher is not an apostle or prophet or pastor. The gift of teaching bears one of the largest responsibilities given by God; therefore, the teacher will be required to give a strict account to God for his faithfulness in using his gift.

The spiritual gift of teaching is the gift of understanding and communicating the Word of God, of edifying believers in the truths of God's Word. It involves understanding, interpreting, arranging, and communicating the Word of God. The gift of teaching is given to the believer who commits his life to the Word of God, to sharing its glorious truths with God's people.

"Go ye therefore, and teach all nations, baptizing them in the name of the Father, and of the Son, and of the Holy Ghost: <u>teaching</u> them to observe all things whatsoever I have commanded you: and, lo, I am with you alway, even unto the end of the world" (Mt.28:19-20).

QUESTIONS:
1. According to Scripture, can men pass on spiritual gifts to other men? Why or why not?
2. What do you think a person can do in order to develop his spiritual gifts?
3. What can a church do to develop the spiritual gifts of its members? Is this being done in your church?

4. EVERY BELIEVER'S GIFT HAS A THREEFOLD PURPOSE (vv.12-16).

Note a significant fact: the five gifts described above are gifts that involve speech or proclamation. They are very specialized gifts, gifts that are usually looked upon as being the official or professional gifts of the church. They are not given in full measure to every believer although every believer...

- should be as an apostle in that he is serving Christ in a very special ministry and faithfully using the gift God has given him
- should be as a prophet in that he is daily proclaiming God's Word
- should be as an evangelist in that he is bearing witness to the lost
- should be as a pastor in that he is shepherding and caring for people all the time
- should be as a teacher in that he is teaching the truths of God's Word to all whom he knows

1. There is an *immediate purpose* for the professional or office-bearing gifts in the church and among God's people. It is to equip believers to do the work of the ministry. The word "perfecting" means to equip for service and ministry. This is critical to see, for the office bearer in the church *is not* to be the only one who goes about doing the work of the ministry. In fact, his *primary task* is to be an equipper, a person who makes disciples and *prepares others* to serve Christ. Note another critical point: the very purpose for equipping laymen is so that the body of Christ, the church, may be built up. This is a significant point, for it means that the church cannot be built up without the members themselves doing the work of the ministry. All believers within a church must be involved in the work of the ministry.

If the work of the ministry were left up to the professional ministers, the task would never get done, for there are too few official ministers. Lay persons must be equipped to reach the lost and to minister to the needs of a world reeling under the weight of evil and suffering and death.

ILLUSTRATION:
Is every member of your church a minister? Look at this challenging story about a group of Christians who discovered their spiritual gifts and began to minister:

> *A church of my observation had experienced consecutive years of progressive growth. As attendance increased, buildings were added and the ministerial staff was enlarged. It appeared that there would never be an end to financial increase, but then the bottom dropped out of oil prices and the area slipped rapidly into its own recession.*
>
> *Every possible cost-cutting measure was implemented, including drastic staff reductions. The pastor expected severe negative responses from the congregation when services that they had taken for granted were no longer available. Instead, the people testified, "We are spoiled brats who have been waited on hand and foot by our paid staff. Now it's time for us to go to work."*
>
> *...The church not only went on, but it strengthened its family relationships and drew new members into its ranks even though most of the professionals were gone. Getting the people involved in the work of the ministry proved to be a needed tonic for that congregation, for they had been overfed and underexercised for a long season.* [2]

APPLICATION:
Let's examine God's provision for building (*perfecting*) ministers. The term that Paul chose is a medical term that implies the "setting of a bone." This is very

[2] Judson Cornwall. *Leaders Eat What You Serve.* (Shippensburg, PA: Destiny Image Publishers, 1988), p.5.

significant because no one comes into the Kingdom of God with his act together. Everyone needs to be perfected or equipped. In order to be equipped, each one must realize that:

1. All of us are broken people on the mend.
2. No one knows it all.
3. In order to be equipped, we must be teachable.
4. Everyone needs a mentor to hold himself accountable. Who holds your walk accountable?

2. There is an *eternal purpose* for the office-bearing or professional gifts. It can be stated no clearer than what the verse itself says. It says three things:

a. The servant of God works to bring about a perfect unity among God's people. The servant of God is called...
   - to bring peace and reconciliation to the church
   - to lead people into perfect harmony and oneness of spirit
   - to shepherd people out of cliques, divisiveness, murmuring, grumbling, griping, and all the other sins that militate against a perfect unity

"Now I beseech you, brethren, by the name of our Lord Jesus Christ, that ye all speak the same thing, and that there be no divisions among you; but that ye be perfectly joined together in the same mind and in the same judgment" (1 Co.1:10).

b. The servant of God works to bring about the knowledge of the Son of God.

"Then shall we know, if we follow on to know the Lord: his going forth is prepared as the morning; and he shall come unto us as the rain, as the latter and former rain unto the earth" (Ho.6:3).

c. The servant of God works to bring about a perfect man, a man who measures up to the stature of Christ Himself—to the fulness of His stature.

"But strong meat belongeth to them that are of full age, even those who by reason of use have their senses exercised to discern both good and evil" (He.5:14).

3. There is the *personal purpose* for the professional or office-bearing gifts. This purpose also involves three parts.

a. That we no longer be children and immature, being led astray by false teaching. Again, the verse is the best commentary on itself. Ministers are given to keep us from being "children, tossed to and fro, and carried about by every wind of [false] doctrine" or false teaching. We must always remember, there is such a thing as...
   - "the sleight of men": deceivers, cheaters in the faith, men who will cheat us out of the truth
   - "cunning craftiness": deceivers who act clever and have novel ideas that sound correct, but they are only deceptions of the truth

Note that such men are plentiful, so plentiful that they are just lying, waiting to deceive.

"Beware of false prophets, which come to you in sheep's clothing, but inwardly they are ravening wolves" (Mt.7:15).

b. That we grow up in all things—in Christ. Note there is only one way to do this: by speaking and proclaiming the truth. This is our task as believers.

"Now ye are clean through the word which I have spoken unto you" (Jn.15:3).

c. That we do our part in building up the church. Note that *every joint or every believer "supplies"* something to the body of Christ (the church). And what every joint or believer supplies is very significant. Note how the significance is stressed: Christ takes every joint or believer and the believer…
- is fitly joined together with all the other believers
- has his work compacted with that supplied by other believers
- has an effective and productive work along with that of other believers
- helps to increase the body
- helps to edify the body in love

What more could be said about the contribution made by every believer? What greater challenge could be given to a believer? We must give all we are and have to get the job done. Much is at stake for each of us.

An eternal weight of responsibility rests upon every single believer, for each one is responsible for reaching people and building them up. Some people will never be reached and ministered to if a single one of us comes up short. For this reason, everyone of us is gifted by Christ Jesus our Lord.

"Now there are diversities of gifts, but the same Spirit. And there are differences of administrations, but the same Lord. And there are diversities of operations, but it is the same God which worketh all in all. But thc manifestation of the Spirit is given to every man to profit withal" (1 Co.12:4-7).

APPLICATION:

1. The Scripture literally says that "the saints are to be prepared for *practical* service" (v.12). There is a big difference between a program-generated church and a Spirit-led program in a church. The former saps the life out of people while the latter gives life.
2. Whatever you do for the Lord, ask yourself this question, "Is this *practical* service? Will it really do good?" There is danger when you become consumed with doing a lot of things and justify your walk as being worthy when in actuality you have lost your joy in serving and are burned out.

QUESTIONS:

1. What can you do that would be practical ministry?
2. Here are some suggestions for you to consider:
   a. Befriend a single parent and find ways to serve them.
   b. Do you know someone who has just gone through a divorce? Reach out to them and keep them in the flock of God's church. They need love…not rejection.
   c. Do you know a family that is "losing it" with the kids? Offer them your listening ear and offer to share with them some Christian resources on parenting.
   d. Do you know of a marriage on the rocks? Are you willing to pray and do all you can to help the couple? What are some practical things you can do to help them?
3. The suggestions could go on and on. Ask the Lord this question right now: *what would You have me do?*

EPHESIANS 4:7-16

SUMMARY:

By now, you should have been challenged to learn just what your spiritual gifts are, and to use your gifts to reach and minister to people. Let's review the major points of the study again:

1. Every believer is gifted.
2. Every believer's gift has cost the greatest possible price.
3. Every believer's gift is Christ-centered.
4. Every believer's gift has a threefold purpose:
   a. An immediate purpose: to equip others
   b. An eternal purpose: to become a mature person like Christ
   c. A personal purpose
      1) to no longer be as children—immature
      2) to grow up in all things—mature
      3) to do one's part in building up the church

PERSONAL JOURNAL NOTES:
(Reflection & Response)

1. The most important thing that I learned from this lesson was:

2. The area that I need to work on the most is:

3. I can apply this lesson to my life by:

4. Closing Statement of Commitment:

	C. The Believer is to Walk Differently From the Gentiles, 4:17-24		
1. The believer is not to walk or live as the Gentiles do, that is, as ungodly men a. With emptiness of mind b. With dark understanding c. Being separated from God 1) Because they are ignorant of God 2) Because their hearts are hard d. Being insensitive, past all feeling e. Being given over to gross sensuality	17 This I say therefore, and testify in the Lord, that ye henceforth walk not as other Gentiles walk, in the vanity of their mind, 18 Having the understanding darkened, being alienated from the life of God through the ignorance that is in them, because of the blindness of their heart: 19 Who being past feeling have given themselves over unto lasciviousness,	to all uncleanness with greediness. 20 But ye have not so learned Christ; 21 If so be that ye have heard him, and have been taught by him, as the truth is in Jesus: 22 That ye put off concerning the former conversation the old man, which is corrupt according to the deceitful lusts: 23 And be renewed in the spirit of your mind; 24 And that ye put on the new man, which after God is created in righteousness and true holiness.	f. Indulging in every kind of impurity & greed **2. The believer is to walk as Christ walks** a. The reason: He has learned about Christ—heard & been taught about Him b. The way to walk in Christ 1) Put off the old man—the old person, the old self 2) Recommit your spirit, your mind 3) Put on the new man—the new person, the new self

Section IV
THE WALK OF THE CHRISTIAN BELIEVER
Ephesians 4:1–6:9

(Note: Because of the length of this outline and commentary, you may wish to split this passage into two or three studies).

Study 3: **THE BELIEVER IS TO WALK DIFFERENTLY FROM THE GENTILES**

Text: **Ephesians 4:17-24**

Aim: To make absolutely sure that your Christian walk matches your Christian talk.

Memory Verse:

"And that you put on the new man, which after God is created in righteousness and true holiness" (Ephesians 4:24).

INTRODUCTION:

Most people are familiar with the expression "practice what you preach." This is a very convenient cliche to use, but it proves to be a shallow saying when the rubber of life hits the road. The truth is this: doing what we should is always more difficult than saying what we should do.

What can you do to match your walk with your talk? What makes a Christian believer distinctive from the non-believer? A non-believer seldom gets involved in someone else's life unless there is something in it for him. But the Christian believer does not learn about Christ in that way. The challenge for each of us is to put off the old and put on the new. This session will teach us how to enhance our walk with Christ.

This passage contains an astounding truth—believers are neither Gentiles nor Jews; they are a *third race* of people. Therefore, they are not to walk like men (natural, ungodly men); they are to walk like Christ.

OUTLINE:
1. The believer is not to walk or live as the Gentiles do, that is, as ungodly men (vv.17-19).
2. The believer is to walk as Christ walks (vv.20-24).

1. THE BELIEVER IS NOT TO WALK OR LIVE AS THE GENTILES DO, THAT IS, AS UNGODLY MEN (vv.17-19).

This is very significant. Remember: Paul is writing to Gentiles. The church at Ephesus was a Gentile church. Now note the verse. In the authorized version (King James) believers are told to no longer walk as "other Gentiles" walk, as though they were still classified as Gentiles. But the word "other" is not in the best and oldest manuscripts. Thus, the exhortation is to "no longer walk as Gentiles walk." That is, believers are set off and set apart from Gentiles. They are no longer classified as Gentiles or Jews (see 1 Co.10:32). Who then are believers? The point being made is that they are a *third race on earth*. They are the *new creation*; the creation of a *new body* of people, a *new nation*, a *new race*. They are the children of God who are to inhabit the *new heavens and earth*.

The point is this: believers are not to walk as *other men* walk. Why? Because believers are new creatures in Christ Jesus, and the walk of other men does not please God. What is it that other men do that does not please God? This passage gives five traits about unbelievers that displease God. Remember: believers are to have nothing to do with any of these. They are never to return to the paths of their former life.

1. Unbelievers walk in the *vanity of their mind* (v.17). The *mind* includes the ability to will and to do the truth as well as know the truth; it includes morality as well as reasoning and understanding. The word "vain" means empty, futile, senseless, aimless, unsuccessful, worthless.

When men push God out of their minds, their minds are void and empty of God and of His truth and morality. *God is not in their thoughts*. Their minds are ready to be filled with some other god or supremacy, that is, with the things of the world:

⇒ wordly pleasures	⇒ wordly religions
⇒ wordly possessions	⇒ wordly ideas
⇒ wordly power	⇒ wordly honor
⇒ wordly position	⇒ wordly gods

> **"And God saw that the wickedness of man was great in the earth, and that every imagination of the thoughts of his heart was only evil continually" (Ge.6:5).**

The mind of man walks after these things, neglecting, ignoring, and rejecting God. The believer must never return to the *walk of an empty mind*; he must never again allow his mind to become empty of God.

2. Unbelievers walk with their *understanding darkened* (v.18). To *understand* means to grasp, comprehend, perceive. To be *darkened* means to be blinded and unable to see. The unbeliever does not grasp or understand God; his understanding is darkened and blinded and unable to see God. He often understands this world and the things of this world, and he gives his life over to the things of this world. But he is not able to understand God and His eternal plan for the world through the Lord Jesus Christ.

The believer is not to allow his understanding to become darkened. He is not to return to the world of the spiritually blind, the world of those who walk with darkened understanding.

> **"Ever learning, and never able to come to the knowledge of the truth" (2 Ti.3:7).**

3. Unbelievers walk *alienated from the life of God.* Unbelievers are spiritually dead and doomed to eternal death. "Alienated" means to be estranged, separated, cut off, detached. There are always unfriendly or hostile feelings involved in alienation. The unbeliever is *alienated* from the life of God. He is...

- estranged from God with unfriendly or hostile feelings
- separated from God with unfriendly or hostile feelings
- cut off from God with unfriendly or hostile feelings
- detached from God with unfriendly or hostile feelings

Why? Not because of God. The Bible is clear about this issue. Unbelievers are alienated from God because of their own wilful ignorance and hardness of heart. The word "blindness" is the word hardness in the Greek. Note the words "in them." The cause is "in them":

⇒ They choose to be ignorant within their minds—choose to be ignorant of God.
⇒ They choose to harden their own hearts.

Unbelievers are responsible for their own death. God has provided the fountain of youth for man, the way for man to live forever. God has given His life, that is, eternal life, to man. The only way man can ever miss God's gift of eternal life is to reject God and His gift.

> **"This people draweth nigh unto me with their mouth, and honoureth me with their lips; but their heart is far from me" (Mt.15:8).**

4. Unbelievers are *past feeling;* that is, they reach a point where they no longer have feelings for God and His standard of morality. To be *past feeling* means to become callous, insensible, hardened. The more a person walks without God, the more callous a person becomes to God. The more a person walks in sin, the more callous his conscience becomes to righteousness. Sin becomes more and more acceptable. The person's conscience no longer bothers him. He reaches a point of being *past feeling*. The believer is not to return to sin. He is not to walk as other men walk—in sin, becoming callous and insensitive to God.

> **"For the heart of this people is waxed gross, and their ears are dull of hearing, and their eyes have they closed; lest they should see with their eyes and hear with their ears, and understand with their heart, and should be converted, and I should heal them" (Ac.28:27).**

5. Unbelievers give themselves over to *lasciviousness*, to all forms of sensual living.

6. Unbelievers indulge in all uncleanness with greediness. The word "uncleanness" means to be dirty and filthy; to be infested with every kind of unclean, immoral, dirty, and polluted behavior. It is the most immoral behavior imaginable. It is *unbridled lust* turned loose.

> **"For God hath not called us unto uncleanness, but unto holiness" (1 Th.4:7).**

7. The word "greediness" means avarice, coveting, craving, grasping, desiring to have more and more; hoarding all one can get and still craving more. It is being enslaved and held in bondage by the things of this earth: for example, food, drink, and a host of fleshly sins and self-centered behavior.

Believers are not to walk in such a life. They are not to walk as other men walk.

> **"Thou shalt not covet thy neighbour's house, thou shalt not covet thy neighbour's wife, nor his manservant, nor his maidservant, nor his ox, nor his ass, nor any thing that is thy neighbour's" (Ex.20:17).**

ILLUSTRATION:

Your witness makes a big difference as you walk with Christ in this world. It is important to guard yourself from the "old man" who wants to represent you. Don't be discouraged! Your Christian life lived out makes an impact on those who are watching you. Look closely at this story and apply it to your walk:

> *An old man, walking the beach at dawn, noticed a young man ahead of him picking up starfish and flinging them into the sea. Catching up with the youth, he asked what he was doing. The answer was that the stranded starfish would die if left until the morning sun.*
>
> *"But the beach goes on for miles, and there are millions of starfish," countered the old man. "How can your effort make a difference?"*
>
> *The young man looked at the starfish in his hand and then threw it to safety in the waves. "It makes a difference to this one," he said.*[1]

QUESTIONS:

1. What draws a Christian to walk like a Gentile (the way of the world)?
2. How does a heart become hardened?
3. What thoughts come to your mind when you hear the word "*vanity*"?
4. What happens when Christians walk like unbelievers? Who is affected?

2. THE BELIEVER IS TO WALK AS CHRIST WALKS (vv.20-24).

He is not to walk as men walk. The reason is clearly stated: believers did not learn such a sinful life from Christ. Christ did not live a sinful life, and He has not taught us to live a sinful life as other men live. If a man has heard Christ and been taught by Christ, then he has heard and been taught *the truth*. Note that the Teacher is Christ Himself, not the minister nor the lay teacher. By the Holy Spirit, Christ uses the body and voice of the minister and teacher to teach people how they are to live. If a person has really heard Christ speaking to their hearts, then what they heard was not the kind of life lived by unbelievers. The true walk is a walk in Christ, and a walk in Christ involves three actions. (Because of their importance and length, the three actions are covered under the heading "A CLOSER LOOK.")

1. The believer is to *put off the old man*—Ep. 4:22.
2. The believer is to be *renewed in the spirit of his mind*—Ep. 4:23.
3. The believer is to *put on the new man*—Ep. 4:24.

---

1 Craig B. Larson, Editor. *Illustrations for Preaching and Teaching*, p.66.

A CLOSER LOOK:

(4:22) **Old Man**: the "old man" refers to what a man is *before he accepts Christ*. It is the very *nature of man*, the *natural*, corruptible seed which is passed on from generation to generation and leads to death. It is what is called the nature of Adam.

Three things are taught about the old man in the Scriptures.

1. The believer's *old man* has already been put to death. It was crucified with Christ (Ro.6:6). When the believer received Christ, God began immediately to count him buried with Christ and united with Christ in the very likeness of His death. This is the meaning symbolized in baptism.

2. The deeds of the old man have been *put off* from the believer (Co.3:9). The power of evil deeds has been broken, and the believer is no longer in bondage to them.

3. In this passage, the believer himself is exhorted to *put off the old man*. He is told to exercise his own will in putting off the *old man*. He so wills by realizing and acting upon three truths.

a. The old man, from God's perspective, is counted dead. Therefore, the believer *counts* his old man as already being dead.

> **"Likewise reckon ye also yourselves to be dead indeed unto sin, but alive unto God through Jesus Christ our Lord" (Ro.6:11).**

b. The old man is recognized as being very much alive. The old man is tempted to *look, taste, feel, think*—to *experience sin*. But the believer rejects the temptation. He refuses to participate in sin. He puts off the old man as he walks day by day.

> **"Let not sin therefore reign in your mortal body, that ye should obey it in the lusts thereof. Neither yield ye your members as instruments of unrighteousness unto sin: but yield yourselves unto God, as those that are alive from the dead, and your members as instruments of righteousness unto God" (Ro.6:12-13).**

c. The old man (including all creation) is seen aging and dying day by day. The believer realizes that this world and all that is within it, including his old man, is in a constant process of dying. He knows that all is dying because the evil desires of nature are deceitful, and deceit disturbs and destroys relationships—the very nature of things (Ep.4:22). Such destruction deteriorates and corrupts; it eats away at life and at the balance of things until all things become nothing but decayed matter. Therefore, the believer puts off the old man and puts on the new man—by faith in the love of God. When a person believes in the love of God, God responds by loving him so much that He makes a permanent man out of him, a new man who is to live eternally and become a citizen of the new heavens and earth.

> **"Knowing this, that our old man is crucified with him, that the body of sin might be destroyed, that henceforth we should not serve sin" (Ro.6:6).**
>
> **"But he that lacketh these things is blind, and cannot see afar off, and hath forgotten that he was purged from his old sins" (2 Pe.1:9).**

QUESTIONS:
1. According to Scripture, is this "old man" still alive in you?
2. What instuctions is the Christian given in dealing with the "old man"?
3. Give some examples of how the "old man" acts when he doesn't get his way?

A CLOSER LOOK:

(4:23) **Mind**: the believer's mind is to be renewed, which means to be made new, readjusted, changed, turned around, and regenerated.

a. The mind of man has been affected by sin. It desperately needs to be renewed. The mind is far from perfect. It is *basically worldly*, that is...
   - selfish
   - self-centered
   - self-seeking
   - centered on this world
   - centered on the flesh
   - centered on this life

Scripture is clear about the corruption of man's mind. The human mind has just been tragically corrupted by man's selfishness and sin.

⇒ Man's mind has become *vain*, empty, and futile in its *imaginations*.

"Because that, when they knew God, they glorified him not as God, neither were thankful; but became vain in their imaginations, and their foolish heart was darkened" (Ro.1:21).

⇒ Man's mind has become *reprobate*.

"And even as they did not like to retain God in their knowledge, God gave them over to a reprobate mind, to do those things which are not convenient" (Ro.1:28).

⇒ Man's mind has become carnal and full of enmity against God.

"Because the carnal mind is enmity against God: for it is not subject to the law of God, neither indeed can be" (Ro.8:7).

⇒ Man's mind has become blinded by Satan lest it believe the glorious gospel of Christ.

"In whom the god of this world hath blinded the minds of them which believe not, lest the light of the glorious gospel of Christ, who is the image of God, should shine unto them" (2 Co.4:4).

⇒ Man's mind has become *full* of vanity, futility, emptiness.

"This I say therefore, and testify in the Lord, that ye henceforth walk not as other Gentiles walk, in the vanity of the mind" (Ep.4:17).

⇒ Man's mind has become focused upon earthly things.

"For many walk, of whom I have told you often, and now tell you even weeping, that they are the enemies of the cross of Christ:

whose end is destruction, whose God is their belly, and whose glory is in their shame, who mind earthly things" (Ph.3:18-19).

⇒ Man's mind has become alienated from God and an enemy to God.

"And you, that were sometime alienated and enemies in your mind by wicked works, yet now hath he reconciled" (Co.1:21).

⇒ Man's mind has become fleshly.

"Let no man beguile you of your reward in a voluntary humility and worshipping of angels, intruding into those things which he hath not seen, vainly puffed up by his fleshly mind" (Co.2:18).

⇒ Man's mind has become defiled.

"Unto the pure all things are pure: but unto them that are defiled and unbelieving is nothing pure; but even their mind and conscience is defiled" (Tit.1:15).

b. The mind is renewed by the presence of Christ in the life of the believer. When a person receives the Lord Jesus Christ as His Lord, the man is *spiritually*...
- born again (Jn.3:3-8; 1 Pe.1:23)
- made into a new man (Ep.4:24; Co.3:10)
- made into a new creature (2 Co.5:17)
- given the mind of Christ (1 Co.2:16; see vv.9-15)

What this means is a most wonderful truth, and it is easily seen. When a person receives Jesus Christ into his life, he receives the mind of Christ as well. Christ places His mind into the believer's mind; that is, Christ changes the believer's mind to focus upon God. Whereas the believer's mind used to be centered upon the world, it is now centered upon spiritual matters. The believer's mind is renewed, changed, turned around, and regenerated to focus upon God. However, it is critical to remember that only Christ can renew the human mind. Only Christ can implant *the mind of Christ* within a person. Only Christ can give a person His thoughts and the spirit to *live out* His thoughts.

c. The believer is to live a transformed life; that is, he is to walk day by day *renewing his mind more and more*. He is to allow the Spirit of Christ (the Holy Spirit) to focus his mind more and more upon God and spiritual things.

⇒ The believer is to love the Lord with all his mind.

"Jesus said unto him, Thou shalt love the Lord thy God with all thy heart, and with all thy soul, and with all thy mind" (Mt.22:37).

⇒ The believer is to keep his mind upon spiritual things, not carnal things.

"For they that are after the flesh do mind the things of the flesh; but they that are after the Spirit the things of the Spirit.

For to be carnally minded is death; but to be spiritually minded is life and peace" (Ro.8:5-6).

⇒ The believer is to cast down imaginations and every thought that interrupts his knowledge of God, and he is to captivate every thought for Christ.

"Casting down imaginations, and every high thing that exalteth itself against the knowledge of God, and bringing into captivity every thought to the obedience of Christ" (2 Co.10:5).

⇒ The believer is not to let his mind be corrupted.

"But I fear, lest by any means, as the serpent beguiled Eve through his subtlety, so your minds should be corrupted from the simplicity that is in Christ" (2 Co.11:3).

⇒ The believer is not to fulfill the desires of the flesh and of the mind.

"Among whom also we all had our conversation in times past in the lusts of our flesh, fulfilling the desires of the flesh and of the mind; and were by nature the children of wrath, even as others" (Ep.2:3).

⇒ The believer is not to walk as the world walks, in the vanity of their mind.

"This I say therefore, and testify in the Lord, that ye henceforth walk not as other Gentiles walk, in the vanity of their mind" (Ep.4:17).

⇒ The believer is to be renewed in the spirit of his mind.

"And be renewed in the spirit of your mind" (Ep.4:23).

⇒ The believer is to let the mind of Christ be in him by walking humbly before God and men.

"Let this mind be in you, which was also in Christ Jesus" (Ph.2:5).

⇒ The believer is to think only upon the things of praise and virtue.

"Finally, brethren, whatsoever things are true, whatsoever things are honest, whatsoever things are just, whatsoever things are pure, whatsoever things are lovely, whatsoever things are of good report; if there be any virtue, and if there be any praise, think on these things" (Ph.4:8).

⇒ The believer is to live by the laws of God which God has put into his mind.

"For this is the covenant that I will make with the house of Israel after those days, saith the Lord; I will put my laws into

their mind, and write them in their hearts: and I will be to them a God, and they shall be to me a people" (He.8:10).

⇒ The believer is to arm himself with the same mind as Christ in bearing suffering.

"Forasmuch then as Christ hath suffered for us in the flesh, arm yourselves likewise with the same mind: for he that hath suffered in the flesh hath ceased from sin" (1 Pe.4:1).

QUESTIONS:

1. Who actually renews the mind, you or God? Explain your answer.
2. What sorts of things do you have to avoid in order to protect your mind from contamination?
3. Give some examples of how your mind is renewed.
4. What keeps you from having a renewed mind? What can you do in order to overcome these barriers?

A CLOSER LOOK:

(4:24) **New Man**: man is *regenerated, renewed, born again* who has become spiritually minded. It is a *new man* created by Christ; he has been given a holy nature and an incorruptible life. It is opposed to the *old man* with a corrupt nature. It is a man who is...

- in fellowship with God
- obedient to God's will
- devoted to God's service

There are two Greek words translated by the English word *new*. There is the word *neos* which refers to something new that has just been made, but there are already many others existing just like it. There is the word *kainos* which refers to something new, something just made, and there is nothing like it in existence. *Kainos* is the word used here. Jesus Christ makes a *new man* entirely—a creation unlike any other creation existing. The Gentile believer is not made into a Jew; neither is a Jewish believer made into a Gentile. Each, through the Lord Jesus Christ, is made into a *new kind of person—a new man in God*. Every person *can begin life all over again*; every person can have a new beginning, a new life by coming to Jesus Christ.

How is this possible? By the power of God. When a person believes in and entrusts his life into the hands of Jesus Christ, God's Son, God creates the spirit of the person in righteousness and true holiness. God actually credits the person's faith *as the perfect righteousness and holiness of Jesus Christ*. But note: this is not all that God does. He does more marvellous things for the believer—all having to do with creating the believer into a new person.

1. God quickens the spirit of the believer and makes his spirit alive. Whereas the believer's spirit was dead to God, God creates it and makes it alive to God.

"And you hath he quickened, who were dead in trespasses and sins" (Ep.2:1).

2. God causes the believer to be born again spiritually.

"Jesus answered, Verily, verily, I say unto thee, Except a man be born of water and [of] the Spirit, he cannot enter into the kingdom of God" (Jn.3:5).

"Being born again, not of corruptible seed, but of incorruptible, by the word of God, which liveth and abideth for ever" (1 Pe.1:23).

3. God actually places His divine nature into the heart of the believer.

Whereby are given unto us exceeding great and precious promises: that by these ye might be partakers of the divine nature, having escaped the corruption that is in the world through lust" (2 Pe.1:4).

4. God actually creates a new man out of the believer.

"Therefore if any man be in Christ, he is a new creature: old things are passed away; behold, all things are become new" (2 Co.5:17; see Ro.12:2; Ep.4:24; Co.3:10).

5. God renews the believer by the Holy Spirit.

"Not by works of righteousness which we have done, but according to his mercy he saved us, by the washing of regeneration, and renewing of the Holy Ghost" (Tit.3:5, see Ep.1:13; 4:30).

APPLICATION:
Some people are constantly changing their outward appearance by varying their style of clothes, wearing a different hairstyle, or even focusing on different jewelry or makeup. But underneath, they are still the same people. Who have they fooled? What looks good to them now will be dissatisfactory to them in a week or two or maybe a month. Then they will change their appearance again. There is an ongoing lack of contentment with their looks. But our heavenly Father has given us a new life in Him that never tarnishes or looks bad or wears out. It is the inward man that is changed; it is the new man. The new man is a permanent part of our lives; the old way of sin is no longer acceptable. And it is only through Christ that we can receive this new nature. It is up to us to accept or reject what God has offered us.

QUESTIONS:
1. How does a person become a *new man*?
2. What happens to that person when he puts on the *new man*?
3. Why do you think some Christians continue to put on the old man?
4. What area of your spiritual life needs a new start? How can you do a better job of putting on the new man?

SUMMARY:

The believer *is* to walk differently from the Gentiles, from ungodly men. Let's review the major points again:
1. The believer is not to walk or live as the Gentiles, that is, as ungodly men.
2. The believer is to walk as Christ walks. How?
    a. Put off the old man
    b. Recommit your spirit, your mind
    c. Put on the new man

EPHESIANS 4:17-24

PERSONAL JOURNAL NOTES:
(Reflection & Response)

1. The most important thing that I learned from this lesson was:

2. The area that I need to work on the most is:

3. I can apply this lesson to my life by:

4. Closing Statement of Commitment:

	D. The Believer is to Walk Putting Off the Garments of the Old Man, 4:25-32	29 Let no corrupt communication proceed out of your mouth, but that which is good to the use of edifying, that it may minister grace unto the hearers.	**4. The garment of worthless talk** a. The charge: Do not use foul, unclean language b. The reason: To build up others
1. The garment of lying a. The charge: Stop lying; speak the truth b. The reason: Believers are one body	25 Wherefore putting away lying, speak every man truth with his neighbour: for we are members one of another.	30 And grieve not the holy Spirit of God, whereby ye are sealed unto the day of redemption.	**5. The garment of disobedience** a. The charge: Do not grieve the Spirit b. The reason: He seals us
2. The garment of anger a. The charge: Deal with your anger b. The reason: So the devil does not get control	26 Be ye angry, and sin not: let not the sun go down upon your wrath: 27 Neither give place to the devil.	31 Let all bitterness, and wrath, and anger, and clamour, and evil speaking, be put away from you, with all malice:	**6. The garments of unkindness** a. Charge 1: Get rid of bitterness, anger, evil speaking
3. The garment of stealing a. The charge: Work for what you need & more b. The reason: To support yourself & to help the needy	28 Let him that stole steal no more: but rather let him labour, working with his hands the thing which is good, that he may have to give to him that needeth.	32 And be ye kind one to another, tenderhearted, forgiving one another, even as God for Christ's sake hath forgiven you.	**7. The garments of the new man** b. Charge 2: Be kind, tenderhearted, forgiving c. The reason: God forgave you; you are a new person

Section IV
THE WALK OF THE CHRISTIAN BELIEVER
Ephesians 4:1–6:9

Study 4: THE BELIEVER IS TO WALK PUTTING OFF THE GARMENTS OF THE OLD MAN

Text: Ephesians 4:25-32

Aim: To strip off your old nature and put on the new.

Memory Verse:

> **"Let no corrupt communication proceed out of your mouth, but that which is good to the use of edifying, that it may minister grace unto the hearers" (Ephesians 4:29).**

INTRODUCTION:

Have you heard the phrase: "Clothes make the man"? A lot of money is spent on clothes throughout the world. The right combination of clothes can enhance a person's appearance. The right color and style go a long way toward the process of dressing up properly.

Of course, the reverse is true as well. The wrong combinations, colors, and styles will be offensive to many who have different tastes.

Therefore, when a person clothes himself, he wants to be sure to put on the right clothes. If he dresses improperly, putting on clothes that clash or are unsuitable, he is frequently unacceptable and shunned. Most people avoid the person who is improperly dressed, for he embarrasses them. So it is with God. There are things that we are to put on and things that we are not to put on, things that are to clothe our lives and things that are not to clothe our lives. The believer's duty is to discover those things that are to be stripped off, allowing the Lord to cleanse Him through and through. The believer is to put off the garments of the old man.

OUTLINE:

1. The garment of lying (v.25).
2. The garment of anger (vv.26-27).
3. The garment of stealing (v.28).
4. The garment of worthless talk (v.29).
5. The garment of disobedience (v.30).
6. The garments of unkindness (v.31).
7. The garments of the new man (v.32).

1. THE GARMENT OF LYING (v.25).

The believer is to strip away the garment of lying. The word lying means that which is false. It is untruthfulness, deception, misrepresentation, exaggeration.

1. A lie does at least three things.
   a. Lying misrepresents the truth. It camouflages and hides the truth. The person being lied to does not know the truth; therefore, he has to act or live upon a lie. If the lie is serious, it can be very damaging:
      ⇒ A lie about a business deal can cost money and cause terrible loss.
      ⇒ A lie about the salvation of the gospel can cost a person the hope of eternal life.
      ⇒ A lie about loving someone can stir emotions that lead to destruction.

   b. Lying deceives a person. It leads a person astray. A person deceives...
      - to get what he wants
      - to seduce someone
      - to cover up or hide something
      - to cause harm or hurt

      The point to see is that lying is a deception, and deception eventually causes misunderstanding, disappointment, bewilderment, helplessness, and emotional upheaval.

   c. Lying builds a wrong relationship, a relationship built upon sinking sand. Two people cannot possibly be friends or live together if the relationship is based upon lies. Lying destroys...
      ⇒ confidence
      ⇒ assurance
      ⇒ security
      ⇒ love
      ⇒ trust
      ⇒ hope

2. Scripture gives one strong reason for believers to speak only the truth: they are members of one another. Every believer is a member of the great body of people which God is building, the body of Christ, that is, the church. William Barclay has an excellent description of this point.

> *We can only live in safety because the senses and the nerves pass true messages to the brain. If in fact the senses and the nerves took to passing false messages to the brain, if, for instance, they told the brain that something was cool and touchable when in fact it was hot and burning, life would very soon come to an end. A body can only function accurately and healthily when each part of it passes true messages to the brain and to the other parts. If then we are all bound into one body, that body can only function when we speak the truth. All deception impairs the working of the body of Christ.*[1]

---

1 William Barclay. *The Letters to the Galatians and Ephesians*, p.184.

3. The believer is to be altogether what he says. There is to be nothing covered, nothing hid, no shame, no pretense. He is to be exactly the same before men as he is in private and the same in private as he is before men. His life is not to be a lie.

⇒ Lying or bearing false witness is one of the sins included in the Ten Commandments.

> **"Thou shalt not bear false witness against thy neighbor" (Ex.20:16).**

⇒ Lying is one of the gross sins that defile men.

> **"For out of the heart proceed evil thoughts, murders, adulteries, fornications, thefts, false witness, blasphemies" (Mt.15:19).**

⇒ Lying takes its stand with the father of lies, the devil.

> **"Ye are of your father the devil and the lusts of your father ye will do. He was a murderer from the beginning, and abode not in the truth, because there is no truth in him. When he speaketh a lie, he speaketh of his own: for he is a liar, and the father of it" (Jn.8:44).**

⇒ Lying is closely associated with idolatry. It causes a person to profess something other than the truth.

> **"And there shall in no wise enter into it any thing that defileth, neither whatsoever worketh abomination, or maketh a lie: but they which are written in the Lamb's book of life" (Re.21:27).**

⇒ Lying or deceiving men is to be a characteristic of the antichrist.

> **"Even him, whose coming is after the working of Satan with all power and signs and lying wonders" (2 Th.2:9).**

⇒ Lying is not what it professes to be.

> **"I have not written unto you because ye know not the truth, but because ye know it, and that no lie is of the truth" (1 Jn.2:21).**
>
> **"Even him, whose coming is after the working of Satan with all power and signs and lying wonders" (2 Th.2:9).**

⇒ Lying is opposed to the truth.

> **"But the anointing which ye have received of him abideth in you, and ye need not that any man teach you: but as the same anointing teacheth you of all things, and is truth, and is no lie, and even as it hath taught you, ye shall abide in him" (1 Jn.2:27).**

QUESTIONS:

1. How do you get into the habit of telling the truth?
2. Give some examples of how some Christians 'bend the truth.' How does God feel about Christians telling 'white lies'?
3. Can you remember a time when you failed to tell the truth. What was the end result? What would you do differently today?

2. THE GARMENT OF ANGER (vv.26-27).

The believer is to strip away the garment of anger. Men do become angry: note that Scripture recognizes this. There are times when anger is called for, but we are to guard against sinning when we become angry. Anger causes us to either react, lash out and hurt others, or else it motivates us to right wrongs and correct injustices.

1. There is wrong anger, or what may be called unjustified or selfish anger.
   a. There is the anger that broods, that is selfish. It harbors malice; it will not forget; it lingers; it broods; it wills revenge and sometimes seeks revenge.
   b. There is the anger that holds contempt. It despises; it ridicules; it arrogantly exalts self and calls another person empty and useless. This is an anger that is full of malice. It despises and scorns. It arises from pride—a proud wrath (Pr.21:24). Such feelings or anger walk over and trample a person. It says that whatever ill comes upon a person is deserved.
   c. There is the anger that curses. It seeks to destroy a man and his reputation morally, intellectually, and spiritually.

2. There is right anger, or what may be called justified anger. The believer must be an angry person—angry with those who sin and do wrong and who are unjust and selfish in their behavior. However, a justified anger is always disciplined and controlled; it is always limited to those who do wrong either against God or against others. The distinguishing mark between justified and unjustified anger is that a justified anger is never selfish; it is never shown because of what has happened to oneself. It is an anger that is purposeful. The believer knows that he is angry for a legitimate reason, and he seeks to correct the situation in the most peaceful way possible.

> **"Be ye angry, and sin not: let not the sun go down upon your wrath" (Ep.4:26).**
>
> **"If it be possible, as much as lieth in you, live peaceably with all men" (Ro.12:18).**

APPLICATION:

1) Anger is cast against many. Too often hurt feelings exist between those who are supposed to be the closest: husband and wife, parent and child, neighbor and friend, employer and employee. The Lord is clear about the matter: we must never allow anger to take hold of us without just cause.
2) Note that the devil exploits selfish anger, using it for his own ends. He sows discord and disturbance and dissension. Paul usually prefers to use the word "satnas" for Satan, but here he uses "diabolos." "Diabolos" means slanderer, a tale-bearer who murders reputations.

> **"But now ye also put off all these; anger, wrath, malice, blasphemy, filthy communication out of your mouth" (Co.3:8).**

ILLUSTRATION:

Do you know any angry people? You know, those people who are volcanoes just waiting to erupt on anyone who happens to be near. Everyone around them walks on eggshells. Practically everything that is said to them is taken personally. Take a look at such a man probably familiar to many of us.

> *Rusty was an angry man. The son of a stern military father, he grew up being yelled at most of the time. There was never any physical abuse, but there was verbal and emotional abuse aplenty. Rusty lived for the day when he would be old enough to leave home.*
>
> *Well, he finally left home and got married while in college. He had grown up with one agenda only: never to be controlled again by anyone. His father*

had taught him the secret of gaining control: yell and yell a lot. All his associates kept out of his way. His new wife learned quickly never to cross him. A son was born a few years later and become a mirror-image of his father and his father before him. Another generation was being formed into the shape of anger.

How do you channel your anger? Rest assured you are making an impact on someone—either good or bad.

QUESTIONS:
1. If someone like Rusty came to you for help in overcoming his anger, what would you do?
2. What are some examples of justified anger?
3. What is the secret to controlling your anger?
4. Complete the following statement: I am most angry when... How does trusting God help you with this anger?

3. THE GARMENT OF STEALING (v.28).

The believer is to strip away the garment of stealing. The word "steal" means to cheat, to take wrongfully from another person, *either legally or illegally*. Note that the laws of men are not the determining rule governing whether a person is stealing or not. This is what is so often misunderstood about stealing.

⇒ Men can sometimes use the law to steal.
⇒ Men can take from others without ever breaking a law.
⇒ Men can secure too much of something, well beyond what they need; and when they hoard, they are taking something that by nature belongs to others.

Very simply stated, the Bible teaches that stealing is the taking of anything that *rightfully or by nature* belongs to others. There are at least three forms of stealing.

1. A person steals by taking something which is *actually possessed or personally owned* by another person. If a person owns it and we take it, then we are guilty of stealing. It may be something as simple as a pencil from the office or an answer to a test from a fellow student, or it may be something as complex as embezzlement of funds through bookkeeping procedures. If we take it, we have broken God's commandment and stand guilty as thieves.

> **"A false balance is abomination to the LORD: but a just weight is his delight" (Pr.11:1).**

2. A person steals by hoarding and banking more than he needs. *Keeping back* is stealing. It is...

- keeping what is not needed for one's own needs
- keeping back what is desperately needed by others
- taking away what nature and the earth have provided to meet the needs of the human population
- hoarding the knowledge and gifts and blessings God gave to be used for the welfare of a desperate world filled with so many who are less privileged and gifted

We may call it by whatever name we wish, but to God it is stealing. God has put within the earth enough resources to meet the needs of His people, and He has given men both the *ability and command to subdue and have dominion over the earth*. Look closely at His command:

> **"And God blessed them [man and woman], and God said unto them, Be fruitful, and multiply, and replenish the earth, and subdue it; and have dominion over the fish of the sea, and over the fowl of the air, and over every living thing that moveth upon the earth" (Ge.1:28).**

The earth is to be subdued and taken dominion over by men. Men are commanded by God to develop the technology to explore the universe and to control nature, and to feed, clothe, house and give health to people. Note what God is saying. He is not saying some are to have the benefits and blessings of the earth. He is saying that men are to love each other and *share* the blessings of the earth together. When men use their God-given ability to make money and produce goods, and then begin to keep back and hoard, they are stealing; they are keeping for themselves what rightfully belongs to others. Therefore, they will suffer catastrophic loss in the next world. They will suffer total devastation (Lu.12:20; 16:22-23). Why? Because they did not *love enough* to do what they and their particular talents were put on earth to do: provide for those who were less gifted and less fortunate.

> **"Lay not up for yourselves treasures upon earth, where moth and rust doth corrupt, and where thieves break through and steal: but lay up for yourselves treasures in heaven, where neither moth nor rust doth corrupt, and where thieves do not break through nor steal: for where your treasure is, there will your heart be also" (Mt.6:19-21).**

3. A person steals by living extravagantly, beyond what he needs. There are some who give to meet the crying needs of the world, yet they do not live sacrificially. They *keep plenty* for themselves, indulging their flesh...

- in clothing
- in food
- in jewelry
- in housing
- in transportation
- in recreation
- in possessions
- in property

Many within industrialized nations are guilty of *selfishness* despite a tenderness and concern for the needy in the world. However, *concern and some giving* are not enough to fulfill the demand of God that we share and meet the needs of our fellow men throughout the world. Every day that we awaken and arise out of bed, the world is reeling under the weight of *masses*...

- who are hungry and starving to death
- who are without drinking water
- who are without adequate clothing
- who are diseased and without medicine
- who have no roof over their heads
- who have no one to teach them

There is no question, the means to help meet the needs of the world exist today. The lack is not manpower and resources; the lack is *sacrificial commitment* to give the resources and to go and become personally involved. The extravagant and indulgent are stealing from the needy, and the gifted are not meeting the needs of the less gifted. The scene is tragic, for God put the gifted upon earth to *sacrificially* meet the needs of the less gifted. But instead of meeting their needs, the gifted are living in excessive comfort and pleasure, indulging the whims of their flesh.

"Woe unto you, scribes and Pharisees, hypocrites! for ye make clean the outside of the cup and of the platter, but within they are full of extortion and excess" (Mt.23:25).

What is the answer? Diligent work—working and working so that we can have enough to help others. This is the will of God: working in order to have enough to give away. Work is to be honest and to meet the necessities of one's family; however, working just for self is selfish. And selfishness corrupts, leaving a person's heart and work empty and aimless. But working in order to help others in the name of Christ—this is the will of God. This is the only way the needs of the world can be met. Work is to be for the Lord's purpose and cause—the cause that provides the means to reach and to help people (1 Jn.3:17).

QUESTIONS:

1. Why is living extravagantly considered to be stealing?
2. What is the purpose of work?
3. What is the difference between a "want" and a "need"? Why do you think many Christians do not know the difference?
4. Are you comfortable with how you share from your abundance? What one thing needs to be improved?

4. THE GARMENT OF WORTHLESS TALK (v.29).

The believer is to strip away filthy and foul talk. The word "corrupt" means rotten, foul, putrid and polluting. Corrupt talk, of course, would include cursing and unholy talk and even the worthless conversation that is so often carried on by people. The Amplified New Testament has a good description.

"Let no foul or polluting language, nor evil word, nor unwholesome or worthless talk [ever] come out of your mouth" (Ep.4:29). (Amp.N.T.).

Scripture says that a man with a foul mouth has a mouth that is "an open sepulchre [grave]" (Ro.3:13). An open grave is foul, and it is a symbol of corruption. So is a man with a sinful mouth. His mouth is...

- foul
- dirty
- obscene
- polluted
- filthy
- detestable
- profane
- dishonorable
- offensive

The obscene mouth may range from off-colored humor to dirty jokes, from immoral suggestions to outright propositions for sex. But no matter, a man with a foul mouth stinks just like an open grave; his filthiness causes corruption, the decay of character. The filth from his mouth eats away at his character and at the character of his listeners—so much so that he becomes as offensive as that of a decayed corpse. The foul, filthy mouth kills character, its attractiveness, trust, faithfulness, morality, honor, and godliness.

"O generation of vipers, how can ye, being evil, speak good things? for out of the abundance of the heart the mouth speaketh" (Mt.12:34).

The believer is to speak only that which is good and which will edify or build up people. Speech is for the purpose of...

- sharing good things
- building up and strengthening people
- ministering grace (favor, blessings) and helping each other as we plow through life

"Speaking to yourselves in psalms and hymns and spiritual songs, singing and making melody in your heart to the Lord" (Ep.5:19).

QUESTIONS:
1. If you are close by when a dirty joke is told, how do you react?
2. Are there any areas of your talk which require some change? What are they? What kinds of things can you do in order to change?
3. How do you feel when someone goes out of their way to speak kind words to you?
4. Who needs to hear kind words from you today? Why? How will they feel if you do this?

5. THE GARMENT OF DISOBEDIENCE (v.30).

The believer is to strip away the garment of being contrary or of grieving the Holy Spirit. "Grieving" means to pain; to offend; to vex; to sadden the Holy Spirit. When a child acts contrary to the counsel of his parents, he hurts and grieves them. So when a person acts contrary to the counsel of the Holy Spirit, he hurts and grieves Him. Note three points.

1. The command is very forceful. This is seen in the name of the Holy Spirit. He is not only called the Holy Spirit here, He is called both the Holy Spirit and "the Spirit of God"—a double reference.

2. There are at least four ways the Holy Spirit can be grieved.

a. He is *grieved* when believers allow impure things to penetrate their life or thoughts.

"For they that are after the flesh do mind the things of the flesh; but they that are after the Spirit the things of the Spirit. For to be carnally minded is death; but to be spiritually minded is life and peace. Because the carnal mind is enmity against God: for it is not subject to the law of God, neither indeed can be" (Ro.8:5-7).

b. He is *grieved* when believers behave immorally.

"Therefore, brethren, we are debtors, not to the flesh, to live after the flesh. For if ye live after the flesh, ye shall die: but if ye through the Spirit do mortify the deeds of the body, ye shall live" (Ro.8:12-13).

c. He is *grieved* when believers act unjustly.

"But Peter said, Ananias, why hath Satan filled thine heart to lie to the Holy Ghost, and to keep back part of the price of the land? Whiles it remained, was it not thine own? and after it was sold, was it not in thine own power? why hast thou conceived this thing in thine heart? thou hast not lied unto men, but unto God" (Ac.5:3-4).

d. He is *grieved* when believers participate in anything contrary to the nature of the Holy Spirit. Note the context of this passage: the command to "grieve not the Spirit" is surrounded by a series of negative commands.

"So then they that are in the flesh cannot please God. But ye are not in the flesh, but in the Spirit, if so be that the Spirit of God dwell in you. Now if any man have not the Spirit of Christ, he is none of his. And if Christ be in you, the body is dead because of sin; but the Spirit is life because of righteousness" (Ro.8:8-10).

3. The reason we should not grieve the Spirit of God is because of His great ministry to us: He has sealed us until the day of redemption.

APPLICATION:
This word *grieve* was used in classical Greek literature when speaking of the severe humiliation or outrage experienced by a king who had been deposed by his subjects. In a very strong sense, the Holy Spirit feels betrayed when a Christian grieves Him.

QUESTIONS:
1. What are some ways that you can grieve the Holy Spirit?
2. What do you feel like inside when you grieve the Holy Spirit? How do you think He feels when you grieve Him?
3. Do you think it is possible to hurt the Holy Spirit's feelings? To drive Him away?

6. THE GARMENTS OF UNKINDNESS (v.31).

The believer is to strip off the garment of unkindness.

1. There is "*bitterness*": resentment, harshness. A man who is bitter is often…

- sharp
- cold
- intense
- distasteful
- resentful
- harsh
- relentless
- unpleasant
- cynical
- stressful

Any expression involving any of these is sin to God. God desires men to be filled with love and joy and peace and to express such. Anything less than the expression of these is sin.

2. There is "*wrath*": anger, rage, fury.
3. There is "*anger*": passion, fury, hostility.
4. There is "*clamor*": arguing, fussing, quarrelling, brawling. It means insulting, boisterous behavior, and loud talking.
5. There is "*malice*": slander, hurtful, injurious speech.

QUESTIONS:
1. What sort of circumstances tempt Christians to put the garment of unkindness on? What kind of things can you do to avoid these circumstances?
2. What are some of the natural results of bitterness? Is it possible for the Christian to become bitter?
3. What do you think your role is when you meet a bitter friend?

7. THE GARMENTS OF THE NEW MAN (v.32)

The believer is to put on the garments of the new man. Frankly, this verse speaks for itself more forcefully than any commentary ever could.

1. The word "*kind*" means to be gentle, caring, helpful, courteous, good, useful, giving, and showering favors upon people. It is the opposite of being neglectful, harsh, sharp, bitter, and resentful. Lehman Strauss points out that kindness comes from such

words as *kin* and *kindred* which means that it treats a person as one's own kin. Believers are brothers in the Lord.[2]

> **"Be kindly affectioned one to another with brotherly love; in honour preferring one another" (Ro.12:10).**

2. The word "*tenderhearted*" means to show compassion, mercy, understanding, love, tenderness, and warmth. It means to *be aware* of a person's hurts and sufferings, problems and difficulties, emotions and mental state, physical and spiritual condition. It means to be tenderhearted toward them.

> **"Blessed are the merciful: for they shall obtain mercy" (Mt.5:7).**

3. The word "*forgiving*" means to be gracious to a person, to pardon him for some wrong done. Note that the person has done wrong; he has hurt us, causing us pain. But the command is to still forgive him.

4. The reason we should forgive each other is because God has forgiven us. No matter how much a person has done against us, it does not come close to what we have done against God. Yet, God has forgiven us. Why? For Christ's sake. Jesus Christ died for us—died for our sins so that we could be forgiven. Therefore, God forgives us. No matter what we have done, God forgives us when we want forgiveness. He forgives us despite our having rejected, cursed, ignored, neglected, and rebelled against Him.

The point is this: because of what Christ has done for us, we should forgive others no matter what they have done.

> **"Forbearing one another, and forgiving one another, if any man have a quarrel against any: even as Christ forgave you, so also do ye" (Co.3:13).**

QUESTIONS:

1. Think a moment. What was the worst thing that was ever done to you by another person? Have you truly forgiven that person?
2. Why is it important for you to be kind, tenderhearted, and forgiving?
3. How does this verse help your Christian walk?

ILLUSTRATION:

The excellent expositor John R.W. Stott says this in his writings:

> *I find it helpful to think in these terms. Our biography is written in two volumes. Volume one is the story of the old man, the old self, of me before my conversion. Volume two is the story of the new man, the new self, of me after I was made a new creation in Christ. Volume one of my biography ended with the judicial death of the old self. I was a sinner. I deserved to die. I did die....Volume two of my biography opened with my resurrection. My old life having finished, a new life to God has begun.*
>
> *We are simply called to "reckon" this—not to pretend it, but to realize it. It is a fact. And we have to lay hold of it. We have to let our minds play upon these truths. We have to meditate upon them until we grasp them firmly. We have to keep saying to ourselves, "Volume one has closed. You are now living in volume two. It is inconceivable that you should reopen volume one. It is not impossible, but it is inconceivable.*[3]

---

2 Lehman Strauss. *Devotional Studies in Galatians and Ephesians*, p.189.

3 John R.W. Stott. *Men Made New: An Exposition of Romans 5-8.* (Grand Rapids, MI: Baker Book House, 1978), pp.49-50.

EPHESIANS 4:25-32

SUMMARY:

Don't be like so many people who return to the old clothes thinking they are more attractive and acceptable to people. It is just inconceivable that any of us would get back into the clothes of the old man. The believer, the new man, must put off:

1. The garment of lying.
2. The garment of anger.
3. The garment of stealing.
4. The garment of worthless talk.
5. The garment of being contrary.
6. The garments of unkindness.
7. The garments of the new man.

PERSONAL JOURNAL NOTES:
(Reflection & Response)

1. The most important thing that I learned from this lesson was:

2. The area that I need to work on the most is:

3. I can apply this lesson to my life by:

4. Closing Statement of Commitment:

	CHAPTER 5 **E. The Believer is to Walk Following God, 5:1-7**	2 Neither filthiness, nor foolish talking, nor jesting, which are not convenient: but rather giving of thanks.	**4. By being clean-mouthed: Using only clean, wholesome speech**
1. By being a follower of God	**B**e ye therefore followers of God, as dear children;	3 For this ye know, that no whoremonger, nor unclean person, nor covetous man, who is an idolater, hath any inheritance in the kingdom of Christ and of God.	**5. By knowing God's solemn warning** a. Uncleanness has no part with God
2. By loving as Christ loved a. Christ made an offering to God—sacrificed Himself b. Christ became a sweet fragrance to God	2 And walk in love, as Christ also hath loved us, and hath given himself for us an offering and a sacrifice to God for a sweet smelling savour.	4 Let no man deceive you with vain words: for because of these things cometh the wrath of God upon the children of disobedience.	b. There are deceivers c. The wrath of God is coming
3. By being clean-bodied, that is, morally pure & without any greed	3 But fornication, and all uncleanness, or covetousness, let it not be once named among you, as becometh saints;	5 Be not ye therefore partakers with them.	**6. By separating oneself from the unclean**

Section IV
THE WALK OF THE CHRISTIAN BELIEVER
Ephesians 4:1–6:9

Study 5: **THE BELIEVER IS TO WALK FOLLOWING GOD**

Text: **Ephesians 5:1-7**

Aim: To encourage a closer walk with God.

Memory Verse:

"Be ye therefore followers of God, as dear children" (Ephesians 5:1).

INTRODUCTION:

All of us would probably agree with this statement: you are likely to follow someone whom you trust. Relate this story to your life as you read along:

The night was pitch black, as if every star in the heavens had been snuffed out. And there I was: holding on to the side of a dirt bank waiting for the general's orders to attack an enemy I could not see. The waiting was eating me alive. For days my division had been unable to go forward because of the enemy's intense fire. All I wanted to do was turn around and go back home.

While I was waiting, I began to reflect on all of my training. Follow the leader was a theme that was hammered into each recruit. From the first day, my leader promised to teach me everything that I would need before I fought my first battle.

As I was lost in my thoughts, the command finally came to leave the dirt bank and charge the enemy's position. Are they serious? Do they know something that I do not know? Do they know what they are doing? I could not move. Victory might be just ahead, but I'm afraid if I follow my leader's orders…What if he is wrong?

Like this soldier, we have been trained as Christians to follow orders. There are many times that we do not fully understand why God would have us do certain things. In the final analysis, we must conclude that God is always right, and so we must trust Him—even when the way ahead appears hard. Battles are never won by running backwards. For the Christian, the victory comes when we choose to follow God.

The challenge of this passage is one of the greatest challenges in all the Word of God. Just imagine—the great Pattern for the believer is God Himself. The believer is to follow the Person of God. The believer is to walk through life following God.

OUTLINE:
The believer is to walk following God:
1. By becoming a follower of God (v.1).
2. By loving as Christ loved (v.2).
3. By being clean-bodied, that is, morally pure and without any greed (v.3).
4. By being clean-mouthed: using only clean, wholesome speech (v.4).
5. By knowing God's solemn warning (vv.5-6).
6. By separating oneself from the unclean (v.7).

1. BY BECOMING A FOLLOWER OF GOD (v.1).

The believer follows God, first, by *becoming* a follower of God. Note the word "be." It means *to become* a follower of God. The idea is that of commitment, attachment, devotion, allegiance, attention. Before a person can be a follower of God, he must commit and attach himself to God. He must surrender and devote his life to God and then begin to follow after God.

The word "followers" means imitators. Some prefer this translation, that we are to become imitators of God. Note the phrase "as dear children." Just as children learn by imitating their parents, so we are to learn by imitating God. The very idea that we are to be *followers and imitators* of God is a bold idea. Just imagine, Scripture boldly proclaims that we are to become *like God*!

⇒ Christ said: **"Be ye therefore perfect, even as your Father which is in heaven is perfect" (Mt.5:48).**
⇒ God demanded: **"Ye shall be holy: for I the LORD your God am holy" (Le.19:2).**
⇒ Paul declared: **"But we all...are changed into the same image [of Christ] from glory to glory" (2 Co.4:18).**
⇒ Peter charged: **"But as he which hath called you is holy, so be ye holy in all manner of conversation; because it is written, Be ye holy; for I am holy" (1 Pe.1:15-16)**
⇒ The early church saint, Clement of Alexandria said: "The Christian practices being God"[1]

QUESTIONS:
1. What must a Christian first do before he or she can become a follower of God? Have you personally made this decision?
2. What is the ultimate goal of becoming a follower of God?
3. Do you think it is possible for you to follow God without knowing where He is going? How do you know His direction?

[1] Quoted by William Barclay. *The Letters to the Galatians and Ephesians*, p.190.

2. BY LOVING AS CHRIST LOVED (v.2).

The believer follows God, second, by loving as Christ loved. Two things about the death of Christ should be noted here.

1. The phrase "gave Himself for us" is a simple phrase with profound meaning. It does not mean that Christ died only as an example for us, showing us how we should be willing to die for the truth or for some great cause. What it means is that Christ died in our place, as our substitute. This meaning is unquestionably clear.

a. The idea of sacrifice to the Jewish and pagan mind of that day was the idea of a life given in another's place. It was a substitutionary sacrifice.

b. The idea of sacrifice is often in the very context of the words, **"Christ gave Himself for us" (Ep.5:2).**

> **"I am the living bread which came down from heaven: if any man eat of this bread, he shall live for ever: and the bread that I will give is my flesh, which I will give for the life of the world" (Jn.6:51).**

2. The words "Christ gave Himself...an offering...to God for a sweet-smelling savour [smell]" gives a higher meaning to the death of Christ than just meeting our need. The word "offering" refers to the burnt offering of the Old Testament (Le.1:1f). The burnt offering was given to God not merely because of sin but because a person wished to glorify and honor God. A person wished to show his love and adoration to God. This is an aspect of Christ's death that is often overlooked—an aspect that rises far above the mere meeting of our need. In giving Himself as an "offering to God," Christ was looking beyond our need to the majestic responsibility of glorifying God. This means that His first purpose was to glorify God. He was concerned primarily with doing the will of God—with obeying God. God had been terribly dishonored by the first man, Adam, and by all those who followed after him. Jesus Christ wished to honor God by showing that at least one man thought more of God's glory than of anything else. Christ wished to show that God's will meant more than any personal desire or ambition that He might have.

He said: "That the world may know that I love the Father, and as the Father hath given commandment [to die for man], even so I do. Arise, let us go hence" (Jn.14:31; cp. Lu.2:42; Jn.5:30).

The point is this: the believer is to walk in love, *just as Christ has loved us and has given Himself as an offering and a sacrifice to God.* There is to be no limit to the offering and sacrifice of our lives to God and to men. Remember: God's love—agape love—is always an acting love.

> **"This is my commandment, That ye love one another, as I have loved you" (Jn.15:12).**

ILLUSTRATION:

The hardest thing for any person to do is to deny his selfish desires and offer his life as a sacrifice. All of us can relate to the following story:

> *Once upon a time a pig and a chicken went for a walk together down the main street of town. As they were walking, the chicken noticed a sign in the restaurant that looked like a pretty good deal to him.*
>
> *"Hey, pig. Look at that sign in the window: 'Ham and eggs—all that you can eat.' That's a great deal."*
>
> *The pig paused for a moment while he carefully chose his words. "A good deal you say. Well, for you its only an offering; but for me its a sacrifice."*

APPLICATION:
The million dollar question is how do you walk in a sacrificial kind of love? We must first of all look to Jesus' example. He loves us in very practical ways:
⇒ He forgives our sin.
⇒ He comforts us.
⇒ He provides for us.
⇒ He answers our prayers.
⇒ He grants us peace.

How then, do you walk in love?
⇒ Forgive those who hurt you.
⇒ Give comfort to those who are hurting.
⇒ Share out of your resources to those in need.
⇒ Be willing to become an answer to someone's prayer.
⇒ Be a witness to those who need the gospel of peace.

If you really want to follow God, you must be willing to totally sacrifice yourself to God for His cause: to reach and minister to those who are lost and hurting.

QUESTIONS:
1. When do you feel most loved by the body of Christ? Why is this true?
2. What thoughts come to your mind when you hear the word "sacrifice?"
3. Give an example of a time recently when you experienced sacrificial love? Were you the recipient or did you give this love to someone else?

3. BY BEING CLEAN-BODIED, THAT IS, MORALLY PURE AND WITHOUT ANY GREED (v.3).

The believer follows God, third, by being clean-bodied, that is, morally pure. If a believer is to follow and imitate God, he has to be morally pure; he has to keep his body clean. He cannot let it become dirty and spotted.
⇒ He has to keep his body free of fornication.
⇒ He has to keep his body free of uncleanness.
⇒ He has to keep his body free of covetousness.

Note the importance of rejecting these sins: they are not to be named *even once* among us. And the command is an imperative: "Let it not be *once named*"—not even *mentioned once*. You, that is, your body, are never to engage in fornication, uncleanness, or covetous acts. Note another fact: such things are not even to be talked about. They are not to be named, talked about, or mentioned in our conversation. Immorality and indecent conversation and jokes are to be the farthest thing from the mind of the believer who follows God. God has nothing to do with such dirt and filth.

"Blessed are the pure in heart: for they shall see God" (Mt.5:8).

ILLUSTRATION:
If we are going to follow the Lord, we must do it on His terms and not on ours. Read this sobering thought from *Disciplines of a Godly Man* by R. Kent Hughes:

Recently Leadership Magazine commissioned a poll of a thousand pastors. The pastors indicated that 12 percent of them had committed adultery while in the ministry—one out of eight pastors!—and 23 percent had done something they considered sexually inappropriate. Christianity Today surveyed a thou-

sand of its subscribers who were not pastors and found the figure to be nearly double, with 23 percent saying they had had extramarital intercourse and 45 percent indicating they had done something they themselves deemed sexually inappropriate. One in four Christian men are unfaithful, and nearly one half have behaved unbecomingly! Shocking statistics! Especially when we remember that Christianity Today readers tend to be college-educated church leaders, elders, deacons, Sunday school superintendents, and teachers. If this is so for the Church's leadership, how much more for the average member of the congregation? Only God knows![2]

APPLICATION:
Continuing on with Hughes' analysis of the above statistics, he makes the following conclusions:

This leads to an inescapable conclusion: The contemporary evangelical Church, broadly considered, is 'Corinthian' to the core. It is being stewed in the molten juices of its own sensuality so that it is:

⇒ *No wonder the Church has lost its grip on holiness.*
⇒ *No wonder it is so slow to discipline its members.*
⇒ *No wonder it is dismissed by the world as irrelevant.*
⇒ *No wonder so many of its children reject it.*
⇒ *No wonder it has lost its power in many places—and that Islam and other false religions are making so many converts.*

Sensuality is easily the biggest obstacle to godliness among men today and is wreaking havoc in the Church.[3]

QUESTIONS:
1. What can you do to keep from becoming morally impure?
2. How can you guard your thoughts?
3. How can you help others who have fallen into a sinful lifestyle?
4. What are some natural results of sin that becomes public knowledge?

4. BY BEING CLEAN-MOUTHED: USING ONLY CLEAN, WHOLESOME SPEECH (v.4).

The believer follows God, fourth, by being clean-mouthed. If a believer is to follow and imitate God, he has to be pure in speech and conversation; he has to keep his mouth or tongue clean. He cannot let his mouth become foul and polluted, filthy and vile.

1. He is never, not once, to be engaged in "filthiness": using the mouth in obscene, shameful, foul, polluted, base, immoral conduct and conversation. What an indictment of our day—a day of sodomy and perversion. And note: the word refers to both conduct and speech. How polluted and foul-mouthed so many have become—so much so that society could easily be known as a second Sodom and Gomorrah.

"For this cause God gave them up unto vile affections: for even their women did change the natural use into that which is against nature: and likewise also the men, leaving the natural use of the woman, burned in their lust one toward another; men with men working that which is unseemly, and receiving in themselves that recompence of their error which was meet" (Ro.1:26-27).

---

2 R. Kent Hughes. *Disciplines of a Godly Man.* (Wheaton, IL: Crossway Books, 1991), pp.23-24.
3 ibid., p. 24.

2. The believer is *never once* to engage in "foolish talking": empty, unthoughtful, senseless, wasted, idle, aimless, or purposeless talk; talk that just fritters away and wastes time, that has absolutely no purpose to it. It also means sinful, foolish, silly and corrupt talk.

> **"In the multitude of words there wanteth not sin: but he that refraineth his lips is wise" (Pr.10:19).**

3. The believer is *never once* to engage in "jesting": to joke, talk foolishly, poke fun, act or speak without thought; to be suggestive in conversation; to make wisecracks. It also has the idea of being cunning and clever, of being polished in suggestive and off-colored joking and using it to attract attention and win favors.[4] Jesting is often used in off-colored jokes or conversation, at parties or breaks in order to be suggestive.

> **"As a mad man who casteth firebrands, arrows, and death, so is the man that deceiveth his neighbor, and saith, Am not I in sport [joking]?" (Pr.26:18-19).**

Note that such talk is not fitting or becoming to believers. Believers are to be engaged in conversation that builds people up and offers thanks and praise to God.

> **"Let your speech be alway with grace, seasoned with salt, that ye may know how ye ought to answer every man" (Co.4:6).**

QUESTIONS:
1. Do Christians ever get involved in 'idle' or 'off-colored' conversations?
2. What would you say to a Christian who tried to tell you a crude joke?
3. What happens to a Christian whose speech is foul?
4. Are there areas of your speech and conversation that are less than desirable? How can you go about changing those areas?

5. BY KNOWING GOD'S SOLEMN WARNING (vv.5-6).

The believer follows God, fifth, by knowing God's solemn warning. Note three significant points.

1. *Uncleanness has no part with God*. The profession of a person does not matter: if he practices these things, he will not share in the kingdom of Christ and of God. And, note, *the doom* pronounced is not future, it is present. It does not say, "he shall not have," but rather, "he does not have an inheritance with God." He may have houses, lands, and all kinds of possessions; but he does not have one scrap of the kingdom. He has lost all that is really worth having. Note the specific sins mentioned that doom a person.

⇒ Being a "*whoremonger*": illicit sexual intercourse; fornication; prostitution; immoral behavior.
⇒ Being an "*unclean person*": unclean, immoral, dirty thoughts or behavior.
⇒ Being a "*covetous person*": desirous, greedy.
⇒ Being an "*idolater*": worshipper of idols, heathen.

2. *There are deceivers walking all around us*. There are people who will tell us...

- that sex is the normal and natural thing for man—that a one-time affair will not hurt—that it is acceptable and will not harm us.

---

4 Kenneth S. Wuest. *Ephesians and Colossians*. "Word Studies in the Greek New Testament," Vol.1. (Grand Rapids, MI: Eerdmans Publishing Co., 1953), p.121.

- that securing possessions is normal behavior and banking and storing up is acceptable. It builds position, ego, and self-image, and that could never be wrong; and having more than what we need enables us to give to help the needy as we desire.

"For they that are such serve not our Lord Jesus Christ, but their own belly; and by good words and fair speeches deceive the hearts of the simple" (Ro.16:18).

3. William Barclay points out that there were and still are two main deceptions about Christianity.[5]

a. There were those who felt that they could say and do anything and still be acceptable to God. This argument came primarily from those *outside* the church, although there were some within the church who held the same argument. This idea finds its roots in the philosophy of Gnosticism. Gnosticism said that man is both body and spirit. Gnostics felt that...
- the spirit was the only important part of man—the only part that really mattered
- the spirit was the only part that really concerned God. What a man did with his body did not matter; the body was not important
- it made no difference whatsoever if a man abused his body: gorged, dirtied, and fouled it

However, Christianity counters, "Never!" Both body and soul are important. We see this in Jesus Christ. He honored the body by taking a body upon Himself (He.2:14). Today He honors the body by making it the "holy temple" for His presence in the person of the Holy Spirit (1 Co.6:19). Jesus Christ is interested in the body of man as well as the spirit of man. He is interested in the whole man, and He saves the whole man.

b. There were those primarily within the church who felt that sin was irrelevant. How much a person sinned just did not matter. God is love, and He forgives and forgives no matter how much wrong we do. In fact, some argued that the more we sin, the more God is able to forgive and demonstrate His mercy in us. So why not live the way we want? Why not sin and let God's mercy and love shine through us, for the more we sin the more God's grace will be seen. But Christianity counters, "Never!" God's love and grace are not only a gift and a privilege, but a responsibility and an obligation.

However, note what God says: "Because of these things the wrath of God comes upon the children of disobedience" (v.6; see Ep.2:2). The wrath of God is a deliberate anger that arises from His very nature of holiness. It is an anger that is *righteous, just, and good*—that stands against the sins and evil of men—their dirt and pollution and immoralities—their injustices and neglect of a world that reels under the weight of lost, starving, diseased, and dying masses. God could never overlook the whoremonger who destroys family life nor the covetous man who overlooks the needy. He would not be God; He would not be loving or just if He overlooked such evil persons.

"For the wrath of God is revealed from heaven against all ungodliness and unrighteousness of men, who hold the truth in unrighteousness" (Ro.1:18).

5 William Barclay. *The Letters to the Galatians and Ephesians*, p.192f.

QUESTIONS:
1. How can the Christian abuse the grace of God?
2. How can the Christian identify a deceiver?
3. How meaningful is God's Word in showing you how to act?
4. How do Christian believers sometimes act like Gnostics? How do believers show that they treat sin as irrelevant? How can we avoid this kind of thinking?

6. BY SEPARATING HIMSELF FROM THE UNCLEAN (v.7).

The believer follows God, sixth, by separating himself from the unclean. No believer is to take part in the sins discussed in these verses. In fact, he is to separate himself from all who do take part in such sins.

> **"Love not the world, neither the things that are in the world. If any man love the world, the love of the Father is not in him. For all that is in the world, the lust of the flesh, and the lust of the eyes, and the pride of life, is not of the Father, but is of the world" (1 Jn.2:15-16).**

APPLICATION:
Beware of the trap of being a co-conspirator with those who rebel against God. Remember that "birds of a feather flock together." Or using a more Biblical reference:

> **"Do not be deceived: Bad company corrupts good morals" (1 Co.15:33 NASB).**

ILLUSTRATION:
We cannot follow God and walk closely with Him if we are not tuned in to what He is telling us. Listen to this story.

> *A former park ranger at Yellowstone National Park tells the story of a ranger leading a group of hikers to a fire lookout. The ranger was so intent on telling the hikers about the flowers and animals that he considered the messages on his two-way radio distracting, so he switched it off. Nearing the tower, the ranger was met by a nearly breathless lookout, who asked why he hadn't responded to the messages on his radio. A grizzly bear had been stalking the group, and the authorities were trying to warn them of the danger.*
>
> *Any time we tune out the messages God has sent us, we put at peril not only ourselves, but also those around us. How important it is that we never turn off God's saving communication!*[6]

QUESTIONS:
1. When we "tune out God," the only signal left to be heard belongs to the world. What practical things can you do in order to tune out the world's signal?
2. What changes can you make in your lifestyle in order to separate yourself from unclean things?
3. As you think about your lifestyle, what are your biggest concerns? Are you committed to obeying this verse? Would you make a commitment right now to separate yourself from the unclean? To turn your life over to God, to follow Him and His righteousness?

---

6 Craig B. Larson, Editor. *Illustrations for Preaching & Teaching*, p.238.

Ephesians 5:1-7

Summary:

The believer is to walk following God. We have discovered that there are many things that can disrupt our walk with Him. Thankfully, God has graciously provided a way for us to keep up with the pace that He has set:

1. By becoming a follower of God
2. By loving as Christ loved
3. By being clean-bodied, that is, morally pure
4. By being clean-mouthed
5. By knowing God's solemn warning
6. By separating ourselves from the unclean

Personal Journal Notes
(Reflection & Response)

1. The most important thing that I learned from this lesson was:

2. The area that I need to work on the most is:

3. I can apply this lesson to my life by:

4. Closing Statement of Commitment:

	F. The Believer is to Walk as a Child of Light, 5:8-14	fruitful works of darkness, but rather reprove them. 12 For it is a shame even to speak of those things which	a. The charge: Have no fellowship with darkness b. The reason: It is a shame to even speak of the things done in secret
1. Light, not darkness, is the nature of believers	8 For ye were sometimes darkness, but now are ye light in the Lord: walk as children of light:	are done of them in secret. 13 But all things that are reproved are made manifest by the	**5. Light reveals & converts everything it touches**
2. Light bears the things of life—the fruit of the Spirit	9 (For the fruit of the Spirit is in all goodness and righteousness and truth;)	light: for whatsoever doth make manifest is light. 14 Wherefore he	**6. Light awakens the sleeping**
3. Light shows what is acceptable, pleasing to God	10 Proving what is acceptable unto the Lord.	saith, Awake thou that sleepest, and arise from the dead, and	a. The challenge: Awake from the darkness of sin
4. Light exposes the deeds of darkness	11 And have no fellowship with the un-	Christ shall give thee light.	b. How: Accept the light of Christ

Section IV
THE WALK OF THE CHRISTIAN BELIEVER
Ephesians 4:1–6:9

Study 6: **THE BELIEVER IS TO WALK AS A CHILD OF LIGHT**

Text: **Ephesians 5:8-14**

Aim: To make sure that you walk in God's light and not in darkness.

Memory Verse:

"And have no fellowship with the unfruitful works of darkness, but rather reprove them" (Ephesians 5:11).

INTRODUCTION:

Have you ever groped around in the dark to find a light switch? As you carefully stepped, you were fearful of what might be in your path or of some unseen danger. You felt you would never get where you were going. But what happened when you turned on the light? Your fears were erased, your heart calmed, and you got your bearings back. The same is true in our Christian walk. When we grope around in the dark, it is a scary world out there. But when we walk in God's light, He helps keep us on the right path!

Two walks through life are available to men. There is the life and walk of darkness or the life and walk of light. There is a world of difference between the two. In fact, a person's eternity is determined by which life and walk he pursues.

OUTLINE:

1. Light, not darkness, is the nature of believers (v.8).
2. Light bears the things of life—the fruit of the Spirit (v.9).
3. Light shows what is acceptable, pleasing to God (v.10).
4. Light exposes the works of darkness (vv.11-12).
5. Light reveals and converts everything it touches (v.13).
6. Light awakens the sleeping (v.14).

1. LIGHT, NOT DARKNESS, IS THE NATURE OF BELIEVERS (v.8).

1. Before a person is saved, he is in darkness. What does this mean? Think for a moment: a person who does not know God is all alone. He may have plenty of people and friends moving around him, but they will soon die and be gone. In fact, so will he, and he will have died in darkness—never having known God. A person who does not know God is in darkness:

⇒ *He does not know where he has come from.* To him everything is the result of a human and natural process. It is the way of the world and of man: we are born and here we are. Man is blind—in darkness about the truth of where he and his world originated.

⇒ *He does not know why he is on earth*—not really. He arises in the morning, goes about his daily affairs, and retires at night. Arises the next morning, goes about his daily affairs, and retires at night. Arises the next morning, and on and on. Where he is heading and why he is here—the inner core of life—is all a mystery. The real purpose, meaning, and significance of life are not understood. He lives in darkness as to why he and everyone else are really on earth.

⇒ He does not know where he is going—not after death. Is there actually a God or not, a heaven or not? How can he know and be absolutely sure? He is in darkness about the future, that inevitable day of death and eternity that rushes ever so rapidly toward every one of us.

This is what is meant about man's being in darkness. He is wrapped up in darkness: past, present, and future. Apart from God, no man knows the truth: no man knows where he has come from, why he is here, or where he is going. His whole life is shadowed and covered, permeated and filled with darkness. He is not walking as light; he is walking as darkness.

> **"But if thine eye be evil, thy whole body shall be full of darkness. If therefore the light that is in thee be darkness, how great is that darkness!" (Mt.6:23).**

2. However, the truth is glorious: the believer was darkness, *but now* he is light *in the Lord*. Jesus Christ said: "I am the light of the world: he that followeth me shall not walk in darkness, but shall have the light of life" (Jn.8:12). It is Christ who brings light to life. He shows us the truth of life, of God, of creation, of death, and of destiny. He shows us…

- the beginning and origin of all things
- the purpose, meaning, and significance of all things
- the truth of death and eternity

But note: Jesus Christ has not only shown us light; He has made us light. He has changed our nature from darkness to light; we shall live eternally. We are the light of the eternal God in the midst of a world of darkness. Therefore, we are to walk as children of light.

> **"Ye are the light of the world. A city that is set on a hill cannot be hid" (Mt.5:14).**

QUESTIONS:
1. What does verse eight say about man's ability to save himself?
2. What was the source of your illumination before you made a decision to follow Christ?
3. You are charged to walk as a child of light. How should this affect the things you do?

2. LIGHT BEARS THE THINGS OF LIFE—THE FRUIT OF THE SPIRIT (v.9).

Light bears all good things—the fruit of the Spirit. A life that illuminates light will give off three things in particular.

1. *Goodness*
2. *Righteousness*
3. *Truth*

APPLICATION:
Have you ever known someone who was always full of joy and kindness no matter the circumstances? There is only one thing that can give a person that kind of glow—that is Jesus Christ. He fills us with His light, and we bear the fruit of the Spirit. Is the fruit of the Spirit alive and abundant in your life?

In order to understand the source of this glow and warmth, we need to investigate this point a little more closely.

A CLOSER LOOK:

(5:9) **Goodness:** being full of virtue and excellence, kindness and helpfulness, peace and consideration. It means that a person…

- has a good heart and good behavior
- is good and does good
- is a quality person

Note that a good person lives and treats everyone just as they should be treated. He does not take advantage of any person nor does he stand by and let others take advantage of anyone. He stands up and lives for what is right and good and just. This means that goodness involves discipline and rebuke, correction and instruction as well as love and care, peace and conciliation. A good person will not give license to evil, will not let evil run rampant. He will not allow evil to indulge itself and treat others unjustly. He will not allow others to suffer evil. Goodness steps forward and does what it can to stop and control evil.

> **"And I myself also am persuaded of you, my brethren, that ye also are full of goodness, filled with all knowledge, able also to admonish one another" (Ro.15:14).**

- God is full of goodness

> **"O taste and see that the Lord is good: blessed is the man that trusteth in him" (Ps.34:8).**

- Believers are to be full of all goodness

> **"And I myself also am persuaded of you, my brethren, that ye also are full of goodness, filled with all knowledge, able also to admonish one another (Ro.15:14).**

A CLOSER LOOK:

(5:9) **Righteousness:** means two simple but profound things. It means both *to be right and to do right.*

1. There are those who stress *being righteous and neglect doing righteousness.* This leads to two serious errors.

a. *False security*. It causes a person to stress that he is saved and acceptable to God because he has *believed in* Jesus Christ. But he neglects doing good and living as he should. He neglects obeying God and serving man.

b. *Loose living*. It allows one to go out and do pretty much as he desires. He feels secure and comfortable in his *faith in Christ*. He knows that what he does may affect his fellowship with God and other believers, but he thinks his behavior will not affect his salvation. He thinks that no matter what he does he is still acceptable to God.

The problem with this stress is that it is a false righteousness. Righteousness in the Bible means *being righteous*, but it also means *doing righteousness*. The Bible knows nothing about being righteous without living righteously.

2. There are those who stress *doing righteousness and neglect being righteous*. This also leads to two serious errors.

a. *Self-righteousness and legalism*. It causes a person to stress that he is saved and acceptable to God because he does good. He works and behaves morally, keeping certain rules and regulations. He does the things a Christian should do by obeying the main laws of God. But he neglects the basic law: the law of love and acceptance—that God does not love him and accept him because he does good, but because he loves and trusts the righteousness of Christ.

b. *Being judgmental and fault-finding*. A person who stresses that he is righteous (acceptable to God) because he keeps certain laws often judges and finds fault with others. He feels that rules and regulations can be kept. *He* keeps them; therefore, anyone who fails to keep them is judged, criticized, and censored.

The problem with this stress is that it, too, is a false righteousness. Again, righteousness in the Bible is *being righteous as well as doing righteousness*. The Bible knows nothing of being acceptable to God without *being made righteous in Christ Jesus*.

> **"For I say unto you, That except your righteousness shall exceed the righteousness of the scribes and Pharisees, ye shall in no case enter into the kingdom of heaven" (Mt.5:20).**

A CLOSER LOOK:

(5:9) **Truth:** means moral truth, saving truth, working truth, living truth. It is not simply something to be *known*; it is something to be *done* (Jn.8:31). It is the knowledge and the experience of true reality as opposed to false reality. It is truth in "the inward parts" (cp. Ps.51:6; Eph.5:9). It is diametrically opposed to sham and hypocrisy. It permits no compromise with evil. It even abstains from the appearance of evil (1 Th.5:22). It is a regard for truth in every respect: believing it, reverencing it, speaking it, acting it, hoping in it, and rejoicing in it. Such truthful behavior frees one from all the bondages and impediments of life.

> **"Jesus answered them, and said, My doctrine is not mine, but his that sent me. If any man will do his will, he shall know of the doctrine, whether it be of God, or whether I speak of myself" (Jn.7:16-17).**

God's Word is said to be the truth (Jn.17:17), and Jesus Christ Himself claimed to be the Truth (Jn.14:6). To distinguish between the two, God's Word is sometimes said to be the Written Truth or Word, and Jesus Christ is sometimes said to be the Living Truth or Word.

1. *The truth sets man free from the shadow of doubt and despair*. Man no longer has to grasp and grope about to know the truth, whether it be the truth of God or of

his own world. Jesus Christ has revealed the truth: the nature, the meaning, and the destiny of all things.

> **"That was the true Light, which lighteth every man that cometh into the world....And the Word was made flesh, and dwelt among us, (and we beheld his glory, the glory as of the only begotten of the Father,) full of grace and truth" (Jn.1:9, 14).**

2. *The truth sets men free from the bondages of sin.* Man no longer has to grasp after the power to overcome; nor does he have to struggle against the weight of guilt. The search for deliverance and for the power to conquer, to overcome, to attain, and to live is now over. It is all found in Jesus Christ (see Ro.6:1f).

> **"But as many as received him, to them gave he power to become the sons of God, even to them that believe on his name" (Jn.1:12).**

3. *The truth sets man free from the bondage of death.* Man no longer has to be subjected to the fear of death. By His death and resurrection, Jesus Christ has now conquered death. And in His death and resurrection man now has the most glorious hope: he can now live eternally (Heb.2:14-15).

> **"For the law of the Spirit of life in Christ Jesus hath made me free from the law of sin and death" (Ro.8:2).**

4. *The truth sets man free from the bondage of judgment and hell.* The darkness of an unknown future and the apprehension of an impending judgment constantly faces man. At best, man can only hope for annihilation, and he shudders at the thought. At worst, he can expect torture by the gods that be, and he trembles at the possibility. But Jesus Christ has revealed the truth. He Himself has borne the judgment and the punishment of judgment for man.

> **"For Christ also hath once suffered for sins, the just for the unjust, that he might bring us to God, being put to death in the flesh, but quickened by the Spirit" (1 Pe.3:18).**

5. *The truth sets man free to be saved to the uttermost.* Existence, love, joy, peace, satisfaction, pleasure, hope—nothing has to be incomplete any longer. No good thing ever again has to be denied man. Jesus Christ, the Truth, is able to save man to the uttermost—completely, perfectly, finally, and for eternity. All a person has to do is to come to Christ for salvation, Who lives forever to intercede for every man.

> **"Wherefore he is able also to save them to the uttermost that come unto God by him, seeing he ever liveth to make intercession for them" (He.7:25).**

QUESTIONS:

1. How do you cultivate the fruit of the Spirit in your life? What fruit of the Spirit are you lacking? What do you need to do to begin bearing this fruit?
2. What kind of characteristics does a Christian have who bears the fruit of the Spirit? How will you know if this fruit appears in your life?
3. Do you ever experience uneasy feelings when you see the truth being compromised by someone you know? How do you handle those feelings?

3. LIGHT SHOWS WHAT IS ACCEPTABLE, PLEASING TO GOD (v.10).

Light proves things; it shows what is acceptable. What does this mean? As the believer walks in the light…

- he proves what is acceptable and not acceptable to the Lord
- he discriminates between what is acceptable and not acceptable to the Lord
- he shows to the world what is acceptable and not acceptable to the Lord
- he shows what path to take and what path not to take
- he shows what a person should do and not do

APPLICATION:
Everything the believer does is to be "unto the Lord"; that is, he is to set his attention and energy upon pleasing the Lord. He is to strive to do the pleasure of the Lord. He is to struggle to bring his will under control and to control his behavior in order to fulfill the joy of the Lord. Why? Because the Lord loved and gave Himself for the believer; therefore, the believer is to love and give himself to please the Lord.

> **"Furthermore then we beseech you, brethren, and exhort you by the Lord Jesus, that as ye have received of us how ye ought to walk and to please God, so ye would abound more and more" (1 Th.4:1).**

QUESTIONS:
1. Does God have a right to tell you what is acceptable to Him? Why?
2. Why do some people tend to think there are no absolute standards to live by? What is the Christian's source for those standards?
3. Why do you think God wants you to walk in the light?

4. LIGHT EXPOSES THE WORKS OF DARKNESS (vv.11-12).

1. The charge is clear and forceful: believers are to have no fellowship with the unfruitful works of darkness. Note that the works of darkness are…

- dark: leaving a man stumbling and groping about in the world, lost and unable to see where he is going
- unfruitful: bearing no lasting fruit beyond this world when death overtakes him

The unfruitful works of darkness are those works covered in the previous passage (Eph.5:3-6) and in the works of the flesh (Ga.5:19-21). They lead to death; therefore, the believer is to have no fellowship whatsoever with the unfruitful works of darkness.

> **"Be ye not unequally yoked together with unbelievers: for what fellowship hath righteousness with unrighteousness? and what communion hath light with darkness?" (2 Co.6:14).**

2. The believer's task on earth is striking: he is not to fellowship with the works of darkness; he is to live in so much light that his life reproves (exposes, rebukes, and convicts) people of their sins or dark works.

APPLICATION:
Sin is never to be taken lightly. The very fact that we are charged to reprove it is clear evidence. Our task is to reflect so much light that all the works of darkness around us are exposed and expelled. Remember when light appears, the darkness is always extinguished. But if the light leaves or is turned off, the darkness reappears.

> **"Take heed to yourselves: If thy brother trespass against thee, rebuke him; and if he repent, forgive him" (Lu.17:3).**

3. The reason why we should not have fellowship with the dark works of the world is this: it is a *shame* to even speak of those things which are done by them in secret. What a rebuke! We are not even to talk about dark works! We are not to be sharing conversation about the dark works of this world.

> **"Let your speech be alway with grace, seasoned with salt, that ye may know how ye ought to answer every man" (Co.4:6).**

ILLUSTRATION:
Does the darkness of sin ever overwhelm you? The gospel of Christ illuminates the way for the Christian believer.

> *A father took his son into an art shop to buy a picture of Christ for him. The boy was shown different pictures of Christ but he didn't like any of them. "No, Daddy, these are not what I want." The father, thinking that his son didn't want a picture of Christ after all, asked, "What kind of picture of Christ do you want?" Promptly the boy replied, "I want a Christ who shines in darkness!" The boy had seen a luminous picture of Christ which shone in darkness.*
>
> *We greatly need Christ to shine in the night of sorrow, suffering, testing and temptation. Only He can illumine life's dark pathway. As we follow Him, our way grows increasingly bright.*[1]

QUESTIONS:
1. What do these verses tell you about God's promise to give you direction?
2. Why do you suppose God wants you to have no fellowship with darkness?
3. Have you failed to walk in the light in some area of your life? What was the outcome?
4. What is the secret to staying in the light?

5. LIGHT REVEALS AND CONVERTS EVERYTHING IT TOUCHES (v.13).

Note two things.

1. When light touches something, it becomes light. It is lit up; and, to some degree, the object gives off light itself. It is converted and changed. When the light of Jesus Christ touches the life of a person in darkness, that life is changed: it becomes light. The darkness is done away with and eliminated. Note another fact as well: that person begins to touch the lives of those in darkness who surround him.

2. So long as evil is done in secret it thrives, but when it is dragged out of the dark corners and closed rooms into the light, it dies. When a person confronts Christ, his dark works are exposed in all their hurt, damage, filth, and corruption. We must always remember, this is the very reason many refuse to confront Christ. They prefer their dark works (Jn.3:20f). But when a man confronts Christ and abandons his dark sins, he becomes "light in the Lord" (Ep.5:8). He is transformed by the person of Christ. William Barclay points out that this is seen in the *healing* that is found in the rays of the sun. The light of Jesus Christ is like the rays of the sun. The light of Jesus Christ not only illuminates and reveals, it also cleanses. The light of Jesus Christ is not only a revealing and condemning thing, it is a healing thing as well.[2]

---

1 *W.B.K.* Walter B. Knight. *Knight's Treasury of 2,000 Illustrations*, p.203.

2 William Barclay.*The Letters to the Galatians and Ephesians*, p.195f.

APPLICATION:
One of the great truths of the Gospel of Jesus Christ is its power to change dark hearts into hearts of light. When we offer Christ to a world that is in darkness, we are offering light.

QUESTIONS:
1. What barriers do those in darkness try to erect in order to prevent the light from shining into their hearts?
2. Are you committed to being a light for the gospel? How can you be a better witness?
3. What are some dark areas in your community that need the light of Jesus Christ? What are some ways that you could make a difference?

6. LIGHT AWAKENS THE SLEEPING (v.14).

Light awakens the sleeping, those who are spiritually dead. Most people in the world are as sleeping men when it comes to walking in the light of God. They are living in the darkness of spiritual sleep and spiritual death—rushing on to that inevitable day of eternal darkness and death. Note an unfortunate fact: this passage is being written to believers. Too many professing believers are passing through life just like unbelievers: asleep—living in the darkness of spiritual sleep and spiritual death—fellowshipping with and, too often, participating in the works of darkness. They are unaware and ignorant of the great heritage and promises God has given us in Christ Jesus.

> **"And that, knowing the time, that now it is high time to awake out of sleep: for now is our salvation nearer than when we believed" (Ro.13:11).**

APPLICATION:
Note that the only Source to awakening out of spiritual sleep and death is Jesus Christ and Him alone.

> **"In him was life; and the life was the light of men" (Jn.1:4).**
>
> **"Then spake Jesus again unto them, saying, I am the light of the world: he that followeth me shall not walk in darkness, but shall have the light of life" (Jn.8:12).**

ILLUSTRATION:
For many of us, there is a struggle to get up and go in our Christian walk and service. This is not the time to just lay around and appear dead. Listen to this:

> *Winston Churchill had planned his funeral, which took place in Saint Paul's Cathedral. He included many of the great hymns of the church and used the eloquent Anglican liturgy. At his direction, a bugler...intoned...the sound of "Taps", the universal signal that says the day is over.*
>
> *But then came a dramatic turn: as Churchill instructed, after "Taps" was finished, another bugler...played the notes of "Reveille"—"It's time to get up. It's time to get up. It's time to get up in the morning."*[3]

Isn't it time for you to get up to serve the Lord with all of your might?

---

3 Craig B. Larson, Editor. *Illustrations for Preaching and Teaching*, p.52.

EPHESIANS 5:8-14

QUESTIONS:

1. In your Christian life, where do you stand right now?
   - ⇒ I'm in the light—I am wide awake.
   - ⇒ I'm in the shadows—I am taking a nap and do not really want to be disturbed.
   - ⇒ I'm in the dark—leave me alone; I'm sleeping.
2. What can you do that will help stir you and get you excited in your service for the Lord?
3. Why are some Christians asleep in the light? How does God feel about them?

SUMMARY:

As you examine your own spiritual life and walk with Christ, remember these facts:

1. Light, not darkness, is the nature of believers.
2. Light bears the things of life—the fruit of the Spirit.
3. Light shows what is acceptable.
4. Light exposes the works of darkness.
5. Light reveals & converts everything it touches.
6. Light awakens the sleeping.

PERSONAL JOURNAL NOTES (Reflection & Response)

1. The most important thing that I learned from this lesson was:

2. The area that I need to work on the most is:

3. I can apply this lesson to my life by:

4. Closing Statement of Commitment:

	G. The Believer is to Walk Carefully & Strictly, 5:15-21	is excess; but be filled with the Spirit;	**5. By being filled with the Spirit**
		19 Speaking to yourselves in psalms and hymns and spiritual songs, singing and making melody in your heart to the Lord;	a. A singing spirit
1. By looking around & watching every step	15 See then that ye walk circumspectly, not as fools, but as wise,		
2. By redeeming the time, making the most of every opportunity	16 Redeeming the time, because the days are evil.	20 Giving thanks always for all things unto God and the Father in the name of our Lord Jesus Christ;	b. A thankful & praying spirit
3. By understanding the Lord's will	17 Wherefore be ye not unwise, but understanding what the will of the Lord is.		
4. By rejecting drunkenness	18 And be not drunk with wine, wherein	21 Submitting yourselves one to another in the fear of God.	c. A submissive & respectful spirit

Section IV
THE WALK OF THE CHRISTIAN BELIEVER
Ephesians 4:1–6:9

Study 7: **THE BELIEVER IS TO WALK CAREFULLY AND STRICTLY**

Text: **Ephesians 5:15-21**

Aim: To set a dynamic example in the way you walk.

Memory Verse:

"Wherefore be ye not unwise, but understanding what the will of the Lord is" (Ephesians 5:17).

INTRODUCTION:

The Christian believer's life is a visual sermon, whether he wants it to be or not! Whether you are walking sharply in the Spirit or failing in the flesh, you are providing an example which will be copied. Listen to this short, but pointed poem:

"Walk A Little Plainer Daddy"

Walk a little plainer Daddy, said a little boy so frail.
I'm following in your footsteps and I don't want to fail.

Sometimes your steps are very plain.
Sometimes they are hard to see.
So walk a little plainer Daddy for you are leading me.

I know that once you walked this way many years ago
And what you did along the way I'd really like to know;
For sometimes when I am tempted I don't know what to do.
So walk a little plainer Daddy for I must follow you.

Some day when I grow up you are like what I want to be.
Then I will have a little boy who will want to follow me.

EPHESIANS 5:15-21

And I would want to lead him right and help him to be true.
So walk a little plainer Daddy; for we must follow you.[1]

How the believer walks day by day throughout life is crucial to the cause of Christ and to the welfare of society. He either contributes to the building up of society or to the tearing down of society. He either carries the message of life to the world, or he carries the message of silence and death. For this reason, it is important that the believer walk carefully and strictly throughout life.

OUTLINE:

1. By looking around and watching every step (v.15).
2. By redeeming the time, making the most of every opportunity (v.16).
3. By understanding the Lord's will (v.17).
4. By rejecting drunkenness (v.18).
5. By being filled with the Spirit (vv.18-21).

1. BY LOOKING AROUND AND WATCHING EVERY STEP (v.15).

Life is a walk, a path that we trod every day. When we arise in the morning, we begin to walk around. God expects us to walk carefully and accurately, exactly as we should. Note: there are two kinds of persons who walk throughout life.

1. *There is the fool or unwise person*: this simply means the person who is unthinking, thoughtless, careless, uncaring, and worldly minded.

The unwise is the person who gives little thought about where he should go and where he should not go. He just arises in the morning and goes to work or about his daily routine, with little thought about God and about what happens beyond this life. If he makes a mistake here and there, it does not matter that much, not to him. Making mistakes is just the way of all human life.

He thinks that he will be acceptable to God if he just lives a life...

- that is fairly decent, honorable, and useful
- that pays its dues to God here and there

The unwise person is not concerned about watching every step and being alert to every temptation and pitfall in life. He could care less about struggling and being exact and strict in life. Living a careful, accurate, strict, disciplined, controlled life is not that important to him.

2. *There is the wise person*: the thinking, thoughtful, careful, caring, spiritually minded person. This is the person on a mission. He knows God personally. He knows that he is on earth to live a righteous and godly life, to bear testimony to the Lord Jesus Christ. Therefore, when he arises in the morning and goes to work or about his daily affairs, he walks in the presence and praise of God. His thoughts are upon God all day long. Mistakes matter to him. It all matters—the daily reports and talk about man's...

- sin
- cursing
- murder
- immorality
- drunkenness
- war
- hunger
- divorce
- suffering
- power struggle
- drugs
- evil
- off-colored jokes
- illnesses
- selfishness
- shame
- neglect
- hate

The wise man is not only concerned about every step of life, he struggles to watch every step—to make sure that he walks through life in a disciplined and controlled

---

[1] Author Unknown.

manner. He knows that the only answer to the evil and problems of life is Jesus Christ and His righteousness.

> **"This I say then, Walk in the Spirit, and ye shall not fulfil the lust of the flesh" (Ga.5:16).**

QUESTIONS:
1. What positive words and acts do you pass on which are imitated by someone else? What negative words and acts?
2. Do you ever experience feelings of "being on the spot"—like your life is being examined under a microscope? How do you handle these feelings?
3. Which person do you identify with the most—the unwise or wise? Why?

2. BY REDEEMING THE TIME, MAKING THE MOST OF EVERY OPPORTUNITY (v.16).

The idea is not to *buy* time. Time is the gift of God; a man has time. What man must do is use his time to buy things of value. This means two things.

1. *A person is to use his time wisely; he is not to waste time.* Time is a gift of God. Time exists—it is here with or without us. What we have to do is use time wisely, use it *to do* the best we can.

APPLICATION:
The choice is ours. We can sit and twiddle away hours, engaging in activity and conversation that are of little, if any, value or worth; or we can use time wisely, keeping our thoughts and hands busy...
- in our profession and work, contributing to the good of society
- in our worship and service for Christ—all day long—joining with others of God's church in witnessing and ministering to the lost and needful of our communities and cities
- in meeting the needs of a world reeling under the weight of suffering, sin, and death

2. *A person is to use his time by taking advantage of the opportunities that arise throughout the day.* This, too, is what redeeming the time means. The believer is to redeem the opportunities...
- to live righteously and godly
- to witness and share Christ
- to be diligent on the job
- to set an example of commitment and discipline with work, at home and at play
- to be faithful to God and family
- to speak up for Christ and righteousness
- to pray instead of allowing time to be wasted. (If a believer commits himself to pray as Christ and Paul prayed, he will find that he has no time to waste.)

Note why we are to redeem the time: because the days are evil. This refers to all the evil that confronts the believer as he walks day by day—so much evil that he must stay alert to keep from falling and failing. He must be alert to live righteously and to bear testimony to Christ. The evil can range from mild temptations to persecutions, from small money problems to a world economic collapse, from a minor family squabble to war. The evil of the world is ever before us—small and great. The task of the believer is to redeem the time—make the most use of what time he has. The opportunity will soon pass because the days are evil.

⇒ The opportunity to witness will pass.
⇒ The opportunity to show diligence will pass.
⇒ The opportunity to speak up will pass.
⇒ The opportunity to love will pass.
⇒ The opportunity to minister will pass.
⇒ The opportunity to work hard will pass.
⇒ The opportunity to pray will pass.
⇒ The opportunity to give will pass.

APPLICATION:
How many of us waste time? Much time is wasted...

- not being efficient
- watching television
- reading unsuitable literature
- sitting in restaurants
- loafing around at home
- not working diligently
- engaging in unprofitable activity on weekends
- sitting around in useless activity and talk

Each of us needs to take a moment to think through where we waste so much time and correct it. More than ever, we need to give ourselves to make a significant contribution to our work and society, to our church and community, to living righteously and godly, to witnessing and helping a world of people who are discouraged and lonely, hungry and cold, hurting and suffering, needy and helpless—all lost in sin—all without the knowledge of Christ and of eternal life. The call of the hour is to redeem the time.

> **"Casting down imaginations, and every high thing that exalteth itself against the knowledge of God, and bringing into captivity every thought to the obedience of Christ" (2 Co.10:5).**
>
> **"So teach us to number our days, that we may apply our hearts unto wisdom" (Ps.90:12).**

QUESTIONS:

1. In a typical 24-hour day, how much of your time is spent doing these activities:

ACTIVITY	# OF HOURS
Prayer/worship:	
Work:	
Family Time:	
TV/Videos:	
Recreation:	
Sleep:	

   Which area needs to be adjusted first?
2. Why is it important to redeem the time? What kind of things can you do in order to be a better steward of your time?

3. BY UNDERSTANDING THE LORD'S WILL (v.17).

Note how both the unwise man and the wise man are defined in this verse.

⇒ The unwise man is a man who does not understand the will of the Lord.
⇒ The wise man is a man who does understand the will of the Lord.

The word "understand" means to grasp, perceive, see with the mind and comprehend. As stated in the previous verse, the days are full of all sorts of evil. The believer must understand what God's will is in order to conquer the evil. If he does not, then he is as a fool and acting unwisely. How can a person know what the will of the Lord is?

⇒ By knowing the Word of God—by knowing it so well that he can apply it to the situations that confront him every day.

"Then said Jesus to those Jews which believed on him, If ye continue in my word, then are ye my disciples indeed; and ye shall know the truth, and the truth shall make you free" (Jn.8:31-32).

⇒ By being sensitive to the leadership of the Holy Spirit.

"Teach me to do thy will; for thou art my God: thy spirit is good; lead me into the land of uprightness" (Ps.143:10).

ILLUSTRATION:
Are you prone to make daily decisions without knowing God's will? Bob Mumford gives the following advice:

A certain harbor in Italy can be reached only by sailing up a narrow channel between dangerous rocks and shoals. Over the years, many ships have been wrecked, and navigation is hazardous.

To guide the ships safely into port, three lights have been mounted on three huge poles in the harbor. When the three lights are perfectly lined up and seen as one, the ship can safely proceed up the narrow channel. If the pilot sees two or three lights, he knows he's off course and in danger.

"God has also provided three beacons to guide us. The same rules of navigation apply—the three lights must be lined up before it is safe for us to proceed. The three lights of guidance are:

1. *The Word of God (objective standard).*
2. *The Holy Spirit (subjective witness).*
3. *Circumstances (divine providence).*

Together they assure us that the directions we've received are from God and will lead us safely along His way"[2]

QUESTIONS:
1. How much of your life is planned without considering God's will? Are there any areas of your life that are not in God's perfect will? What must you do to have those areas subjected to God's will?
2. Why is it important for you to understand God's will?
3. How do you feel about having to make an important decision without knowing God's will?

4. BY REJECTING DRUNKENNESS (v.18).

Drunkenness means to be intoxicated with drink or drugs. The word "excess" is excessive behavior. The Greek means...

- the dissipation and wasting away of the body
- uncontrolled behavior
- rioting, wild and outrageous behavior and conduct

2 Craig B. Larson, Editor. *Illustrations for Preaching & Teaching*, p.108.

Drunkenness is a work of the flesh, and it often leads to other sins of the flesh: partying, loose behavior, immodest clothing, exposure of the body, sexual thoughts, immorality, wickedness, evil, unfairness, violence, physical abuse, notions of grandeur, strength, or power. The Bible says several things about drunkenness.

1. Drunkenness excludes a person from the kingdom of God.

> **"Nor thieves, nor covetous, nor drunkards, nor revilers, nor extortioners, shall inherit the kingdom of God" (1 Co.6:10).**

2. Drunkenness leads to other forms of misbehavior and sin.

> **"And not many days after the younger son gathered all together, and took his journey into a far country, and there wasted his substance with riotous living" (Lu.15:13).**

3. Drunkenness makes it impossible to grasp the fleeting opportunities of time.

> **"Redeeming the time, because the days are evil. Wherefore be ye not unwise, but understanding what the will of the Lord is. And be not drunk with wine" (Ep.5:16-18).**

APPLICATION:
Is liquor a disease? If it is—

1. *It is the only disease that is contracted by an act of the will.*
2. *It is the only disease that requires a license to propagate it.*
3. *It is the only disease that is bottled and sold.*
4. *It is the only disease that requires outlets to spread it.*
5. *It is the only disease that produces a revenue for the government.*
6. *It is the only disease that provokes crime.*
7. *It is the only disease that is habit-forming.*
8. *It is the only disease that is spread by advertising.*
9. *It is the only disease without a germ or virus cause, and for which there is no human corrective medicine; and*
10. *It is the only disease that bars the patient from heaven."*[3]

ILLUSTRATION:
Does the gospel of Jesus Christ offer any hope at all for those who have fallen into the grips of alcoholism? Listen to this exciting testimony:

As a Christian businessman concluded his business with a lawyer in St. Louis some years ago, he said to the lawyer: "I have often wanted to ask you a question, but I have been a coward." "Why?" replied the lawyer, "I did not think you were afraid of anything. What is the question?" The man said, "Why are you not a Christian?" The lawyer hung his head. He said, "Is there not something in the Bible that says no drunkard shall have any part in the Kingdom of God? You know my weakness." "That is not my question," answered the Christian man. "I am asking you why you are not a Christian?" "Well," answered the lawyer, "I cannot recall that anyone ever asked me if I were a Christian, and I am sure nobody ever told me how to become one."

Then the Christian drew his chair close to the lawyer, read him some passages from the Bible, and said simply, "Let us get down and pray."

3 *The Gospel Banner*. Walter B. Knight. *Knight's Treasury of 2,000 Illustrations*, p.401.

The lawyer prayed first: "O Jesus, Thou knowest what a slave I am to drink. Here this morning Thy servant has shown me the way to God. Oh, break the power of this habit in my life."

Giving his testimony later, this drinking lawyer said, "[Write] it down big, [write] it down plain, that God broke that power instantly." Who was this drunken lawyer? Dr. C. I. Scofield, famous editor of the Scofield Reference Bible![4]

QUESTIONS:

1. Why do some people tend to think that drunkenness is a disease? Do you agree or disagree? Why?
2. Give an example of how drunkenness leads to other sins.
3. Do you think God loves those who are addicted to alcohol or drugs? What do you think your role is in reaching them with the gospel?

5. BY BEING FILLED WITH THE SPIRIT (vv.18-21).

This command is in the present tense which means that the believer is to be *constantly filled* with the Spirit; he is to *keep on being filled.* The Spirit's filling is the personal manifestation of Christ to the believer who walks obediently day by day (Jn.14:21). It is a consciousness of His presence, of His leadership—moment by moment. This consciousness is the believer's privilege. But the Spirit's filling is not an automatic experience. The responsibility of being filled with the Spirit rests upon the shoulders of the believer. He is filled only as he walks obediently with Christ.

In understanding the infilling of the Spirit, it is helpful to review what the Lord had to say about the manifestations of the Spirit in the Gospel of John.

> **"He that hath my commandments, and keepeth them, he it is that loveth me: and he that loveth me shall be loved of my Father, and I will love him, and will manifest myself to him. Judas saith unto him, not Iscariot, Lord, how is it that thou wilt manifest thyself unto us, and not unto the world?" (Jn.14:21-22).**

Note that the Holy Spirit is the very *special manifestation* of Christ within the believer. Apparently, this refers to very special manifestations of the Lord to the heart of the believer, those very special times when there is a deep consciousness of love between the Lord and His dear follower. This is bound to be what Christ meant, for He had already spoken about His personal presence within the believer (Jn.14:18-20). When believers go through terrible trials and severe crises, God knows and He loves and cares; so He moves to meet the need of His dear children. He moves within the believer's heart, manifesting His presence and giving a deep sense of His love and care, helping and giving confidence, forgiveness, and assurance—giving whatever the believer needs. The depth of the experience and the intensity of *the special manifestation* depends upon the need of the believer. God knows and loves His dear child perfectly, so He gives whatever experience and depth of emotion are needed to meet the need of His child. We must always remember that God loves each one of us so much He will do whatever is needed...

- to lift us up
- to strengthen us
- to conform us to the image of His dear Son, the Lord Jesus Christ

---

4 *Dr. P.W. Philpott in Evangelical Christian.* Walter B. Knight. *Knight's Treasury of 2,000 Illustrations*, p.400.

Note that the *special manifestations* of the Lord's presence are given only to the believer who does two things.

⇒ The believer who receives the commandments of Christ, has them in his heart, knows them, and has made them his own (Ps.119:11).
⇒ The believer who keeps the commandments of Jesus.

The believer who does these two things shows that he *truly* loves the Lord Jesus. And it is he who loves and obeys the Lord Jesus who receives the very special manifestations and infillings of the Holy Spirit.

Note an important fact: the special manifestation is questioned. Judas asked the question for the first time, but the special manifestation of Christ's presence has been questioned and doubted by thousands ever since. Judas was thinking like all men think—in terms of a physical manifestation, a visible appearance.

The word "manifestation" means unveiling or revelation. It suggests that a new thing has come to light; that something never known by man before is made known. Some mystery has now been revealed. It is something that cannot be discovered by man's reason or wisdom. It is a mystery that is hidden from man and beyond his grasp.

> **"And when they had prayed, the place was shaken where they were assembled together; and they were all filled with the Holy Ghost, and they spake the word of God with boldness" (Ac.4:31).**

Now, note the three traits of a Spirit-filled person.

1. *A Spirit-filled person has a singing spirit*. This is in contrast to the drunken person. The mention of singing is the picture of joy and happiness. The worldly person often seeks joy and happiness in drinking and partying. This is not to be the case with the true believer. He is to seek his joy and happiness by being filled with the Spirit of God and by singing to himself. Note a crucial point: singing to oneself helps a person to experience the fulness of the Spirit. What do we sing? God tells us:

⇒ *Psalms*: the psalms of the Old Testament. We need to learn them—yes, by memory—so that we can sing them. Think how victoriously we could walk through life if we knew the Psalms.
⇒ *Hymns*: the great hymns of the church. Again we must learn them.
⇒ *Spiritual Songs*: F.F. Bruce suggests that these may refer to songs being made up by the person as he walks along singing praise to the Lord throughout the day.[5] We have all experienced walking along making melody in our hearts to the Lord; therefore, his suggestion makes sense.

It is certainly a good practice.

> **"O come, let us sing unto the LORD: let us make a joyful noise to the rock of our salvation" (Ps.95:1).**

2. *A Spirit-filled person has a thankful spirit*. Note the words "always" and "for all things." Our lives are in God's hands. He guides and directs us through all things. Therefore, we can thank Him for all things—no matter what the things are. He controls all. Giving thanks as we walk along throughout the day helps us to experience the fulness of God's Spirit.

> **"Be careful [anxious] for nothing; but in every thing by prayer and supplication with thanksgiving let your requests be made known unto God" (Ph.4:6).**

---

5 F.F. Bruce. *The Epistle to the Ephesians*, p.111.

3. *A Spirit-filled person has a submissive and respectful spirit.* A Spirit-filled person does not have a spirit of criticism, dissension, envy, divisiveness, or selfishness. The same is true of churches: a Spirit-filled church has a body of people who are submissive—going out of their way to minister and serve each other. There is no dissension or divisiveness, no envy or selfishness among its people. In the fear of God, they submit to each other before they break the fulness of God's Spirit.

> **"Likewise, ye younger, submit yourselves unto the elder. Yea, all of you be subject one to another, and be clothed with humility: for God resisteth the proud, and giveth grace to the humble" (1 Pe.5:5).**

QUESTIONS:

1. Are you experiencing the Spirit-filled life today? In what ways can this life be best cultivated in you?
2. What thoughts come to your mind when you hear the words "filled with the Spirit?"
3. How do you know when you are filled with the Spirit?
4. What happens to Christians when they are Spirit-filled?

SUMMARY:

We understand a little bit better now why it is important for the Christian to walk the narrow path. People everywhere (at home, work, and play) are looking for us to show the way. They are telling us, "Walk a little plainer for we must follow you." How do we walk a little plainer?

1. By looking around and watching every step (v.15).
2. By redeeming the time, making the most of every opportunity (v.16).
3. By understanding the Lord's will (v.17).
4. By rejecting drunkenness (v.18).
5. By being filled with the Spirit (vv.18-21).

PERSONAL JOURNAL NOTES
(Reflection & Response)

1. The most important thing that I learned from this lesson was:

2. The area that I need to work on the most is:

3. I can apply this lesson to my life by:

4. Closing Statement of Commitment:

	H. The Believing Wife & Husband Are to Walk in a Spirit of Submission & Love, 5:22-33
1. The wife is to walk in a spirit of submission a. To submit is God's will	22 Wives, submit yourselves unto your own husbands, as unto the Lord.
b. To submit is God's order for the family 1) The husband is the head 2) The husband is the protector	23 For the husband is the head of the wife, even as Christ is the head of the church; and he is the saviour of the body.
c. To submit is a spiritual mystery comparable to Christ & the church, vv. 23-24	24 Therefore as the church is subject unto Christ, so let the wives be to their own husbands in every thing.
2. The husband is to love his wife a. It means to give yourself for her—sacrificially	25 Husbands, love your wives, even as Christ also loved the church, and gave himself for it;
1) Involves being set apart & cleansed	26 That he might sanctify and cleanse it with the washing of water by the word,
2) Involves having no filth, no deception, no blot on your record	27 That he might present it to himself a glorious church, not having spot, or

wrinkle, or any such thing; but that it should be holy and without blemish.	3) Involves being holy & blameless
28 So ought men to love their wives as their own bodies. He that loveth his wife loveth himself.	b. It means to love her as you love your own body
29 For no man ever yet hated his own flesh; but nourisheth and cherisheth it, even as the Lord the church:	1) To lovingly care for her
30 For we are members of his body, of his flesh, and of his bones.	2) To become one body
31 For this cause shall a man leave his father and mother, and shall be joined unto his wife, and they two shall be one flesh.	c. It means to leave your parents 1) To be united to your wife 2) To become one flesh
32 This is a great mystery: but I speak concerning Christ and the church.	d. It means a mystery—a spiritual love like the love of Christ for the church
33 Nevertheless let every one of you in particular so love his wife even as himself; and the wife see that she reverence her husband.	e. The conclusion 1) Husband: Love your wife 2) Wife: Respect your husband

Section IV
THE WALK OF THE CHRISTIAN BELIEVER
Ephesians 4:1–6:9

Study 8: **THE BELIEVING WIFE AND HUSBAND ARE TO WALK IN A SPIRIT OF SUBMISSION AND LOVE**

Text: **Ephesians 5:22-33**

Aim: To gain a true understanding of what a godly marriage is.

Memory Verse:

"For this cause shall a man leave his father and mother, and shall be joined unto his wife, and they two shall be one flesh" (Ephesians 5:31).

EPHESIANS 5:22-33

INTRODUCTION:
Every day, all over the world, important words are being spoken to some men and women: "*I now pronounce you man and wife.*" And with that charge, married couples make daily discoveries that cloud their ideas on what makes a marriage good. For many, the wedding day was the pinnacle. As they experience trials and tribulations, the promises they made to each other become faint memories. They ignore their vows by going from "until death do us part" to "How soon can I get out of this?"

What has gone wrong with the marriage that God has ordained as His will?

Why are so many missing so much in their marriage? Is a good Christian marriage out of reach? Is Christian marriage just too much of a burden to be endured?

When dealing with wives and husbands, we must always remember that God's instructions are not grievous. In fact, they are easy and light. God instructs and guides us down the easiest and lightest path possible. As Christ said:

> **"Come unto me, all ye that labour and are heavy laden, and I will give you rest. Take my yoke upon you, and learn of me; for I am meek and lowly in heart: and ye shall find rest unto your souls. For my yoke is easy, and my burden is light" (Mt.11:28-30).**

If we walk down the path God has laid for us—if we do just what He says—we can experience the most loving, peaceful, rich, and full life imaginable. This is *doubly true* for husband and wife, for they have the companionship of each other as well as of the Lord.

OUTLINE:

1. The wife is to walk in a spirit of submission (vv.22-24).
2. The husband is to love his wife (vv.25-33).

1. THE WIFE IS TO WALK IN A SPIRIT OF SUBMISSION (vv.22-24).

There are three reasons why the wife is to be submissive to her husband.

1. *To submit is God's will.* In fact, it is a commandment of God. There is to be no equivocation, no argument, not even a question about being submissive: "Wives submit yourselves unto your own husbands."

God is God, and as God, He has the right to demand anything of us. But note the words "as unto the Lord." When we do anything, we are to do it *as to the Lord.* Why? Because we love Him. The Lord has loved us and given Himself for us that He might save us. He loved us; therefore, we love Him. This is always the first reason to obey Him. We love Him; therefore, when He says to do something, we do it *as to Him*—to please Him.

Now, let us ask ourselves: What kind of spirit is the Christian wife to have as she obeys God?

- A spirit of slavery or love?
- A spirit of hostility or love?
- A spirit of resentment or love?
- A spirit of reaction or love?

The answer is obvious: she is to act out of love. She loves the Lord; therefore, to please Him she submits herself to her husband. The point is this: God instructs wives to walk in a spirit of submission to their husbands. Therefore, Christian wives do not obey the Lord out of resentment and reaction because of the commandment. They obey the Lord out of love because they love both the Lord and their husbands. Therefore, they focus and set their lives upon pleasing the Lord and their husbands. If the Lord says do it, then they do it because they love the Lord and want to please Him above all else.

2. *To submit is God's order for the family* (v.2). There is to be a *partnership* and order within the family. This is basic for the family and society to exist. In fact, no organization, no matter what it is, can survive and exist without a spirit of partnership and order. Note three important facts.

a. The husband is the head of the wife. The word "head" in Scripture refers to authority, *not being*. Neither man nor woman is superior to the other in being. Men and women are equal in God's eyes.

⇒ There is an essential partnership between men and women. Neither is independent of the other. Both are from the other, and the relationship that exists between them has come from God.

"Nevertheless neither is the man without the woman, neither the woman without the man, in the Lord. For as the woman is of the man, even so is the man also by the woman; but all things of God" (1 Co.11:11-12).

⇒ There is neither male nor female in God's eyes. He sees both men and women as one, each as significant as the other.

"There is neither Jew nor Greek, there is neither bond nor free, there is neither male nor female: for ye are all one in Christ Jesus" (Ga.3:28).

When God talks about man's being the head of the woman, He is not talking about ability or worth, competence or value, brilliance or advantage. God is talking about function and order within an organization. Every organization has to have a head for it to be operated in an efficient and orderly manner. There are no greater organizations than God's universe, His church, and His Christian family. Within God's order of things there is a partnership, but every partnership must have a head, and God has ordained that man is the head of the partnership.

b. The great pattern for the wife to follow is Christ and the church. Christ is the head of the church. This simply means that Christ has authority over the church. So long as the church lives by this rule, the church experiences love and joy and peace—orderliness—and it is able to carry out its function and mission on earth to the fullest. So it is with the husband; he is the head of the family, the ultimate authority in the family. The wife is to be submissive to that authority just as the church is to be submissive to Christ. So long as she and the rest of the family live by this rule, the family experiences love, joy, and peace—orderliness—and it fulfills its function and purpose on earth. This, of course, assumes that the husband is fulfilling his part in the family. As in any organization, each member must do his part for the organization to be orderly and accomplish its purpose.

c. The husband is the savior of the body just as Christ is the Savior of the church. Christ is the great Protector and Comforter of the church. So the husband is to be the *protector and comforter* of the wife. By nature, that is, by the constitution and build of the body, the husband is stronger than the wife. Therefore, in God's order of things, he is to be the main protector and comforter of the wife. These two functions are two of the great benefits which the wife receives from a loving husband who is faithful to the Lord.

3. *To submit is a spiritual mystery* (v.23). The wife's submission is comparable to Christ and the church. Again, Christ is the pattern for the wife:
as she submits to Christ, so she is to submit to her husband.

⇒ as she depends upon Christ for help and protection, so she is to depend upon her husband for help and protection.

⇒ as she depends upon Christ for companionship and comfort, so she is to depend upon her husband for companionship and comfort.

In summary, the submission that wives are to show to their husbands is an example of the submission that all believers are to show to one another (Ep.5:21). It does not mean that women are inferior to men. It simply means that there is to be an arrangement, an order in the household. Every *body* must have such order, and every *body* must have a head. Two heads in any body or organization would be a monstrosity and make for disorder. Therefore, in God's order of things for the family, the husband is the head over the family. He arranges things in a spirit of *tenderness and love* and the wife is to submit herself in a sweet spirit of *understanding and reasonableness* (see Pr.31:10-31.)

> **"Wives, submit yourselves unto your own husbands, as it is fit in the Lord" (Co.3:18).**

QUESTIONS:

1. What specific things come to your mind when you hear the word "submit"?
2. How good are you at submitting? Why do you suppose that submission runs against the grain of some people?
3. Why do some people tend to think that submission is another word for becoming a doormat?
4. What do these verses teach concerning God's order for the home? If you are married, how easy is it for you to accept this truth and apply it to your marriage?

2. THE HUSBAND IS TO LOVE HIS WIFE (vv.25-33).

Note five significant points.

1. *The love which the husband is to have for his wife is the very love of God Himself* (agape love). *Agape* love is a selfless and pure love, a giving and sacrificial love. It is the love of the mind and will as well as of the heart. It is not only a love of affection and feelings; it is a love of the *will and commitment*. It is a love that wills and commits itself to love a person. It is the love that works for the highest good of the person loved...

- that loves even if the person *does not deserve to be loved*
- that loves even if the person is *utterly unworthy of being loved*

APPLICATION:
Just imagine! What would happen in most marriages if the husband so loved his wife, loved her...

- with a *selfless and unselfish love*
- with a *giving and sacrificial love*
- with a love of the *will as well as of the heart*
- with a love of *commitment as well as of affection*

One thing that would happen in most marriages would be this: the wife would willingly accept his authority as the head of the family.

Note that the standard of the husband's love is the love of Christ for the church. The love of Christ for the church can be described in one simple statement: Christ *gave Himself* for the church. Christ loved the church so much that He gave all He was and had for it, *sacrificed Himself totally*. This is the love the husband is to have for his wife. Chrysostom, a great minister in the early church, said:

> *If it be needful that thou shouldst give thy life for her, or be cut to pieces a thousand times, or endure anything whatever, refuse it not....He brought the Church to His feet by His great care, not by threats nor fear nor any such thing; so do thou conduct thyself towards thy wife.*[1]

The sacrificial love of the husband involves three things. Note that the very things said about Christ and the church are to be true of the husband and wife.

a. The husband's love involves being *set apart and cleansed.* The word *sanctify* means to be set apart. When a young man asks a young lady to be his wife, he sets himself apart for her and for her alone. His word, his act, his promise of marriage also causes her to set herself apart. When he speaks the word and makes the promise of marriage, he and she both are thereafter set apart and cleansed for each other.

   A dirty bride or groom—a dirty, defiled marriage—is unthinkable. The one thing above all else that will keep the marriage sanctified and cleansed is the husband's sacrificial love. If the husband will love his wife to the point that he gives himself sacrificially, his love will not only protect him, but it will go a long way in protecting the sanctity and purity of his wife.

b. The husband's love involves having no spot or wrinkle or any such thing. Spots would mean the mistakes that tarnish one's life and marriage, mistakes so serious that they are very difficult to wash off one's body and out of one's mind. They would include such things as...
   - mistreatment and abuse
   - loose and immoral behavior
   - withdrawal and avoidance

   Wrinkles would mean things that cause friction and rattle the nerves and that need to be ironed out. They would include such things as...
   - bad temper and a reactionary spirit
   - broken promises and serious neglect
   - severe selfishness and rejection

c. The husband's love involves being holy and without blemish. The word "holy" means to be separate and untouched by evil. The husband's love—if it is a real love—will stir him to be holy and unblemished, going a long way in stirring his wife to be holy and without blemish.

APPLICATION:

This point is striking, a real eye-opener. It shows just how dependent the marriage is upon the love of the husband—how much effect the husband's love has upon the marriage. Few wives could reject such love; few wives would refuse to walk hand in hand with their husbands if the husbands truly loved them with the love that is unselfish and sacrificial.

"Husbands, love your wives, even as Christ also loved the church, and gave himself for it" (Ep.5:25).

---

[1] William Barclay. *The Letters to the Galatians and Ephesians*, p.206.

"Likewise, ye husbands, dwell with them according to knowledge, giving honour unto the wife, as unto the weaker vessel, and as being heirs together of the grace of life; that your prayers be not hindered" (1 Pe.3:7).

ILLUSTRATION:

The devil takes great pleasure when a Christian marriage hits the rocks and destroys what God had joined together. Are we at the mercy of the desires of the devil? Only if men fail to put up "hedges" around their marriages. As you listen to this illustration, take care that it does not become your story.

Stanley was a Sunday school teacher who wanted to relate to his adult students. He prided himself on being able to talk up a storm about anything. Through the years, he noticed that his gift of gab appealed to the ladies. Stanley was married and had a couple of kids who wanted to be just like Dad. From all observations, he had the perfect marriage and family. Any one who knew Stanley would agree that he was very relational—a real "touchy-feely" man. It was this attribute which led to his demise.

Mary was in Stanley's class and made it a point never to miss a Sunday or any other time the class met for fellowship. She liked Stanley a lot because he always made it a point to greet her with a warm embrace that tended to linger. Everything appeared to be innocent at first, but the fuse was lit shortly after that first embrace. Without saying a word, they both knew the fire that was burning was rapidly becoming a wildfire which would consume their lives. They tried to fight those feelings...for awhile...sort of...not really. To tell you the truth, they just gave up and gave in to a temptation which would destroy his marriage and devastate the church.

In his book, *Hedges—Loving Your Marriage Enough To Protect It,* Jerry B. Jenkins sheds a warning light on men:

Call it what you will, but a man with as perfect a wife as he could ever want is still capable of lust, of a senseless seeking of that which would destroy him and his family. If he does not fear his own potential and build a hedge around himself and his marriage, he heads for disaster.

Shall we all run scared? Yes! Fear is the essential. "There are several good protections against temptation," Mark Twain said, "but the surest is cowardice."[2]

2. *The love which the husband is to have for his wife is the very same love he has for his own body*. This is a startling statement. Note again what it says: the husband is to love his wife just as much as he loves *his own body*.

a. This means that he is to nourish and cherish his wife as he does his own body.

⇒ The word "nourish" means to feed, clothe, nurture, and look after until she is mature in the marriage and then to continue nourishing her as long as she lives.

⇒ The word "cherish" means to hold ever so dear within the heart; to treat with warmth, tenderness, care, affection, and appreciation.

APPLICATION:

What a difference would exist in marriage if the husband just *nourished and cherished* his wife as he does his own body. Think through the meaning of the two words for just a moment and imagine the difference that could exist.

---

2 Jerry B. Jenkins. *Hedges—Loving Your Marriage Enough To Protect It.* (Chicago, IL: Moody Press, 1989), pp.26-27.

b. This means that the husband is to become one body, one flesh and one set of bones with his wife. Two people could never become any closer. This is complete absorption and assimilation of each into the other, a complete union and oneness...
- of body and spirit
- of mind and thoughts
- of objective and purpose
- of behavior and activity

The husband becomes one with his wife, and the wife becomes one with her husband. The two become one flesh. (This is dealt with more fully in the following point.)

3. *The love which the husband is to have for his wife is to be the love that will stir him to leave his parents and be joined to his wife* (see **"A Closer Look," Joined**—Ep.5:31 for discussion).

4. *The love which the husband is to have for his wife is a spiritual mystery—a spiritual love—a love just like Christ's love for the church* (see **"A Closer Look," Spiritual Union**—Ep.5:32 for discussion).

5. The conclusion is simple and straightforward: *the husband is to love his wife as himself, and the wife is to reverence (respect and esteem) her husband* (v.33).

QUESTIONS:
1. What practical differences do "hedges" make in a Christian marriage? What kinds of hedges are in your marriage?
2. In what area of your marriage are you failing to experience God's love? In what ways would God's love improve those areas?
3. Do you ever worry about losing the love in your marriage? What do these verses instruct you to do in order to guard your marriage from losing its love?

A CLOSER LOOK:

(5:31) **Joined**: to join fast together; to glue together; to cement together; to be joined in the closest union possible; to be bound together; to be so totally united that two become one. Therefore, to join means a spiritual union. It is a union higher and stronger than the union of parent and child. It is a union that means more than living together, more than having sex and bearing offspring. Animals do this. It is a union that can be wrought by God alone (v.11). It is a spiritual union that places man above the physical plane of animals. It is a spiritual fulness, a spiritual sharing of life together: a dedication, a consecration, a completeness, a satisfaction that makes a person the exclusive possession of God and of the spouse. As said, such a cleaving or spiritual union is brought about by God alone. Both husband and wife must be willing and submissive for God to bring about such a cleaving in their lives. **"Submitting yourselves one to another in the fear [trust] of God" (Ep.5:21).**

There are three unions within a true marriage, that is, a marriage that *really cleaves* and is really *joined together* by God (Mt.19:6).

1. *There is the physical union*: the sharing of each other's body (1 Co.7:2-5). But note: physical sharing cannot reach its ultimate fulness unless it is experienced while conscious of God's warm and tender mercies (Ep.5:25-33).

2. *There is the mental union*: the sharing of each other's life, dreams, and hopes, and the working together to realize those dreams and hopes. It is important to note that this union still deals only with the physical and material world.

3. *There is the spiritual union*: the sharing, melting, and molding of each other's spirit. This can be brought about only by God. Therefore, there has to be a sharing together with God for there to be a *nourishing* and *nurturing* of the spirit.

Now here is the point: the greatest thing in the world is to know God personally and to be perfectly assured that we shall live now and eternally—to have life abundant with all the love, significance, meaning, and purpose humanly possible. But a man and a woman cannot experience abundant life of and by themselves. They can only nurture the mind and mesh themselves together mentally and physically. To be meshed together spiritually, the couple must share God and His saving grace together. When a couple shares God together day by day, God works supernaturally within their spirits, *melting* their beings and *molding* them into what He calls *one flesh*. They actually become as *one person*. This is what is meant by "God hath joined together." The Greek word for "joined together" actually means to *yoke together*. It is God's yoking, God's joining, God's binding the couple together into such a spiritual union that causes them to become one person.

A couple who is spiritually united does two very practical things.

1. The couple "submits themselves one to the other in the fear of God" (Ep.5:21). They submit, yield, surrender, sacrifice, give themselves up to the other as they live day by day in the fear (trust) of God. Day by day they deliberately set out to nourish and cherish the other, even as the Lord nourishes and cherishes the church (Ep.5:29). They work to become part of each other—so deliberately that they seek to become part of each other's body, each other's flesh, each other's bones (Ep.5:30). They seek to be joined "as one flesh," no matter the surrender and sacrifice required. The meshing together is done by God. God takes such deliberate purpose and behavior, such a melting of one's being, and molds it into the flesh of the other—so much so the two actually become as one, not only physically and mentally, but spiritually as well.

2. The couple shares the presence of God and His saving grace together. As a result, God gives them a spiritual assurance and strength which they share together throughout life. They share the knowledge and confidence...

- that God shall care for and look after them now and forever
- that God shall carry them through the devastating trials of life that confront all human beings every so often
- that God shall bless them with all that is necessary as they walk through life together
- that God shall give them an abundant entrance into the everlasting kingdom of the Lord Jesus Christ—forever and ever

Again, the point is this: God takes such deliberate sharing of spiritual things to melt and mold the man and woman into *one flesh* spiritually—so much so that they actually become one. A man and a woman being spiritually united by God as one person is what cleaving means. Cleaving to one another in God's Spirit is true marriage—the glorious gift of God.

APPLICATION:

No more beautiful picture of marriage could be painted, yet two serious problems exist in far too many marriages.

1. The problem of one or both of the spouses being unwilling to be bound together by the Spirit of God.
2. The problem of one or both of the spouses being unwilling to break away from dependency upon the parents.

QUESTIONS:

1. In what ways can a marriage become unglued? What is the secret to putting a broken marriage back together? What kinds of things bond you to your spouse?
2. Check the description which best summarizes your marriage:
   ⇒ The glue is still wet: We're not bound together yet.
   ⇒ The glue has dried and it's beginning to crack up: We are facing several serious marital problems.
   ⇒ The glue has dried and we're closer than ever: Life is not perfect, but we are committed to each other and our relationship is growing.
3. What changes can you make to improve the bond in your marriage?

A CLOSER LOOK:

(5:32) **Spiritual Union—Marriage**: Marriage is a spiritual union that can be wrought by God and by God alone. It is much more than two people merely agreeing to live together and to be loyal to one another. It is much more than natural affection or infatuation. It is much more than a mere piece of paper, more than a legal contract, more than bearing offspring. After all, animals do the same. Marriage, when it is brought together and honestly committed to God, is a totally unique union that is unlike any other relationship in life. When consummated by God and placed into the hands of God day by day, it is a *spiritual union* lifted ever so high and full of splendor and warmth and tenderness. It is the real experience of love and warmth and tenderness—the full preciousness and richness of sharing all with one another. In reality, a true marriage is indescribable. For a true marriage is a *spiritual experience* that is beyond anything known in the physical world. It is a spiritual union mutually experienced only by the couples who truly know the love of Christ for His church.

A true marriage is love (v.25). It is sacrificial love (v.25); a love for another person that is just as great as one's love for oneself (vv.28, 33). It is a love that cherishes (v.29).

A true marriage is a union (v.30). It is a union so completely and spiritually wrought that two persons become as one body and as one flesh (vv.30-31).

A true marriage is a mystery (v.32). It is a spiritual fact that has to be revealed by God if it is to be experienced by couples (v.32). It is a spiritual mystery that can be illustrated only by the great love Christ has for His church (vv.23-33).

Christ and His love are the symbolic example for the husband. The church and its love for Christ are the symbolic example for the wife. This picture says several practical things.

1. The Christian home is to be lived in the very presence and atmosphere of the Lord.
2. The Christian home is to be governed by the Lord. Its decisions are to be made in light of the Lord and His will.
3. The Christian home is not to have two partners, but three—husband, wife, and Christ.

ILLUSTRATION:

To whom are we to cleave? Only to each other? A great Christian marriage exists when both the man and the woman cleave to the Lord Jesus. Listen closely as this point is illustrated by Dr. Larry Crabb:

> *Consider what may really be happening when a couple gets married: Two people, each with personal needs pressing for fulfillment, pledge themselves to*

become one. As they recite their vows to love and respect each other, strong but hidden motivations stir inside them. If a tape recorder could somehow tune into the couple's unconscious intentions, I wonder if perhaps we would hear words like these:

Bridegroom: *I need to feel important and I expect you to meet that need by submitting to my every decision, whether good or bad; by respecting me no matter how I behave; and by supporting me in whatever I choose to do...My goal in marrying you is to find my significance through you. An arrangement in which you are commanded by God to submit to me sounds very attractive.*

Bride: *I have never felt as deeply loved as my nature requires. I am expecting you to meet that need through gentle affection even when I'm growling, thoughtful consideration whether I am always sensitive to you or not, and an accepting, romantic sensitivity to my emotional ups and downs. Don't let me down.*

A marriage bound together by commitments to exploit the other for filling one's own needs...can be legitimately described as a "tic on a dog" relationship...The rather frustrating dilemma, of course, is that in such a marriage there are two tics and no dog![3]

QUESTIONS:

1. As you think about your marriage, what are your biggest concerns? Are you and your spouse committed to work these out?
2. How meaningful is having a great Christian marriage to you? What is one thing that you can do to improve it today?
3. Why is it important to have a good Christian marriage?
4. What is the relationship between a Christian marriage and Jesus Christ and His Church? What is your role in both of these relationships?

SUMMARY:

When you say "I do" on your wedding day, you commit to a three-fold contract: You make an agreement with God, an agreement with your spouse, and an agreement with your community that your marriage would be for keeps. In review, a good Christian marriage becomes a reality when:

1. The wife walks in a spirit of submission.
2. The husband loves his wife like Christ loves the Church.

---

3 Dr. Lawrence J. Crabb, Jr. *The Marriage Builder.* (Grand Rapids, MI: Zondervan Publishing House, 1982), pp.31-32.

EPHESIANS 5:22-33

PERSONAL JOURNAL NOTES
(Reflection & Response)

1. The most important thing that I learned from this lesson was:

2. The area that I need to work on the most is:

3. I can apply this lesson to my life by:

4. Closing Statement of Commitment:

	CHAPTER 6 **I. Believing Children & Parents Are to Walk Under God's Authority, 6:1-4**	is the first commandment with promise;)	b. To obey is to honor 1) Assures the care of God 2) Assures long life
		3 That it may be well with thee, and thou mayest live long on the earth.	
		4 And, ye fathers, provoke not your children to wrath: but bring them up in the nurture and admonition of the Lord.	**2. Believing parents are not to provoke, exasperate their children, but to train them up in the Lord**
1. Believing children are to obey their parents a. To obey "in the Lord"	Children, obey your parents in the Lord: for this is right. 2 Honour thy father and mother; (which		

Section IV
THE WALK OF THE CHRISTIAN BELIEVER
Ephesians 4:1–6:9

Study 9: **BELIEVING CHILDREN AND PARENTS ARE TO WALK UNDER GOD'S AUTHORITY**

Text: **Ephesians 6:1-4**

Aim: To use God's model to construct your home.

Memory Verse:

"And ye fathers, provoke not your children to wrath: but bring them up in the nurture and admonition of the Lord" (Ephesians 6:4).

INTRODUCTION:

A strong, Christian family is God's design for the world. God wants every family to be strong and to be a follower of Him. God wants every family to be under His authority, under His care and protection, secure in His love. Day by day, the home is to be a place of safety where mistakes can be made and where love will cover a multitude of sins. How safe is your home?

Think for a moment: What happens in your home when someone spills his drink at the dining room table? Does everybody get uptight and make the offender of this "malicious" crime feel like crawling under the table in shame? One family decided to challenge this emotional event by agreeing together that accidents were simply a part of life. To prove the point in a graphic way, the mother put a table cloth on the table and slowly poured a glass of water on it. Her little child's eyes widened in disbelief! "Mom, you'll get in trouble. You'll get in trouble." She softly responded, "From now on, it's O.K. to make a mistake in our family. We are going to learn to love a lot more and yell a lot less."

Children are a gift from the Lord (Psalm 127:3). What does the Bible have to say about protecting this gift, God's gift of children? It is a crucial issue for every day and time. Every generation has its *problem children and problem parents*, and one of the major causes of the tension is the failure to heed the instructions of God's Word. Children and parents are to walk together under God's authority.

OUTLINE:

1. Believing children are to obey their parents (vv.1-3).
2. Believing parents are not to provoke, exasperate their children, but to train them up in the Lord (v.4).

1. BELIEVING CHILDREN ARE TO OBEY THEIR PARENTS (vv.1-3).

The word "obey" means to submit to; to comply with; to hearken; to heed; to follow the directions or guidance of some instruction. When a parent guides and directs a child, the child is to obey the parent. But what about the problems that are so repulsively evident in society: the problems of parental abuse—physical, sexual, and mental abuse? Is a child to obey a parent when the parent is so devilishly wrong? No! A thousand times no!

1. First, to obey here means to obey *in the Lord*. Note the command again: "Children, obey your parents *in the Lord*." The phrase "in the Lord" means at least two things.

   a. There is a limit to the child's obedience. When a parent is not acting in the Lord, he is not to be obeyed. The Lord has nothing whatsoever to do with the filth of unrighteousness and abuse of precious children. If a child can break away to free himself from such parental corruption, he has every right to be freed from his parent. The Lord came to set men free from the abuse and the filth of sin, not to enslave men to it, and especially not to enslave children to it.

   One of the most severe warnings ever issued in all of history was issued by the Lord Jesus to adults who abuse children:

   > **"And whosoever shall offend one of these little ones that believe in me, it is better for him that a millstone were hanged about his neck, and he were cast into the sea. And if thy hand offend thee [by abusing a child], cut it off: it is better for thee to enter into life maimed, than having two hands to go into hell, into the fire that never shall be quenched: where their worm dieth not, and the fire is not quenched. And if thy foot offend thee [by abusing a child], cut it off: it is better for thee to enter halt into life, than having two feet to be cast into hell, into the fire that never shall be quenched: where their worm dieth not, and the fire is not quenched. And if thine eye offend thee [by lusting after a child], pluck it out: it is better for thee to enter into the kingdom of God with one eye, than having two eyes to be cast into hell fire: where their worm dieth not, and the fire is not quenched" (Mk.9:42-48).**

   The abusing parent had better heed, for one of the things that God will not tolerate is the abuse of a child. We must proclaim the Word of God: children are to obey their parents, but they are to obey only if the parents' desire and instructions are *in the Lord*. If a parent is beating a child black and blue or sexually abusing a child, the child should go to some other adult to whom he feels close, asking for help. And as believers, we are called to proclaim Christ and to do what we can to bring His righteousness to earth.

   b. The phrase "in the Lord" also tells why the child is to obey his parents. "Children, obey your parents in the Lord"—obeying your parents is right; it is of the Lord; it pleases the Lord; therefore, obey them. When they guide and instruct you, follow them (see Co.3:20).

   Note the emphasis here; it is striking. Children are not told to obey parents because it pleases the parent, but because it pleases the Lord. Pleasing one's parents is, of course, a reason for obeying them. But the *first* reason for obeying parents is that it pleases the Lord. The child is to walk so closely to the Lord that his mind is constantly upon what he can do to please the Lord. When the child walks this closely with the Lord, then obeying his parents will become an automatic response.

"Children, obey your parents in all things: for this is well pleasing unto the Lord" (Co.3:20).

2. Second, to obey parents means to honor one's father and mother. The word "honor" means to "esteem and value as precious" (The Amplified New Testament); to show respect, reverence, kindness, courtesy, and obedience.[1] Scripture is not speaking to any certain age child. It is speaking to all of us who are children with parents still living. We are to honor our fathers and mothers: *to esteem and value them as precious*—to respect and reverence them. Tragically, this is a rarity today. Too often a child's response to his parent is that of...

- talking back
- cutting parent down
- ignoring
- grumbling
- disregarding the instruction
- speaking disrespectfully
- not listening
- acting like a "know it all
- calling the parent a *cute, but disrespectful name*
- putting off the instruction

In addition to these, there is the dishonor of delinquency, crime, drugs, alcohol, and the abuse of property; and the list could go on and on. And when it comes to adult children with aged parents, there is the dishonor of neglect, the ignoring of their needs and the shuffling of them to the side, failing to adequately care for them. Too many adult children forget how much their parents have done for them—bringing them into the world and taking care of them for years. Too many children forget the rich experience and knowledge that their parents have gained through the years that could be put to great use in meeting community and world needs. And even if the parents failed to be and to do all they should have, we as Christian children are instructed to honor them as followers of the Lord Jesus Christ.

"Children, obey your parents in the Lord: for this is right" (Ep.6:1).

"But if any widow have children or nephews, let them learn first to show piety at home, and to requite [repay, pay back] their parents: for that is good and acceptable before God....But if any provide not for his own, and specially for those of his own house, he hath denied the faith, and is worse than an infidel" (1 Ti.5:4, 8).

Note the two promises made to children who honor their parents.

⇒ Things will go well for the child. Does this mean that the child will never have problems or have to suffer? No! This is not what the Scripture means. God means that He will be with the child, strengthen and take care of him so that he can *walk through* the trials of life victoriously. The child will be strengthened and made strong *where it counts—in the inner man*. He will be enabled to conquer and be victorious over whatever confronts him as he journeys through life.

⇒ The child is assured that he will live a long life on earth. Frankly, there is little question but that Paul meant this and that we should take it for what it says. If a child honestly obeys and honors his parents faithfully, God will give him a long life on earth.

Is there ever an exception to this? What about small babies and children who are taken on to heaven? Does this violate the promise? No! If a child were really obedient, then all we can say is that God knows what is best, and for some reason God wanted the precious little life with Him now. God just could not wait for the fellowship and joy which the precious life would bring Him.

---

1 Kenneth Wuest. *Ephesians and Colossians*, Vol.1, p.136.

ILLUSTRATION:
How do you get a child to obey you? Parents have a choice either to threaten a child or to train a child to follow willingly. Unfortunately, a lot of us find it easier to threaten our children to obey. For example, let's take a look at a sports field as the little ones practice for the next big game.

"*If you don't pay attention to the game, I'm going to jerk you off the field*!" shouted the coach. He was a pretty intense fellow who hated to lose. In fact, he refused to lose. His philosophy in life was pretty simple: drive people into the ground by yelling at them. Name-calling was a valid part of the menu.

During one of these intense practices, seven year old Andy could not take any more. He was doing the best he could, he really was, but it was not enough to please the coach. "*Be a leader or get out of the way!" the coach yelled. After another verbal barrage, Andy left the field, straining so the tears would not gush out. "I'm no good...I'm a failure...I'll never amount to anything, ever.*"

What Andy did not understand was that the negative messages he had heard were lies. Unfortunately, he grew up with a view that equated being yelled at with obedience. How many "Andy's" do you know?

We need to remember the truth of these proverbs:

"A soft answer turneth away wrath: but grievous words stir up anger" (Pr.15:1).

"Pleasant words are as an honeycomb, sweet to the soul, and health to the bones" (Pr.16:24).

"Death and life are in the power of the tongue: and they that love it shall eat the fruit thereof" (Pr.18:21).

QUESTIONS:
1. What can parents do to teach their children obedience?
2. What can parents do to teach their children to honor adults?
3. What are some things parents are guilty of that cause disobedience and lack of respect?
4. Was there a time when you were verbally abused or witnessed verbal abuse? How did getting yelled at make you feel?
5. Do you worry about verbally abusing your children? What can you do to guard your mouth?

2. BELIEVING PARENTS ARE NOT TO PROVOKE, EXASPERATE THEIR CHILDREN, BUT TO TRAIN THEM UP IN THE LORD (v.4).

Parents are bound to upset and irritate their children sometimes; we are human. Discipline, correction, and reproof are seldom enjoyable experiences. Their very nature is that of disturbance and irritation. This is not what this instruction means. The word "provoke" means to arouse to wrath or anger, to provoke to the point of utter exasperation and resentment. Note two significant discussions.

1. Four things will provoke a child.
   a. Failing to accept the fact that things do change will provoke a child. Time and generations do change. This does not mean that a child should participate nor be allowed to do everything that his generation does. But it does mean that parents need to be alert to the changes between generations, allowing the child to be a part of his own generation instead of trying to conform the child to the parent's childhood generation. The parent's childhood generation does not exist now nor will it ever exist again.

What changes should and should not be allowed by a Christian parent? Three words provide a good guideline: *rebellion*, *immorality*, and *injustice*. Open defiance or resistance to authority and immorality and injustice are contrary to God's Word. Any change that involves rebellion, immorality, or injustice needs to be dealt with and controlled by the parent. We are probably safe to say that any change not involving one of these areas should be allowed. Whether true or not, these three areas provide a good practical guideline.

The point is this: a parent must not resist normal and natural change that takes place between generations. If he resists, forbidding his child to grow up in his own generation, the parent is asking for trouble. Most likely the child will be provoked to wrath—to react.

b. Overcontrolling a child will also provoke a child to wrath. Overcontrol ranges all the way from stern restriction and discipline to child abuse. Disciplining and restricting a child *too much* will either stifle the growth of a child or stir him to react and rebel, causing the child to flee from the parent. What is too much discipline? How much should a child be restricted? Should he be allowed to do everything he wants? No! There is a limit, and the limit must be placed upon the child; discipline must be exercised when the limit is crossed. What Christian parents need to remember is this:

⇒ *Some parents allow their children* to participate in every function and activity offered to the child. They are usually the ones without *proper parental* guidance.

The point is this: there must be a balance between family life and the child's community life. The child should be allowed to do his own thing sometime and should be required to share with the family at other times. As he grows older, he should, of course, be allowed to break away from the family more and more in order to prepare him for the day when he will step out into the world on his own. A child needs free time away from the parent and family as well as some family time in order to grow into a healthy person.

"Fathers, provoke not your children to anger, lest they be discouraged" (Co.3:21).

c. Undercontrolling a child can provoke a child. It should be noted that this is the most prevalent problem in an industrialized society. There is a tendency for those with plenty or with wealth to pamper, indulge, and give a child everything imaginable—well beyond what a child needs and what is really best for him. Parents pamper and indulge a child—give in to a child—for five reasons:

⇒ A parents pampers and indulges a child—gives in to a child—*in order to escape responsibility for the child*: to keep a child from interrupting the parents' time or schedule or desires; to get a child out from under the parents' feet. The parent, of course, needs some free time; but too many parents live selfishly, wanting nothing interfering with their own desires and needs. Too many parents push their children out and away, allowing their children to run around too much. Too few sacrifice their own time and desires to look after their children as much as they should.

⇒ A parents pampers and indulges a child—gives in to a child—*in order to gain social standing or to relive his own childhood.* The parent did not have and was not allowed to do what he wanted as a child; therefore, he sees to it that his child has everything and does everything that everyone else does. He is determined that his child will have everything no matter what it costs.

- ⇒ A parents pampers and indulges a child—gives in to a child—*because he has a false understanding or philosophy of child-rearing*. He gives in to ill behavior, whining, pouting, sulkiness, and temper tantrums just to secure peace and quiet.
- ⇒ A parents pampers and indulges a child—gives in to a child—*because of misguided devotion and love*: to keep from losing the loyalty, quietness, cooperativeness, and affection of the child.
- ⇒ A parents pampers and indulges a child—gives in to a child—*because of insecurity and lack of purpose*. For example, some pamper and cling to a child because they (the parents) are insecure in the world. Others cling and pamper because they lack any other purpose. The child fills the need for security and purpose. *Playing house* is lived to the limit: the parent plays house with his child, clinging and pampering to the limit.

"Chasten thy son while there is hope, and let not thy soul spare for his crying" (Pr.19:18).

"Foolishness is bound in the heart of a child; but the rod of correction shall drive it far from him" (Pr.22:15).

d. Living an inconsistent life before a child can provoke a child. A parent who tells a child one thing and then turns around and does the opposite thing himself is full of hypocrisy and false profession. Yet, how common! How many children are doing things because their parents are doing them:

- ⇒ drinking alcohol
- ⇒ taking drugs
- ⇒ watching sexual scenes on television or movies
- ⇒ reading immoral stories
- ⇒ looking at magazines exposing the human body
- ⇒ eating too much
- ⇒ wasting time
- ⇒ dressing or exposing the body to attract attention
- ⇒ attending socials or parties that are loose on decency, morality, marital faithfulness, and on and on

Seeing an inconsistent life in a parent can provoke children.

"And he did evil in the sight of the LORD, and walked in the way of his father, and in the way of his mother, and in the way of Jeroboam the son of Nebat, who made Israel to sin" (1 K.22:52).

2. A parent is to bring up a child in the ways of the Lord, in the nurture and admonition of the Lord.

- ⇒ The word "nurture" means "the whole training and education of children which [involves]...the cultivation of mind and morals...commands and admonitions...reproof and punishment...correcting mistakes and curbing the passions...the increase of virtue" (Thayers Greek - English Lexicon).
- ⇒ The word "admonition" means counsel, exhortation, correction.

Note that the parent is not to rear the child after his own ideas and notions of what is best for the child, but after the nurture and admonition *of the Lord*. The Lord's Word is to be the guide for Christian parents in rearing their child. The benefits in bringing up a child in the Lord are innumerable. Just a few are as follows:

a. A child who is brought to Christ grows up learning love: that he is loved by God and by all who trust God. He grows no matter how evil some may act, knowing that he is to love even those who do wrong.
b. A child who is brought to Christ grows up learning power and triumph: that God will help His followers through all; that there is a supernatural power available to help, a power to help when mother and dad and loved ones have done all they can.
c. A child who is brought to Christ grows up learning hope and faith: that no matter what happens, no matter how great a trial, we can still trust God and hope in Him. He has provided a very special strength to carry us through the trials of this life (no matter how painful); that He has provided a very special place called heaven where He will carry us and our loved ones when we face death.
d. A child who is brought to Christ grows up learning the truth of life and endurance (service): that God has given us the privilege of life, of living in a beautiful earth and universe; that the evil and bad which exist in the world are caused by evil and bad people; that despite such evil, we are to serve in appreciation for life and the beautiful earth upon which God has placed us. We are to work diligently, making the greatest contribution we can.
e. A child who is brought to Christ grows up learning trust and endurance: that life is full of temptations and pitfalls which can easily rob us of joy, destroying our lives and the fulfillment of our purposes; that the way to escape the temptations and pitfalls is to follow Christ, to endure in our work and purpose.
f. A child who is brought to Christ grows up learning peace: that there is an inner peace despite the turbulent waters of this world, that peace is knowing and trusting Christ.

> **"And these words, which I command thee this day, shall be in thine heart: and thou shalt teach them diligently unto thy children, and shalt talk of them when thou sittest in thine house, and when thou walkest by the way, and when thou liest down, and when thou risest up" (De.6:6-7).**

ILLUSTRATION:
Practically speaking, how are parents to bring their children up in the nurture and admonition of the Lord? "How To" books are helpful but are lacking. Material gifts fail to work. The only way Christian parents can obey this verse is to actively build a *relationship* with their children. Christian child psychologist, Dr. James Dobson, shares a story from his childhood with us:

> *My dad and I would arise before the sun came up on a wintry morning. We would put on our hunting clothes and heavy boots and drive twenty miles from the little town where we lived. After parking the car and climbing over a fence, we would enter a wooded area, which I called the "big woods" because the trees seemed so large to me. We would slip down to the creek bed and follow that winding stream several miles back into the forest.*
>
> *Then my dad would hide me under a fallen tree, which made a little room with its branches. He would find a similar shelter for himself around a bend in the creek. Then we would await the arrival of the sun and the awakening of the animal world. Little squirrels and birds and chipmunks would scurry back and forth, not knowing they were being observed. My dad and I then watched as the breathtaking panorama of the morning unfolded, which spoke so eloquently of the God who made all things.*

But most importantly, there was something dramatic that occurred between my dad and me out there in the forest. An intense love and affection was generated on those mornings that set the tone for a lifetime of fellowship. There was a closeness and a oneness that made me want to be like that man...that made me choose his values as my values, his dreams as my dreams, his God as my God.[2]

Are you making memories that are nurturing?

QUESTIONS:

1. What are some ways you provoke your children? Or how do your parents provoke you?
2. In what ways do you tend to be inconsistent when you discipline your children? What steps do you need to take in order to be more consistent?
3. What sort of nurturing things do you do for your children? Do you think it is possible to do even more?
4. How does this verse help you know how to raise your children?
5. Have your children come to a saving knowledge of Jesus Christ? If not yet, what kinds of things can you do to bring them to Christ?

SUMMARY:

Whether you are a parent, a child, or both, God's simple instructions for you and the believing family are this:

1. Believing children are to obey their parents.
2. Believing parents are not to provoke, exasperate their children, but to train them up in the Lord.

PERSONAL JOURNAL NOTES (Reflection & Response)

1. The most important thing that I learned from this lesson was:

2. The area that I need to work on the most is:

3. I can apply this lesson to my life by:

4. Closing Statement of Commitment:

---

2 Rolf Zettersten. *Dr. Dobson: Turning Hearts Toward Home.* (Dallas, TX: Word Publishing, 1989), pp.25-26.

	J. Believing Slaves and Masters (Employers—Employees) are to Walk Under God's Authority, 6:5-9	heart; 7 With good will doing service, as to the Lord, and not to men: 8 Knowing that whatsoever good thing any man doeth, the	Christ—doing the will of God e. With good will—for the employer f. Result: Will be rewarded by the Lord
1. The workman: To obey a. With respect & fear b. In sincerity of heart—as if it were Christ c. Not with eyeservice, only when they are watching—as menpleasers d. As the servants of	5 Servants, be obedient to them that are your masters according to the flesh, with fear and trembling, in singleness of your heart, as unto Christ; 6 Not with eyeservice, as menpleasers; but as the servants of Christ, doing the will of God from the	same shall he receive of the Lord, whether he be bond or free. 9 And, ye masters, do the same things unto them, forbearing threatening: knowing that your Master also is in heaven; neither is there respect of persons with him.	**2. The employer: To obey** a. Is to do the same things as the Christian workman b. Is not to threaten c. The reason: God is his master & is going to judge everyone

Section IV
THE WALK OF THE CHRISTIAN BELIEVER
Ephesians 4:1–6:9

Study 10: **BELIEVING SLAVES AND MASTERS (EMPLOYEES—EMPLOYERS) ARE TO WALK UNDER GOD'S AUTHORITY**

Text: **Ephesians 6:5-9**

Aim: To carry godly standards into the workplace.

Memory Verse:

"With good will doing service, as to the Lord, and not to men" (Ephesians 6:7).

INTRODUCTION:

Why do you work? Have you ever taken the time to think that question through? Chuck Colson and Jack Eckerd share this story with us from their book, *Why America Doesn't Work*:

> *The story is told of a man who visited a stone quarry and asked three of the workers what they were doing. "Can't you see?" said the first one irritably. "I'm cutting a stone."*
>
> *The second replied, "I'm earning a hundred pounds a week." But the third put down his pick and thrust out his chest proudly. "I'm building a cathedral," he said.*
>
> *People view work in many ways: as a necessary evil to keep bread on the table; as a means to a sizable bank account; as self-fulfillment and identity; as an economic obligation within society; as a means to a life of leisure."*[1]

---

1 Charles Colson and Jack Eckerd. *Why America Doesn't Work.* (Dallas, TX: Word Publishing, 1991), pp.177-178.

Why do *you* work? Is it just a routine, an unwelcome obligation? Is that all there is to life? Or is there a deeper meaning and purpose that gives your work real significance?

This passage points out in strong terms what the world's problem really is. It is not an economic problem; it is a spiritual problem. Hunger and economic relationships between individuals and nations can only be solved when men turn to the Lord Jesus Christ. He is Lord, and when men serve Him as Lord, they serve Him in all they do. This means they work for Him; and in working for Him, they work not only to provide for themselves, but also to secure enough to give to others (Ep.4:29). They work and partake of the fruits of their labor; then they give to others. Such is the will of God for every man and for the world which He made. But remember what it is that stirs men to live such sacrificial lives: Christ—commitment to Him.

The instructions to slaves and masters in the New Testament are applicable to every generation of workman. As Francis Foulkes says, "*...the principles of the whole section apply to employees and employers in every age, whether in the home, in business, or in the state.*"[2]

OUTLINE:

1. The workman: to obey (vv.5-8).
2. The employer: to obey (v.9).

1. THE WORKMAN: TO OBEY (vv.5-8).

The workman is to obey; that is, he is to follow the instructions of the employer. Note the phrase "according to the flesh." This means that employers are to be obeyed in matters involving the workplace. The employer has no authority in the spiritual realm. That authority belongs to Christ and to Christ alone. Six specific instructions are given to the Christian workman.

1. The Christian workman is to work with fear and trembling, but not the fear of a superior nor the trembling that something unpleasant might happen. The Christian workman...

- is to fear and tremble before God lest he perform some irresponsible work that brings reproach upon his Lord's name
- is to respect and be eager to serve his employer

> **"And his mercy is on them that fear him from generation to generation" (Lu.1:50).**

2. The Christian workman is to work in singleness of heart, as to Christ. "Singleness of heart" means with purpose and focused attention, in sincerity and without any pretense or hypocrisy or slack. It means that the workman is totally committed to his work. He does his job and does it well. And note why: because he offers his labor *to the Lord*.

> **"For ye are bought with a price: therefore glorify God in your body, and in your spirit, which are God's" (1 Co.6:20).**

3. The Christian workman is not to work with eyeservice as a manpleaser. He is not to work just when the boss is looking. There are those who slow down when the boss is not looking and speed up when the boss is looking. They are guilty of seeking favor they do not deserve. Such standards rob labor of its dignity and bring ill repute to the

---

2 Francis Foulkes. *The Epistle of Paul to the Ephesians*, p.167.

name of Christ. When a man returns home from a day's work, there is only one question to ask: Has he pleased his Lord?

> **"For they loved the praise of men more than the praise of God" (Jn.12:43).**

4. The Christian workman is to work as the servant of Christ doing the will of God *from his heart*. "From the heart" means with interest and energy. It is the opposite of routineness and listlessness, of having no energy or heart for the work. The Christian workman must always remember this: even if the boss is not looking, Christ sees what kind of work he is doing. Therefore, he must work as though he is working for Christ. He must work...

- to serve Christ
- to do the will of God
- to do both *from the heart*

> **"Wherefore we receiving a kingdom which cannot be moved, let us have grace, whereby we may serve God acceptable with reverence and godly fear" (He.12:28).**

5. The Christian workman is to work *with good will*, and he must do it as to the Lord and not to men. It could be stated no clearer: the Christian workman serves the Lord, not other men. No matter where he works and no matter what he does—if it is not immoral or unjust labor—the Christian workman is to work diligently. He is to work as though his boss were the Lord Jesus Christ, and not man.

> **"Therefore, my beloved brethren, be ye stedfast, unmoveable, always abounding in the work of the Lord, forasmuch as ye know that your labour is not in vain in the Lord" (1 Co.15:58).**

6. The result of such diligent labor is to be a *reciprocal reward*. The Lord is going to give the Christian workman *exactly* what he labored for, no more and no less. There is no respect of persons with God. Everyone is going to get exactly what he has labored for upon this earth...

- regardless of his profession
- regardless of his wealth
- regardless of his position
- regardless of his poverty

A person may have been honest or dishonest, a good or poor workman, a white-collar or blue-collar workman, a professional or laborer, a business man or workman, disabled or gifted—it matters not. Everyone is going to receive from God exactly what he has put into his day-to-day work. If he has diligently worked as though he were working for Christ, he will be abundantly rewarded. If he has been working for men and for self, he will go the way of all men and end up eternally lost. If he has been sometimes slack and sometimes diligent, then he is going to receive a piecemeal reward. "Whatsoever good thing any man does, the same shall he receive of the Lord."

> **"For we must all appear before the judgment seat of Christ; that every one may receive the things done in his body, according to that he hath done, whether it be good or bad" (2 Co.5:10).**

ILLUSTRATION:

Is a Christian's work supposed to be below the world's standard? Of course not, but many Christians work like they believe it to be true. Our witness will have absolutely no validity if we are not good workers.

Anatoly is a Russian Christian whose greatest witness was his work ethic. He always made it a point to go beyond the expectations of his supervisors and fellow peers. Over the course of his career, God also saw his faithfulness and promoted him into positions of greater responsibility. Because of his position as a crane operator, Anatoly was able to provide a pleasant home for his family as well as send his children to quality schools.

One day an American Christian spent a typical day with Anatoly and was amazed at how hard Anatoly worked. At the end of the day, the American asked: "Anatoly, you are no longer a young man, and you have a secure position; yet you work harder than you have to work. Why?"

With a puzzled look that appeared to be searching for an English translation, Anatoly said, "I work for God—aren't Christians supposed to work harder?"

"And whatever you do, do it heartily, as to the Lord, and not unto men" (Co.3:23).

For whom and what are you working?

QUESTIONS:

1. What happens—what are some natural results—when a Christian believer works for the Lord and not for men? Why do you think God wants you to work for Him and not for men?
2. What do you think your role is as a witness at your job? Do you worry about pleasing men more than God? Why?
3. Why are some Christians not good workers? What attitudes do they need to change? Are you comfortable with your work ethic? What can you do to be a better worker?

2. THE EMPLOYER: TO OBEY (v.9)

The employer or manager is given two clear commandments governing how he is to treat the workmen under him.

1. The manager is to do the very same things that are required of the workman. He is to treat the workman just like he expects the workman to treat him. (What a difference this would make in labor-management relations if it were really practiced by both parties!)

The manager or employer must realize that he lives and works...

- to serve both the Lord and the employees with fear and trembling, that is, managing with respect and eager concern (The Amplified New Testament).
- to serve in singleness of heart, managing *as to Christ*.
- to serve not with eye-service, as menpleasers.
- to serve as the servants of Christ, managing and doing the will of Christ from the heart.
- to serve with good will, managing as to the Lord, and not to men.
- to serve knowing that he is to receive a reciprocal reward for how well he managed.

The employer or manager expects at least two things from his workmen: diligence and loyalty. The charge to the employer is the same: be diligent in your management and in your loyalty to the workmen under you. Demonstrate your loyalty with fair wages and job security.

2. The manager is to forbear threats. This does not mean a workman cannot be corrected or released if he is not diligent and loyal. God does not encourage slothfulness nor license nor indulgence. God chastens and disciplines when needed. But note: stern

measures are taken only after all other corrective measures have been taken. Every person—no matter how unproductive—is worth saving and developing into a conscientious workman if possible. He is a fellow human being who is on earth with the rest of us, and as long as he is on earth, God will continue to reach out to him. Therefore, he is worth reaching if we can. For this reason alone, every step should be taken to reach and train even the most unproductive workman.

The point is this: employers and managers must guard against unwarranted threats, for they too have a Master in heaven, and He has no favorites. As employers and managers, we hold every workman accountable to us; so the Lord holds us accountable to Him. Therefore, threats should always be issued courteously and carefully.

> **"Masters, give unto your servants that which is just and equal; knowing that ye also have a Master in heaven" (Co.4:1).**
>
> **"And I will come near to you to judgment; and I will be a swift witness against the sorcerers, and against the adulterers, and against false swearers, and against those that oppress the hireling [the hired workman] in his wages, the widow, and the fatherless, and that turn aside the stranger from his right, and fear not me, saith the LORD of hosts" (Mal.3:5).**

APPLICATION:

Everyone who works either has an employer or is an employer. From a Christian believer's viewpoint, we should be able to expect the same qualities from either position:

⇒ hard work
⇒ fairness
⇒ loyalty
⇒ honesty
⇒ accountability

Think how the world would change if all levels of workers from the common laborer to upper management were to work and serve as if God were their boss!

QUESTIONS:

1. How will an understanding of this verse make you a better worker? What steps do you need to take to become a better employer or worker?
2. Is it easier for you to "push people around" in order to get things done? What are some things you can do in order to be a better leader?
3. As you think about your job, what are your biggest concerns? Do you think your attitude needs to change? What do you think you can do to improve your work environment?

SUMMARY:

Why do we work? We have learned that there is a whole lot more to work than just picking up a paycheck. God has placed each of us in a particular work place to make Christianity practical to the unchurched. Listen to this challenge from J. Vernon McGee:

> *Don't tell me Christianity is not practical. It is practical, and it will work. A great Chinese Christian, who had attended college here in the United States and knew America pretty well said, "It is not that in America Christianity has been tried and found wanting. The problem over there is it never has been tried." That*

is still the problem today—we have kept [Christianity] behind stained glass windows. My friend, if Christianity cannot move out of the sanctuary and get down into the secular, there is something radically wrong. It will work *if it is tried.*[3]

1. The workman must obey.
2. The employer must obey.

Your place of work will never be the same again if the workman and employer work under God's authority.

PERSONAL JOURNAL NOTES
(Reflection & Response)

1. The most important thing that I learned from this lesson was:

2. The area that I need to work on the most is:

3. I can apply this lesson to my life by:

4. Closing Statement of Commitment:

[3] J. Vernon McGee. *Thru The Bible, Vol 5.* (Nashville, TN: Thomas Nelson, 1983), p.276.

V. THE WARFARE OF THE CHRISTIAN BELIEVER, 6:10-24

A. The Armor of the Christian Soldier, 6:10-20

1. The soldier's charge a. Be strong in the Lord—in His mighty power	10 Finally, my brethren, be strong in the Lord, and in the power of his might.
b. Put on the full armor of God **2. The soldier's enemy: The devil & his strategies**	11 Put on the whole armor of God, that ye may be able to stand against the wiles of the devil.
3. The soldier's warfare: Not a human struggle but a spiritual struggle	12 For we wrestle not against flesh and blood, but against principalities, against powers, against the rulers of the darkness of this world, against spiritual wickedness in high places.
4. The soldier's duty: To take the full armor of God a. That he may resist in the day of evil b. That he may stand	13 Wherefore take unto you the whole armor of God, that ye may be able to withstand in the evil day, and having done all, to stand.
5. The soldier's armor a. The belt of truth b. The breastplate of righteousness	14 Stand therefore, having your loins girt about with truth, and having on the breastplate of righteousness;
c. The sandals of the gospel	15 And your feet shod with the preparation of the gospel of peace;
d. The shield of faith	16 Above all, taking the shield of faith, wherewith ye shall be able to quench all the fiery darts of the wicked.
e. The helmet of salvation f. The sword of the Spirit, the Word of God	17 And take the helmet of salvation, and the sword of the Spirit, which is the word of God:
6. The supernatural provision: Prayer—always praying a. With all kinds of prayer b. In the Spirit c. Being alert d. For all saints & for ministers in particular	18 Praying always with all prayer and supplication in the Spirit, and watching thereunto with all perseverance and supplication for all saints; 19 And for me, that utterance may be given unto me, that I may open my mouth boldly, to make known the mystery of the gospel, 20 For which I am an ambassador in bonds: that therein I may speak boldly, as I ought to speak.

Section V
THE WARFARE OF THE CHRISTIAN BELIEVER
Ephesians 6:10-24

Study 1: **THE ARMOR OF THE CHRISTIAN SOLDIER**

Text: **Ephesians 6:10-20**

Aim: To prepare yourself—the Christian soldier—for spiritual warfare.

Memory Verse:

> **"Put on the whole armor of God, that ye may be able to stand against the wiles of the devil" (Ephesians 6:11).**

INTRODUCTION:

On December 7, 1941, the United States was attacked by a surprising blow from Japanese military forces. President Roosevelt called it a "Day of Infamy." The world found itself at war as nations prepared to send their armies into battle. World War II finally ended years later at a great cost to life and property. The world would never again be the same.

But has man learned from history? Learned how to prevent wars? No, history books are filled with wars and rumors of wars. The fact is, war between men is inevitable, and it will be until Jesus returns.

As bad as World War II was, there was an even greater day of infamy many years ago. Satan, in all of his deceptive cunning, convinced Adam and Eve to sin, breaking their fellowship with God. Upon their choice to sin, mankind reeled in suffering.

There are many today who act like this war is over. They do not believe that the devil is real. They do not take the time to put on the armor of God. They do not know how to be strong in the Lord and in the power of His might.

This section of Scripture is a call to arms. To those who rest in the comforts and security of this world, this passage is a shock, an abrupt shock.

Paul has been discussing the believer's walk (Ep.4:1-6:9). Now suddenly he jolts the reader and hearer; he changes course. He says there is another way to look at the believer's life in Christ. The believer's life is a battlefield. Immediately upon receiving Christ, the believer finds himself in a constant struggle. He is engaged in an unceasing fight, an unending war. He is a combatant, a soldier in conflict. His calling is not to a life of enjoyment and ease but to a life of hard conflict. There are foes within and foes without. From the cradle to the grave, there is a constant struggle against the lusts of the flesh and the temptations offered by the world and Satan—a struggle against corruption that leads to a sure death (Ro.7:21; Ga.5:17; 6:8; Ep.4:22[b]; 6:10).

OUTLINE:

1. The soldier's charge (vv.10-11).
2. The soldier's enemy: the devil and his strategies (v.11).
3. The soldier's warfare: not a human struggle but a spiritual struggle (v.12).
4. The soldier's duty: to take the full armor of God (v.13).
5. The soldier's armor (vv.14-17).
6. The supernatural provision: prayer—always praying (vv.18-20).

1. THE SOLDIER'S CHARGE (vv.10-11).

Note the word "brothers." It is Christian believers who need the charge, the instructions, not the world. Christian believers must diligently heed what is about to be said. There is no other way to conquer the enemies who stand so violently opposed to the Christian believer. Unless the believer heeds the charge and message of this passage, he will cave in to temptation and sin and end up walking through life just as most men do:

⇒ not experiencing the abundance and joy of life.
⇒ not experiencing the power and deliverance, care and concern, love and fellowship of God's daily presence.
⇒ being uncertain and unsure of the future.
⇒ not having the confidence of being acceptable to God.
⇒ not being assured of living forever with God.

A believer must heed what God says in this passage; he must do exactly what God says in order to conquer the great enemies of life. The charge is twofold.

1. The believer must *be strong in the Lord and in the power of His might*. Note the stress upon power and strength. Three different words are used:

⇒ be *strong*
⇒ in the Lord's *power*
⇒ in the Lord's *might*

The believer is to be strong in the sovereign, unlimited power of the Lord—in the power of His might—in His ability to use His power exactly as it should be used.

But note the critical point: the believer's strength is not human, fleshly strength; it is not the strength of anything within this world. The believer's strength is found *in the Lord*—in a living, dynamic relationship with Him. The Lord is the source of the believer's strength. There is no other source that can give man the strength to overcome this world with all its trials and temptations and death.

2. The believer must *put on the armor of God*. Once the believer is *strong within*, then he is ready to be clothed with the armor of God. But note: no amount of armor is worth the material it is made of unless the soldier has the heart to fight. The believer must—absolutely must—be strong in the Lord before he can be clothed with the armor of God and wage war against the foes of life. Once a man has the presence and power of God within his heart, it is then that he begins to arm himself to wage war against the spiritual enemies of life. But note a most critical point: he must put on the *whole armor* of God, leaving nothing out. If he leaves a piece of the armor off, he exposes himself to the enemy and stands a good chance of being wounded, perhaps killed.

The charge is to be *strong in the Lord, in the power of His might. Put on the* whole armor of God.

> **"That he would grant you, according to the riches of his glory, to be strengthened with might by his Spirit in the inner man" (Ep.3:16).**
>
> **"Now unto him that is able to do exceeding abundantly above all that we ask or think, according to the power that worketh in us" (Ep.3:20).**

QUESTIONS:

1. How does this verse prepare you for spiritual warfare?
2. Does knowing that you have the Lord's power in your life help you overcome Satan's tricks? How?
3. Have you ever failed to depend upon the Lord's power and might? What is an example? How would you handle it differently now?
4. How will you know that you are strong in the Lord?

2. THE SOLDIER'S ENEMY: THE DEVIL AND HIS STRATEGIES (v.11).

The word "wiles" means the deceits, craftiness, trickery, methods, and strategies which the devil uses to wage war against the believer. He will do everything he can to deceive and capture the believer.

1. There are the strategies that appeal to the lust of the eyes. Satan will see to it that something crosses the eyesight of the believer, something that is very appealing to the flesh and pride of life:

⇒ some delicious food
⇒ some attractive person
⇒ some person who is exposing the body
⇒ some possession: clothing, land, cars, houses, whatever
⇒ some position, authority, or power

Satan will present something to the eyes that is so appealing, the believer is doomed unless he is clothed in the *full armor* of God. Satan will entice the believer to eat the second helping, take the second look, buy the unneeded possession, or begin to selfishly seek more power and more position. He will use all the strategies he can to appeal to the flesh and pride of the believer.

> **"Ye are of your father the devil, and the lusts of your father ye will do. He was a murderer from the beginning, and abode not in the truth, because there is no truth in him. When he speaketh a lie, he speaketh of his own: for he is a liar, and the father of it" (Jn.8:44).**

2. Another strategy of the devil is to send a false teacher, a very impressive teacher, across the path of the believer. We must never forget that Satan is not a fiery red figure with horns, a pointed tail, and a pitch fork in his hands. He is a living being in the spiritual world—a being who is transformed into a *messenger of light*. And he has ministers who walk about as ministers of righteousness, but they proclaim a righteousness other than that of Christ. Their message is that of self-righteousness, that of...

- human goodness and works
- ego and self-image
- personal development and growth
- self-improvement and correction
- mind and will

Such messages appeal to the flesh of man, and they are helpful. This must be realized and acknowledged, but such messages are not the basic power needed by man. They cannot deliver man *from* the great trials and sufferings of life or death. They can only lead man down the path of all flesh—that of death, decay, and eternal judgment.

The point is this: one of the most prominent strategies of the devil is to deceive man with false teachers and ministers and their appealing but false messages. The believer is doomed unless he is clothed in the *full armor* of God.

> **"Lest Satan should get an advantage of us: for we are not ignorant of his devices" (2 Co.2:11).**

ILLUSTRATION:

How often do you attempt to fight off the devil in your own strength? How many times have you won?

> *A little Christian [girl] was once asked if Satan [ever tempted] her to do wrong things and how she kept from doing them.*
>
> *The answer was: "Yes, I know he wants to get me, but when Satan knocks at the door of my heart I just say, 'Jesus, won't You go to the door?' and when Satan sees Jesus, he runs away every time."*
>
> *The strongest man that ever lived is not strong enough to meet Satan alone!!*[1]

QUESTIONS:

1. The devil is just like a fisherman: he has a variety of lures to hook his catch. What lures does he use to hook and catch you?
2. What sort of attitude should you have when you meet a new teacher? Is it possible to tell if a teacher is false? How?
3. Do you think it is possible for you to fall into the clutches of a false teacher? Why or why not?
4. How does this verse drive home the point that Satan deceives? How can you guard against this happening to you?

---

1 *S.S. Quarterly.* Walter B. Knight. *3,000 Illustrations for Christian Service*, p.234.

3. THE SOLDIER'S WARFARE: NOT A HUMAN STRUGGLE BUT A SPIRITUAL STRUGGLE (v.12).

Kenneth Wuest has a descriptive picture of the believer's great spiritual struggle:

> *In the word "wrestle," Paul uses a Greek athletic term....When we consider that the loser in a Greek wrestling contest had his eyes gouged out with resulting blindness for the rest of his days, we can form some conception of the Ephesian Greek's reaction to Paul's illustration. The Christian's wrestling against the powers of darkness is no less desperate and fateful.*[2]

The point to see is that the believer's struggle is not against flesh and blood. His foes are not human or physical; they are spiritual—spiritual forces that possess unbelievable power. Note exactly what is said: the believer fights...

- against principalities
- against power
- against the rulers of darkness
- against spiritual wickedness

This reveals some very clear things to us.

1. *The forces of evil are powerful forces.* The thrust of this verse is to stress the enormous power of evil forces which stand against the believer.
2. *The forces of evil are numerous.* Principalities, powers, rulers—all convey the idea of a large number of evil forces who are struggling against the believer.
3. *The forces of evil are apparently organized into a government or a hierarchy of evil.* Again, principalities, powers and rulers of this world in high places—all point toward a ranking of spiritual forces with enormous authority, position, and rule.
4. *The forces of evil are the rulers of the darkness of this world.* Darkness in the Bible means the ignorance of truth and reality, of the real nature and purpose of things. For example...
    - What is the source of man and his world?
    - Where have man and his world come from?
    - What is the purpose of man and his world? Why are man and his world existing?
    - What is the end of man and his world? Is there even a place to go after this life—another world, another life?

Darkness is not knowing these things; it is being ignorant of them. Light is knowing God and His Son, Jesus Christ—that God and Christ stand as the Source and Purpose and end of man and his world. Light is knowing the truth and reality of man and his world: that God created all for Himself, that He loves and saves all to live with Him eternally—if we will only believe and trust Him.

The forces of evil are the rulers of darkness, the rulers who blind the minds of men lest they believe the glorious gospel of eternal salvation.

5. *The forces of evil are spiritual forces of wickedness.* They seek to receive the loyalty and devotion that is due God. Therefore, they are after the spirit of man—that part of man that is destined to worship and serve God and exist forever. If they can capture the spirit of man, they have him eternally—his life and presence forever and ever. Therefore, they do all they can to lead *man's spirit* into wickedness. They are the *spiritual forces of wickedness.*

---

2 Kenneth Wuest. *Ephesians and Colossians,* Vol.1, p.141.

APPLICATION:

Some people scoff at the idea of a personal devil or demons who actually exist in a so-called spiritual world. They feel they are too educated and intelligent to believe such nonsense. They proclaim that such ideas are outdated and belong to the dark ages. But note a significant fact: man is ever so conscious of what he terms…

- *sub-conscious horrors* that affect both his mind and body
- *unseen and uncontrollable forces* that greatly affect his behavior
- *unregulated behavior* that he cannot control even when he knows better and wills to do differently
- *cosmic forces* that affect and determine his behavior
- *blind fate* that controls his life like a puppet

Think for a moment and be honest. Think of all the wickedness and evil and wrong-doing and selfishness in the world—all the…

- division
- prejudice
- favoritism
- anger
- hate
- pride
- war
- killing
- arguing
- selfishness
- immorality
- arrogance
- stealing
- lying
- cursing
- bitterness

The list could go on and on. The evil of man consumes the news reports every day. Just think about it! Don't we know better? Don't enough of us know better that we could change things? Yes, we do. Why then don't we change the world? This passage tells us why:

> **"For we wrestle not against flesh and blood, but against principalities, against powers, against the rulers of the darkness of this world, against spiritual wickedness in high places" (Ep.6:12).**

God—because He is God—has to tell us the truth. He cannot do otherwise. Therefore, God reveals to us a fact that is as clearly evident as any other single fact on earth: there is an evil force that has access to the spirit of man and can influence and enslave man to do evil. He is called Satan, who rules over *the darkness and spiritual wickedness of this world*. The only hope for the believer is to put on the *whole armor of God*.

> **"And the devil said unto him, All this power will I give thee, and the glory of them: for that is delivered unto me; and to whomsoever I will I give it" (Lu.4:6).**
>
> **"And the Lord said, Simon, Simon, behold, Satan hath desired to have you, that he may sift you as wheat" (Lu.22:31).**
>
> **"Be sober, be vigilant; because your adversary the devil, as a roaring lion, walketh about, seeking whom he may devour" (1 Pe.5:8).**

QUESTIONS:

1. Do you sometimes find yourself fighting spiritual battles by using physical means? How? What are the results?
2. What are some of the spiritual battles that you face in day-to-day life?
3. How can you determine if something is of Satan or of God?

4. THE SOLDIER'S DUTY: TO TAKE THE FULL ARMOR OF GOD (v.13).

Note how the believer's need for the *whole armor* of God is again stressed. This shows how essential the armor is. Why? Because of the "evil day." What is the "evil day"?

⇒ It refers to *today*—to the onslaught of evil that is in the world today: "the days are evil" (Ep.5:16).

⇒ It refers to *any day*—to the onslaught of temptations and trials that confront us at any given moment during a day.

⇒ It refers to the *day of unusual temptation and trial*—to a special onslaught and barrage of evil that is thrown against us.

We must withstand the day of evil. But we cannot withstand unless we have done our duty—unless we have obeyed and prepared ourselves—unless we have taken the *whole armor* of God.

> **"The night is far spent, the day is at hand: let us therefore cast off the works of darkness and let us put on the armor of light" (Ro.13:12).**
>
> **"For the weapons of our warfare are not carnal, but mighty through God to the pulling down of strong holds" (2 Co.10:4).**

QUESTIONS:

1. As you study this verse, what role are you to play? What is God's role?
2. What is the logical conclusion of *not* wearing *all* of the armor of God? What insights can you gain from this verse that will help you be better prepared for spiritual warfare?
3. What should be your greatest concern if you fail to wear the full armor of God? What kinds of things can you do to guard against this?

5. THE SOLDIER'S ARMOR (vv.14-17).

Remember that Paul was in prison and under constant guard when writing the Ephesian church. He was forced to stare at the soldier's armor day in and day out. He had an ideal picture of the armor needed by the Christian believer to combat the forces of evil.

1. *The belt of truth*. The belt was used to hold the soldier's clothing next to his body. This kept his clothing from flapping about, allowing him freedom of movement. The belt was also used to strengthen and support the body. The sign of the Christian soldier is the belt of truth.

a. What specifically is the belt of truth that the believer is to put on?

⇒ *First, Christ is the truth*. The believer is to put on Christ.

> **"And the Word was made flesh, and dwelt among us, (and we beheld his glory, the glory as of the only begotten of the Father,) full of grace and truth" (Jn.1:14).**

⇒ *Second, the Word of God is the truth*. The believer is to put on the Word of God. He is sanctified by the Word of God.

> **"Sanctify them through thy truth: thy word is truth" (Jn.17:17).**

⇒ *Third, speaking and living a life of truthfulness is the truth.*

"The law of truth was in his mouth, and iniquity was not found in his lips: he walked with me in peace and equity, and did turn many away from iniquity" (Mal.2:6).

b. Truth does several things for the Christian soldier.

⇒ It keeps him from flapping about from one thing to another, from being tossed to and fro by every attack of the enemy.

"That we henceforth be no more children, tossed to and fro, and carried about with every wind of doctrine, by the sleight of men, and cunning craftiness, whereby they lie in wait to deceive" (Ep.4:14).

⇒ It keeps him from becoming entangled with the affairs of this life.

"Thou therefore endure hardness, as a good soldier of Jesus Christ. No man that warreth entangleth himself with the affairs of this life; that he may please him who hath chosen him to be a soldier" (2 Ti.2:3-4).

⇒ It supports him in the battles and trials of life.

"For we have not an high priest which cannot be touched with the feeling of our infirmities; but was in all points tempted like as we are, yet without sin. Let us therefore come boldly unto the throne of grace that we may obtain mercy, and find grace to help in time of need" (He.4:15-16).

2. *The breastplate of righteousness.* The breastplate covered the body of the soldier from the neck to the thighs. It was used to protect the heart. The believer's heart is focused upon the Lord Jesus Christ and His righteousness, and that focus must be protected. The sign of the Christian soldier is righteousness. Righteousness keeps the heart from ever being wounded and losing its focus. The Christian soldier is...

- to strive after the very righteousness of Jesus Christ
- to live righteously in this present world

"For I say unto you, That except your righteousness shall exceed the righteousness of the scribes and Pharisees ye shall in no case enter into the kingdom of heaven" (Mt.5:20).

"For he hath made him to be sin for us, who knew no sin; that we might be made the righteousness of God in him" (2 Co.5:21).

3. *The sandals of the gospel.* The sandals were a sign of readiness—readiness to march and to do battle. The Roman sandals were made with nails that gripped the ground firmly even when it was sloping or slippery. The sign of the Christian soldier is readiness—a readiness to march and to bear witness to the gospel. Wherever the Christian soldier's feet take him, he shares the gospel that can firmly ground a world reeling under the weight of desperate need and conflict.

APPLICATION:

Lehman Strauss makes a statement about this point that startles the mind of modern man: "The soldier's shoes are not the dancing slippers of this world or the lounging slippers of the slothful, but the shoes of the Christian warrior who knows Christ and makes Him known."[3]

> **"And he said unto them, Go ye into all the world, and preach the gospel to every creature" (Mk.16:15).**

4. *The shield of faith in God.* The word "shield" does not mean the small round shield which the soldier held in his hand to fight off the weapons of the enemy. It means the great oblong shield worn by the soldier to protect his body from the fiery darts thrown by the enemy. The darts were dipped in some combustible material and set afire. When they struck, they served the purpose of small bombs. Satan has his fiery darts—those things that cause the believer...

- to question his salvation
- to question his call
- to question if he is worthy
- to question if he can really serve
- to question if the project can really be done
- to question, doubt, and wonder
- to become discouraged, depressed, and defeated
- to burn with passion and desire

Such fiery darts often assault the mind—one doubting and evil thought after the other, fighting against the will—struggling to get hold of the mind and subject it to doubt or evil.

However, the sign of the Christian soldier is that of the shield of faith, faith in God—a complete and perfect trust that God will quench the darts of doubt and evil that attack him, that God will help him control his mind to conquer the evil doubts and thoughts. The Christian soldier's consciousness of God's presence is so great that *God's presence* itself becomes his shield and defender (Ge.15:1). As Scripture says, God is his help and shield (Ps.33:20; 84:9).

> **"But thou, O LORD, art a shield for me; my glory, and the lifter up of mine head. I cried unto the LORD with my voice, and he heard me out of his holy hill" (Ps.3:3-4).**

5. *The helmet of salvation.* The helmet covered the head and the mind of the soldier. The head, of course, was the core of a soldier's power to wage war. His thinking ability was the most important factor in determining his victory or defeat. Therefore, the soldier needed a helmet to protect his head and mind. The sign of the Christian soldier is the helmet of salvation (deliverance). He must protect his mind and its thoughts, keeping all thoughts focused upon the Leader, the Lord Jesus Christ, and His objective of reaching the world with the glorious news that men can live forever.

The helmet that protects the mind of the Christian soldier is *salvation*. Unless a man has been saved, his mind cannot be protected from the fiery darts of temptation. The mind of an unsaved man is focused upon this earth; it is normal and natural for him...

- to seek more and more
- to possess more and more
- to look at the opposite sex with desire
- to taste and indulge the good things of the earth
- to feel and experience, satisfying his desires and passions
- to have and hoard even when others have little or nothing

---

3 Lehman Strauss. *Galatians and Ephesians*, p.232f.

The unsaved man sees nothing wrong with being his own person and doing his own thing just so he is reasonably considerate of others. His mind and thoughts are upon the earth; and the fiery darts of extravagance, indulgence, pleasure, self-centeredness, worldliness, license, hoarding, and immorality are a part of the unsaved world's daily behavior.

But this is not so with the saved man. The mind of the saved man is focused upon Christ and His mission of sharing the good news of life, both life abundant and life eternal. Because of this, Satan launches his fiery darts of temptation against the mind of the believer, trying to get his thoughts and attention off of Christ and the conquest and ministry to souls. The Christian soldier desperately needs the helmet of salvation. The *helmet of salvation* means the knowledge and hope of salvation. Knowing that we are saved and hoping for the glorious day of redemption...

- stirs us to keep our minds and thoughts upon Christ instead of on sin and this world
- arouses us to focus upon Christ and His mission to carry the gospel to a needy and dying world

> **"For to be carnally minded is death; but to be spiritually minded is life and peace" (Ro.8:6).**
>
> **"Casting down imaginations, and every high thing that exalteth itself against the knowledge of God, and bringing into captivity every thought to the obedience of Christ" (2 Co.10:5).**

ILLUSTRATION:

Having the right mind-set is important for the Christian. God knew that the battle for the mind would be ferocious at times. What does this helmet of salvation do for Christians? It keeps us focused on our salvation. For example:

> *Take a look around where you're sitting and find five things that have blue in them. Go ahead and do it.*
>
> *With a "blue" mindset, you'll find that blue jumps out at you: a blue book on the table, a blue pillow on the couch, blue in the painting on the wall, and so on...In like fashion, you've probably noticed that after you buy a new car, you promptly see that make of car everywhere. That's because people find what they are looking for.*[4]

What's been getting your attention lately?

> **"If ye then be risen with Christ, seek those things which are above, where Christ sitteth on the right hand of God. Set your affection on things above, not on things on the earth" (Co.3:1-2).**

6. *The sword of the Spirit is the Word of God.* The sword was a weapon used for both defense and offense. The sword was used both to protect and to fight off and slay the enemy. The sign of the Christian soldier is his use of the Word of God. By living in the Scriptures, he protects himself from the onslaught of the enemy; and he fights and wins battle after battle, day after day. Remember: Jesus Christ Himself overcame the onslaught of the devil by using Scripture (Mt.4:4, 7, 10). The written Word is the one weapon that assures victory for the Christian soldier:

> **"For the word of God is quick and powerful, and sharper than any twoedged sword, piercing even to the dividing asunder of soul and**

---

4 Craig B. Larson, Editor. *Illustrations for Preaching & Teaching*, p.243.

spirit, and of the joints and marrow, and is a discerner of the thoughts and intents of the heart" (He.4:12).

QUESTIONS:

1. What are the six pieces of God's armor and their function? A suggestion: memorize the six pieces of God's armor and ask God every day to help you put them on.
2. What does the armor of God teach you about being prepared for spiritual warfare?
3. Are you failing to put on any piece of God's armor as you walk day by day? Which piece? What do you need to do to put on that piece of armor?
4. Has any piece of God's armor been battered in your spiritual battles, battered to the point that it has been weakened? Which piece? What do you need to do to reinforce the armor to strengthen it in your life?
5. Is it possible to put on the whole armor of God all the time? How does trusting God help you in this?
6. What action do you need to take in order to repel the fiery darts that are aimed at you?

6. THE SUPERNATURAL PROVISION: PRAYER—ALWAYS PRAYING (vv.18-20).

The soldier enters the conflict fully dressed and armed, but something else is essential: great confidence and assurance and courage. Such comes from a spirit of prayer.

The following things need to be noted about the soldier's prayer.

1. He must pray—always pray. The soldier who is not always praying is not assured of God's protection. The Christian soldier must pray all the time to maintain a constant unbroken consciousness of God's presence and care. Prayer infuses the needed assurance, confidence, and courage.

> **"Seek the LORD and his strength, seek his face continually" (1 Chr.16:11).**

2. He must pray "in the Spirit," that is, in the Holy Spirit, the Spirit of the only living and true God. Prayer to any other god or to one's own thoughts or to some other man-made *god* is empty and useless.

> **"Likewise the Spirit also helpeth our infirmities: for we know not what we should pray for as we ought: but the Spirit itself maketh intercession for us with groanings which cannot be uttered. And he that searcheth the hearts knoweth what is the mind of the Spirit, because he maketh intercession for the saints according to the will of God" (Ro.8:26-27).**

3. He must be *sleepless in prayer*. The Christian soldier must concentrate and persevere in prayer. He must go to the point of being *sleepless* in prayer—sometimes so intensely involved in prayer that he actually goes without sleep in order to pray.

> **"Watch and pray, that ye enter not into temptation: the spirit indeed is willing, but the flesh is weak" (Mt.26:41).**

4. He must pray unselfishly. The soldier is not in battle alone; many are engaged in the same warfare. The outcome of the battle is determined by the welfare of all involved. The Christian soldier must pray for those who fight with him. The Christian soldier must pray as much and as intensely for his fellow soldiers as for himself.

"Wherefore I also, after I heard of your faith in the Lord Jesus, and love unto all the saints, cease not to give thanks for you, making mention of you in my prayers" (Ep.1:15-16).

5. He must pray for leaders in particular. Leaders, their decisions and example, often determine the outcome of the battle. The Christian soldier has leaders who teach, preach, and administer throughout the church and around the world. Boldness and decisiveness and purity are needed to put the enemy to flight and to capture souls for the gospel (Ac.28:20).

"Now I beseech you, brethren, for the Lord Jesus Christ's sake, and for the love of the Spirit, that ye strive together with me in your prayers to God for me" (Ro.15:30).

"Finally, brethren, pray for us, that the word of the Lord may have free course, and be glorified, even as it is with you" (2 Th.3:1).

ILLUSTRATION:

As a Christian soldier, are you serious about prayer? "How To Pray" books fill the shelves in bookstores, libraries and offices. But the haunting question that we must answer before God is: Are you seriously committed to pray? Listen closely to this story from John R. Rice:

> *I once visited a home in Chicago where for purpose of exercise they had an "electric horse." As a horseman of long experience in my youth, I was asked to ride the electric horse. I got on, pressed the button, and presto, I galloped a fine imitation of the gallop of a horse. But it was only an imitation after all, for when I pressed the button, the galloping stopped, and I got off exactly where I got on! I had not been anywhere at all! That is exactly like the prayer of* [so many]*—purely for exercise, not to get things from a prayer-hearing, prayer-answering God!*[5]

QUESTIONS:

1. What does it mean to "pray in the Spirit"? What does it mean to pray *out* of the Spirit? What difference does it make?
2. Will God protect you against Satan and the world if you fail to pray? Whose responsibility is it to get protection? Explain your answer.
3. How "real" is your prayer-life? Is it mechanical? Routine? Boring? Or is it heartfelt, sincere, and personal? What can you do to strengthen your prayer life?

---

5 John R. Rice. *Prayer: Asking and Receiving.* (Murfreesboro, TN: Sword of the Lord Publishers, 1970), p.48.

SUMMARY:

Like it or not, all of us are in a *spiritual battle* because there is a spiritual war going on. The battle is difficult, and yes, we are suffering because of the sinfulness of man. Thankfully, God has made a way for us to fight and to fight well. Remember, He has given us our battle plans found in this session:

1. The soldier's charge.
2. The soldier's enemy: the devil and his strategies.
3. The soldier's warfare: not a human struggle, but a spiritual struggle.
4. The soldier's duty: to take the full armor of God.
5. The soldier's armor.
6. The supernatural provision: prayer—always praying.

In the end, there will be a day of rejoicing when He returns to rule and reign. Until then, Christian soldier...Carpe Diem! (Seize the day).

PERSONAL JOURNAL NOTES
(Reflection & Response)

1. The most important thing that I learned from this lesson was:

2. The area that I need to work on the most is:

3. I can apply this lesson to my life by:

4. Closing Statement of Commitment:

	B. The Examples of Faithful Christian Soldiers, 6:21-24	sent unto you for the same purpose, that ye might know our affairs, and that he might comfort your hearts.	lievers, a messenger of encouragement
1. The soldier Tychicus a. A beloved brother b. A faithful minister c. A friend of be-	21 But that ye also may know my affairs, and how I do, Tychicus, a beloved brother and faithful minister in the Lord, shall make known to you all things: 22 Whom I have	23 Peace be to the brethren, and love with faith, from God the Father and the Lord Jesus Christ. 24 Grace be with all them that love our Lord Jesus Christ in sincerity. Amen.	**2. The soldier Paul** a. A spiritual brother: Concerned for the peace, love, & faith of others b. A prayer warrior: Prayed that God's grace would rest upon others

Section V
THE WARFARE OF THE CHRISTIAN BELIEVER
Ephesians 6:10-24

Study 2: THE EXAMPLES OF FAITHFUL CHRISTIAN SOLDIERS

Text: Ephesians 6:21-24

Aim: To become a strong and faithful soldier of the Lord.

Memory Verse:

"Grace be with all them that love our Lord Jesus Christ in sincerity. Amen" (Ephesians 6:24).

INTRODUCTION:

The great American General Douglas MacArthur said at the end of his illustrious career: "Old soldiers never die. They just fade away." He was speaking of mortal soldiers who would eventually die. But Christian soldiers are not like mortal soldiers who die; Christian soldiers have the promise of eternal life which will never fade away.

This passage presents two Christian soldiers who were faithful to the Lord Jesus Christ. They are a dynamic example for every person who has enlisted in the great army of the Lord.

OUTLINE:

1. There was the Christian soldier Tychicus (vv.21-22).
2. There was the Christian soldier Paul (vv.23-24).

1. THERE WAS THE CHRISTIAN SOLDIER TYCHICUS (vv.21-22).

Paul says three significant things about this great soldier of Christ.

1. He was a beloved brother, a man who had believed in Jesus Christ and demonstrated it by loving others deeply. He treated others as brothers, loving and helping them as he could. Therefore, others counted him as dear to their heart—as a beloved brother.

"I have showed you all things, how that so labouring ye ought to support the weak, and to remember the words of the Lord Jesus, how he said, It is more blessed to give than to receive" (Ac.20:35).

"As we have therefore opportunity, let us do good unto all men, especially unto them who are of the household of faith" (Ga.6:10).

2. He was a faithful minister, a man called and gifted by Christ to preach the gospel and to minister to the needs of God's dear people. He was a man who had a world-wide vision: he gave his life to reach the people of the world with the glorious news that living forever was now possible. And note: he was faithful. There was no slack or slumber, no routineness or slothfulness, no complacency or neglect, no questioning or weakening; he did not fail in his ministry. He was a faithful minister—faithful *in the Lord*. He knew where his strength came from, and he drew his strength from the Lord day by day.

"I must work the works of him that sent me, while it is day: the night cometh, when no man can work" (Jn.9:4).

"For we cannot but speak the things which we have seen and heard" (Ac.4:20).

3. He was a friend of believers, a messenger of encouragement. Paul was in prison. The believers of Ephesus were concerned about Paul's welfare, and Paul was concerned that they know he was doing well through the strength of the Lord. But how was Paul going to communicate with the church which was so far away? The answer lay in a dear, dear friend and fellow minister, Tychicus. Note this: Tychicus had his own ministry. He could have been out preaching, witnessing, and ministering on his own. Remember he was a world-wide minister, having given his life to world evangelism and missions. Yet, here he was giving his time and energy to helping Paul and serving in Paul's ministry. He is seen giving up a separate ministry in order to serve as a dear friend and fellow minister with Paul. Apparently he was the ideal minister and messenger of encouragement.

"Let nothing be done through strife or vainglory; but in lowliness of mind let each esteem other better than themselves. Look not every man on his own things, but every man also on the things of others" (Ph.2:3-4).

ILLUSTRATION:

An essential quality needed to be a Christian soldier is faithfulness. But no one ever said that faithfulness was an easy assignment.

In the eleventh century, King Henry III of Bavaria grew tired of court life and the pressures of being a monarch. He made application to Prior Richard at a local monastery, asking to be accepted as a contemplative and spend the rest of his life in the monastery.

"Your Majesty," said Prior Richard, "do you understand that the pledge here is one of obedience? That will be hard because you have been a king."

"I understand," said Henry. "The rest of my life I will be obedient to you, as Christ leads you."

"Then I will tell you what to do," said Prior Richard. "Go back to your throne and serve faithfully in the place where God has put you."

When King Henry died, a statement was written: "The king learned to rule by being obedient."

When we tire of our roles and responsibilities, it helps to remember God has planted us in a certain place and told us to be a good accountant or teacher or mother or father. Christ expects us to be faithful where he puts us, and when he returns, we'll rule together with him.[1]

QUESTIONS:
1. How can you be faithful when going through trials and temptations?
2. Why is it important for you to be faithful when things get difficult?
3. What kinds of things can you do to encourage other Christian soldiers? Have you ever failed to encourage someone when there was an opportunity to do so? What feelings did you struggle with? How would you handle it differently now?

A CLOSER LOOK:

(6:21) **Tychicus**: Tychicus was a native of Asia. He was a companion of Paul who often traveled with him (Ac.20:4).

⇒ He was commissioned by Paul as a messenger to various churches (Ep.6:21f; Co.4:7; 2 Ti.4:12; Tit.3:12).
⇒ He was entrusted to deliver the letters of Paul to the Ephesians, Colossians, and Philemon (Ep.6:21-22; Co.4:7-8).
⇒ He was sent on a special mission to Ephesus (2 Ti.4:12).
⇒ He was to be sent to Crete for the purpose of relieving Titus (Tit.3:12).
⇒ He was not only called Paul's beloved brother and faithful minister but also his fellow-slave (Co.4:7).

QUESTIONS:
1. Who do you know personally who reminds you of Tychicus? What things stand out that impress you?
2. What practical differences would be in your life if you were more like Tychicus? What steps do you need to take in order to be more like him?

2. THERE WAS THE CHRISTIAN SOLDIER PAUL (vv.23-24).

A glimpse into Paul's heart can be gleaned from these two verses.

1. Paul was a spiritual brother to other believers. Note that his concern was for the spiritual welfare of others.

   a. He wished for them to have *peace*: security, harmony, freedom from disturbance.
   b. He wished for them to have *love*: tenderness, a warm attachment, enthusiasm, or devotion.
   c. He wished for them to have *faith*: belief and trust, loyalty.

2. Paul was a prayer warrior for other believers. He prayed that God's *grace* would rest upon them.

---

[1] Craig B. Larson, Editor. *Illustrations for Preaching & Teaching*, p.166.

EPHESIANS 6:21-24

ILLUSTRATION:

When God's grace rests upon us, it helps put everything we experience here on earth in a better perspective. Listen to this vivid illustration from the pen of Ray Stedman and his book, *Talking to My Father*:

An old missionary couple had been working in Africa for years, and they were returning to New York City to retire. They had no pension; their health was broken; they were defeated, discouraged, and afraid. They discovered they were booked on the same ship as President Teddy Roosevelt, who was returning from one of his big-game hunting expeditions.

No one paid attention to them. They watched the fanfare that accompanied the President's entourage, with passengers trying to catch a glimpse of the great man.

As the ship moved across the ocean, the old missionary said to his wife, "Something is wrong. Why should we have given our lives in faithful service for God in Africa all these many years and have no one care a thing about us? Here this man comes back from a hunting trip and everybody makes much over him, but nobody gives two hoots about us."

"Dear, you shouldn't feel that way," his wife said.

"I can't help it; it doesn't seem right."

When the ship docked in New York, a band was waiting to greet the President. The mayor and other dignitaries were there. The papers were full of the President's arrival, but no one noticed this missionary couple. They slipped off the ship and found a cheap flat on the East side, hoping the next day to see what they could do to make a living in the city.

That night the man's spirit broke. He said to his wife, "I can't take this; God is not treating us fairly."

His wife replied, "Why don't you go in the bedroom and tell that to the Lord?"

A short time later he came out from the bedroom, but now his face was completely different. His wife asked, "Dear, what happened?"

"The Lord settled it with me," he said. "I told Him how bitter I was that the President should receive this tremendous homecoming, when no one met us as we returned home. And when I finished, it seemed as though the Lord put His hand on my shoulder and simply said, 'But you're not home yet!'"[2]

APPLICATION:

As a Christian soldier, your mission may be long, hard, and unheralded. But at all times the grace of God is there to see you through. As you serve day by day, you are, above all else, to be concerned about the spiritual welfare of others and be a prayer warrior for other believers.

QUESTIONS:

1. How can these verses help you become a stronger soldier for Christ? What do you personally need to do to become stronger?
2. Share a time when you experienced the grace of God. What is the secret of keeping strong in His grace?
3. Briefly describe your reaction to the illustration above. What were your thoughts before the missionary went to the Lord with his concern? How does trusting God ease the pain?

---

2 Craig B. Larson, Editor. *Illustrations for Preaching & Teaching*, pp.197-198.

EPHESIANS 6:21-24

SUMMARY:

Old soldiers die and fade away. But the faithful Christian soldier looks toward a homecoming with the Lord and with all the saints in glory. We have the strong example and testimony of two faithful soldiers:

1. There was the Christian soldier Tychicus.
2. There was the Christian soldier Paul.

What will keep you going until that glorious homecoming? God's grace will, just as it did Paul and Tychicus.

PERSONAL JOURNAL NOTES
(Reflection & Response)

1. The most important thing that I learned from this lesson was:

2. The area that I need to work on the most is:

3. I can apply this lesson to my life by:

4. Closing Statement of Commitment:

OUTLINE & SUBJECT INDEX

EPHESIANS

OUTLINE & SUBJECT INDEX

EPHESIANS

REMEMBER: When you look up a subject and then turn to the Scripture reference, you have not only the Scripture but also *an outline and a discussion* (commentary) of the Scripture and subject.

This is one of the *GREAT VALUES* of *THE TEACHER'S OUTLINE & STUDY BIBLE*™. Once you have all the volumes, you will have not only what all other Bible indexes give you, that is, a list of all the subjects and their Scripture references, *BUT* you will also have...

- an outline of *every* Scripture and subject in the Bible
- a discussion (commentary) on every Scripture and subject
- every subject supported by other Scriptures or cross-references

DISCOVER THE GREAT VALUE for yourself. Quickly glance below to the very first subject of the Index of *Ephesians*. It is:

ACCESS
Discussed. 2:18

Turn to the reference. Glance at the Scripture and the outline of the Scripture, then read the commentary. You will immediately see the GREAT VALUE of the INDEX of *THE TEACHER'S OUTLINE & STUDY BIBLE*™.

OUTLINE AND SUBJECT INDEX

Outline & Subject Index

OUTLINE & SUBJECT INDEX

OUTLINE & SUBJECT INDEX

Illustration Index

Ephesians

ILLUSTRATION INDEX

ILLUSTRATION INDEX

ILLUSTRATION INDEX

ILLUSTRATION INDEX

OUTLINE BIBLE RESOURCES

This material, like similar works, has come from imperfect man and is thus susceptible to human error. We are nevertheless grateful to God for both calling us and empowering us through His Holy Spirit to undertake this task. Because of His goodness and grace, ***The Preacher's Outline & Sermon Bible***® New Testament is complete in 14 volumes, and the Old Testament volumes are releasing periodically.

The **Minister's Handbook** and other helpful ***Outline Bible*** materials are available in print form as well as releasing electronically on **POSB-CD** and our **Website**.

God has given the strength and stamina to bring us this far. Our confidence is that as we keep our eyes on Him and grounded in the undeniable truths of the Word, we will continue working through the Old Testament volumes and the second series known as *The Teacher's Outline & Study Bible*™. The future includes helpful ***Outline Bible*** books and **Handbook** materials for God's dear servants.

We offer this material first to Him in whose Name we labor and serve and for whose glory it has been produced and, second, to everyone everywhere who preaches and teaches the Word.

Our daily prayer is that each volume will lead thousands, millions, yes even billions, into a better understanding of the Holy Scriptures and a fuller knowledge of Jesus Christ the incarnate Word, of whom the Scriptures so faithfully testify.

You will be pleased to know that a small portion of the purchase price has gone to underwrite and provide similar volumes in other languages (Russian, Korean, Spanish, and others yet to come). A preacher, pastor, teacher, lay leader, or Bible student somewhere around the world will be more able to present God's message with clarity, authority, and understanding beyond his or her own power. *Amen.*

LEADERSHIP MINISTRIES WORLDWIDE
PO Box 21310 • Chattanooga, TN 37424-0310
(423) 855-2181 • FAX (423) 855-8616
info@outlinebible.org
www.outlinebible.org - FREE Download materials

LEADERSHIP MINISTRIES WORLDWIDE

PURPOSE STATEMENT

LEADERSHIP MINISTRIES WORLDWIDE

exists to equip ministers, teachers, and laymen in their understanding, preaching and teaching of God's Word by publishing and distributing worldwide. *The Preacher's & Sermon Bible®* and related ***Outline Bible*** materials, to reach & disciple men, women, boys and girls for Jesus Christ.

MISSION STATEMENT

1. To make the Bible so understandable – its truth so clear and plain – that men and women everywhere, whether teacher or student, preacher or hearer, can grasp its message and receive Jesus Christ as Savior, and...

2. To place the Bible in the hands of all who will preach and teach God's Holy Word, verse by verse, precept by precept, regardless of the individual's ability to purchase it.

The ***Outline Bible*** materials have been given to LMW for printing and especially distribution worldwide at/below cost, by those who remain anonymous. One fact, however, is as true today as it was in the time of Christ:

THE GOSPEL IS FREE, BUT THE COST OF TAKING IT IS NOT

LMW depends on the generous gifts of believers with a heart for Him and a love for the lost. They help pay for the printing, translating, and distributing of ***Outline Bible*** materials into the hands of God's servants worldwide, who will present the Gospel message with clarity, authority, and understanding beyond their own.

LMW was incorporated in the state of Tennessee in July 1992 and received IRS 501 (c)(3) nonprofit status in March 1994. LMW is an international, nondenominational mission organization. All proceeds from USA sales, along with donations from donor partners, go directly to underwrite our translation and distribution projects of ***Outline Bible*** materials to preachers, church and lay leaders, and Bible students around the world.